D1562555

JOURNEY
IN
TEARS

JOURNEY IN TEARS

Memory of a Girlhood in China

BY

Chow Ching-li

McGRAW-HILL BOOK COMPANY
New York   St. Louis   San Francisco
Düsseldorf   Mexico   Toronto

1234567890 DODO 78321098

Library of Congress Cataloging in Publication Data

Chow, Ching Lie, 1936-
  Journey in tears.
  Translation of Le palanquin des larmes.
  1. Chow, Ching Lie, 1936-   2. China—Social
life and customs.   3. China—Biography.   I. Title.
CT1828.C544A3413   951.05'092'4 [B]   78-18171
ISBN 0-07-010818-8

Originally published in French under the title *Le Palanquin des Larmes*, As Told to
Georges Walter, © Opera Mundi, 1975.

Translated from the French by Abby Israel.

JOURNEY
IN
TEARS

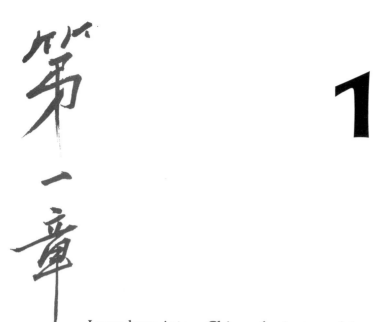

I was born into a China of misery and tears. The China of my birth was a vast, undeveloped country, where poverty, banditry, and civil war were rife, and where it was particularly unwise to be born female.

The year was 1936. But even as late as then, poverty-stricken families were not averse to following the time-worn custom of bundling up their female infants, like a sack of unwanted kittens, and tossing them into the river to drown. For those who were unlucky enough to escape this early fate, a more brutal destiny awaited: sale as a slave into a brothel or rich household when your family could no longer feed you.

Such was the fate that befell many Chinese women through the centuries until as late as 1950, when the new regime, led by Mao Tse-tung, outlawed the murder of newborn female babies, slavery, forced marriages, and other similar cruel and barbaric customs. Although an earlier law against forced marriages had been passed in 1931, it was ignored by many, and this was the first time such a law was being aggressively disseminated, supported, and enforced by the government.

To be sure, the family into which I was born never considered selling me in the conventional way. On the contrary, my childhood in Shanghai was filled with the love and affection of my parents. But I had my fair share of tears, primarily because I was pretty—which in China was more a curse than a blessing, at least for me. Ugly, or even simply plain, I might not have been forced as a child of thirteen into a marriage in one of the richest families in Shanghai; thus I was indeed sold, albeit under the more honorable guise of marriage.

By the time of my birth my parents were reasonably well-to-do. But the memory of their peasant origins, and particularly their poverty, was never far off.

My childhood was full of contradictions. My mother, a peasant girl from Chao-chou, was a fervent believer in Buddha; my father was from Shanghai, where he had received a Western education at St. John's University. And although I was brought up strictly, in the old-fashioned Chinese way, indoctrinated by both parents in Chinese culture and tradition—and by my mother in Chinese superstition—my father nevertheless insisted I attend an American school. There, as a little girl, I ended up praying both to Buddha, because of my mother, and to Jesus, because of the school.

As far back as I can remember, my family was dominated by the figure of my grandfather, Chow Tso-hung, who was born during the nineteenth century, toward the end of the last dynasty, known as Ching (or Manchu), which fell in 1912.

China was still very much under corrupt dynastic control at the time of Chow Tso-hung's birth in 1885, in Chao-chou, a town in the southern part of Kwangtung, some sixty miles from Canton. A microcosm of villages everywhere, Chao-chou was typically impoverished and illiterate. Made mean by poverty and stingy in the extreme, some of its natives specialized in the sale of female children. Girls were never in short supply, and people came from far and wide to buy. A few children were lucky enough to be acquired for the Chinese opera, but in most cases the girls were purchased as servants or, worse, sold as possible "concubines" who would actually later be resold into houses of prostitution.

During Chow Tso-hung's youth, numerous traveling opera troupes roamed like circuses from village to village, setting up their tents in the center of the town. My grandfather had

2

joined one such troupe, but they were so poor they couldn't afford any mules, and each player had to hitch himself to a cart, piled high with props, and pull it to the next village.

My grandfather, however, was responsible for the costumes, which were packed into two huge wicker baskets hung on each end of a bamboo pole slung over my grandfather's shoulders. Still in his teens, his feet in thin straw sandals, Chow Tso-hung covered on foot hundreds of miles of bad trails and treacherous paths that wound around the mountains above Canton. For this arduous work he earned a daily bowl of thin rice gruel, occasionally enriched by a salted turnip—barely enough to keep him alive.

Despite his extreme poverty, my grandfather was married at the age of eighteen to Li Hsing-lan, a pretty peasant girl of fifteen from a neighboring village who, as was customary at the time, moved in with her husband's family in Chao-chou. Apart from the young couple, my grandfather's family consisted of his parents and a younger brother. Eventually, a sixth member was added to the household.

Much to Chow Tso-hung's and Li Hsing-lan's joy, a baby boy was born. There was much rejoicing throughout the village.

And then tragedy struck.

The largest room in the house was the kitchen, which was used as the family room and dominated by an earthen stove, into which was set a huge concave iron pot, a *yü* or *wok*, constantly simmering with the rice gruel known in Cantonese as *chou* or *jook*. Mixed with a great deal of water, a small quantity of rice could be stretched to feed a whole family; and if that family were lucky, bits of salted turnips, dried fish, or whatever else might be handy could be thrown in to make a more wholesome meal, or at least fill the belly.

One day, Chow Tso-hung's younger brother was left at home to tend the baby and look after the *jook*, which needed an occasional stir. The young boy unthinkingly held the baby in one arm while using the other to stir the gruel. To the boy's horror, his squirming nephew slipped out of his arm and into the scalding *jook*.

The baby died of his burns.

3

A few months later, while Chow Tso-hung and Li Hsing-lan were still recovering from the terrible loss of their firstborn, the opera troupe was playing sufficiently close to Chao-chou for grandfather to return home every night. One evening, he was late. Li Hsing-lan was beside herself with worry—the roads around Chao-chou, as elsewhere, were notoriously unhealthy at that time. Bandits abounded and were one of China's chief torments during this period. Circulating in well-organized bands, they victimized even the poor, killing indiscriminately. Although bandits were by imperial edict subject to beheading, regardless of whether the crime was robbery or murder, there were simply too many for the authorities to cope with, and most were never caught.

As dawn approached the next morning, the neighbors came to the house carrying what appeared to Li Hsing-lan to be a corpse. It was her husband, very nearly dead. The bandits had beaten him mercilessly on the head with clubs before fleeing with his costumes, and his queue had become so caked with blood that my grandmother had great difficulty in untangling his braid and cleaning his wounds.

This final outrage, coupled with both his and Li Hsing-lan's inability to forget their son's tragic death as long as they stayed in Chao-chou, forced Chow Tso-hung to reach an inevitable decision. They would leave the village.

Illiterate and without any skills, my grandfather proposed to try his luck in Shanghai, where he had a cousin, and where he had heard that even unskilled peasants could find a job. At first reluctant to leave all that was familiar and dear to her, grandmother finally acquiesced. After all, so many others had successfully sought their fortune elsewhere, from as nearby as Hong Kong to as far away as Singapore—even America. Thus, why not Shanghai?

Once known as the "City of the Mudbank," Shanghai is located in central China, on the Whangpoo River, near the rich delta area of the lower Yangtze. At the time of Chow Tso-hung's arrival in 1903, the city had grown rich on foreign trade and opium, and already had a population of close to a million.

Moreover, the city to which Chow Tso-hung fled was dominated by foreigners, living in enclaves conceded to them fol-

4

lowing a series of wars with China in which China had come out the loser. There was the International Settlement, primarily administered by the British, who shared their privileges with the Americans and other, smaller Western nations. There was the French Concession, governed by the French consul, and also the Japanese-controlled section of Hongkew. While the vast majority of the residents of these enclaves were Chinese, they lived under foreign consular law, maintained by foreign or foreign-dominated courts and police, working for foreign commercial enterprises or Chinese-established offshoots of these enterprises. Surrounding these concessions were suburbs and older Chinese settlements under Chinese administration.

It was in this second Shanghai, the Chinese Shanghai, that Chow Tso-hung, taking advantage of his cousin's hospitality, settled with his young wife. Here the houses were pressed tightly together, the narrow streets flanked by shacks and mud houses, and filled with a noisy and unending sea of people: merchants, housewives, hawkers, coolies, beggars, prostitutes, and sailors of all complexions.

At first it was difficult for Chow Tso-hung to find work, and in desperation he became a street porter, making barely enough to keep himself and his wife alive; nevertheless, they had three sons in quick succession, the second of whom, Chow Hui-i, was to become my father.

With so many mouths to feed, Chow Tso-hung, in addition to his regular day job as a street porter—which required him to pull a handcart filled with heavy packages for delivery from one place to another—also took any other jobs he might still have the energy left to perform.

Scrimping and saving, Chow Tso-hung finally managed to put aside enough money to lease (and later purchase) a small grocery store. At last he would be able to give his children the chance to escape the poverty he had known only too well.

In the ensuing years the store prospered and Chow Tso-hung was able to purchase a larger store in a better location and add more variety to the merchandise he sold. He was becoming a wealthy man, affluent enough to return to Chao-chou to build a home for his old age. For although he would continue to live in Shanghai, my grandfather, like all Chinese who leave home to seek their fortune, wished to return finally to his birthplace, where he could spend his declining years in comfort, his home a testimonial to his success in life.

When he returned to Chao-chou to build his house, grandfather decided it would be a good idea to take both my father, Chow Hui-i, then six, and the youngest son, Chow Hui-ying, who was five.

One day, when the two boys were swimming in the river, they were spotted by an old woman known as Aunt Ma, who happened to be the village marriage broker. Until 1950, the vast majority of marriages in China were "matched marriages" arranged by marriage brokers such as Aunt Ma, a barbaric practice perpetuated not only in China, but by second- and third-generation Chinese in Southeast Asia and as far away as the United States. In some instances, these marriages were arranged between families of long acquaintance, but too often they were made between total strangers, often children, for reasons of money or position, or both. The marriage broker, of course, always received a handsome fee.

Knowing that both Hui-i and Hui-ying were the sons of Chow Tso-hung, who was considered a very rich man by Chao chou standards, Aunt Ma seized upon the opportunity to seek a match between one of the boys and the girl-child of a widow of modest means in the village.

My father, Chow Hui-i, was selected by the widow—who had been dragged by Aunt Ma to the river bank to view the two little boys—simply because he had fair skin, a Chinese ideal. The widow's choice was fortuitous, as the other boy, my uncle Chow Hui-ying, was born simpleminded, and remained so all his life.

The marriage broker, Aunt Ma, then sped to Chow Tso-hung, claiming that "there's an adorable little girl in the neighborhood. Her name is Chung-ai, and her mother's a widow and not rich, but she's hardworking and serious, and her daughter will be, too. As such, Chung-ai will prove a definite advantage to your family." As Chow Tso-hung found nothing objectionable about either mother or daughter—indeed, the little girl was quite nice—grandfather agreed.

Aunt Ma was paid by both families when the negotiations were completed and the children betrothed. Thus my father and mother became engaged at the ages of six and four, respectively. Neither Chow Hui-i nor Chung-ai was aware of the arrangement at the time and, in the years to come, they scarcely saw one another until the day of their wedding.

Whether the two would find themselves compatible—let alone fall in love—when they grew up was unimportant. A betrothal was a betrothal, and it would be unthinkable for anyone on either side to break such a contract.

And so Chow Hui-i returned to Shanghai with his father, while Chung-ai remained in Chao-chou. My grandfather sent Chung-ai's mother money for the "education" of his future daughter-in-law in school, albeit for only six years, it being common wisdom that females shouldn't burden themselves with too much study. As the saying went, She who has little knowledge has great virtue. An education would merely distract a woman from the virtues of humility and submission; her only purpose being to serve her husband and his family and bear children.

Thus, while Chung-ai remained at home to learn to cook, weave, and sew, her fiancé, Chow Hui-i, not only completed preparatory school but continued his studies at St. John's University, a venerable institution comparable to Princeton or Harvard. As a result, my father became Westernized and sophisticated while my mother remained an abysmally ignorant peasant, interested only in money and things material. This difference between them would become increasingly acute over the years, creating much misunderstanding and unhappiness, but no such problems were foreseen when Chow Hui-i, the eighteen-year-old student son of Chow Tso-hung, married the pretty little sixteen-year-old peasant girl, Chung-ai.

The year was 1923. The Ching Dynasty had been forced into abdication some twelve years earlier, and the Republic declared under the leadership of Dr. Sun Yat-sen. Unfortunately, the new republic had in fact been something less than successful, plagued as it was by foreign imperialism, party disunity, and civil strife. Oddly enough, the Bolshevik Revolution in

Russia had inspired both the establishment of the Chinese Communist Party in 1921 and, earlier, the reorganization of the Chinese Revolutionary Party into the Chinese Nationalist Party, or Kuomintang, in 1919. By 1923, Sun Yat-sen succeeded in achieving a temporary coalition with the Chinese Communists, the purpose of which was national unification, much needed in the face of internal warlordism and foreign encroachment.

By 1923, Shanghai had also changed. The European concessions, thanks to foreign profiteering in everything from opium to silk, had built tall and impressive buildings in imitation of those in Paris, London, and New York. Highly polished brass plaques glittered on the façades of the buildings. This Shanghai was now as elegant and fashionable as Paris. Its women were dressed in *haute couture*, or a reasonable facsimile thereof, and life was an unending and mindless round of teas, dinners, parties, tennis, horse racing, and gambling of every sort, or whatever else might amuse.

Cheap Chinese labor, and an unshakeable sense of superiority, made life exceedingly comfortable for even those foreigners who in their own countries might have been considered somewhat *déclassé*.

As was customary, the young newlyweds settled in Shanghai in the home of Chow Tso-hung, in the Chinese quarter, above grandfather's store. Chow Tso-hung and Li Hsing-lan occupied the second floor, while my parents occupied the third. My father, Chow Hui-i, continued his studies at St. John's, where he mingled freely with American professors and the sons of British diplomats and businessmen.

On the Bund, along the Whangpoo, Shanghai might have passed for any European city. The brass plaques multiplied rapidly, and everyone ignored the fact that the prosperity of these respectable houses of commerce—guarded by Indian police, tall Sikhs with red turbans, whom my mother called "the redheads" (and to whom she threatened to turn me over if I didn't behave properly)—was historically based on the opium trade, introduced and imposed upon the Chinese by the English.

During the summer, the *taipans* and their wives went to Jessfield Park to hear the Municipal Orchestra play Mozart and other classical selections. For bachelors, the distractions were as diverse as the beautiful women—Russian, Korean, Japanese, and Chinese—who danced at the Ambassador, the Parliament, and the Venus Café. If these smart night spots palled, "ticket girls" awaited them in less elegant places, where they could explore more exotic experiences, including drugs. The real masters of Shanghai came from the underworld. Their leader was Tu Yüeh-sheng, the most powerful head of the Green Gang, an offshoot of the Triads, a secret society not unlike the Mafia, dating back to 1645. It was thought that since Tu Yüeh-sheng had the monopoly on opium traffic, he also controlled all the rackets in Shanghai, which included everything from dog racing to assassins for hire; and the rumor went around that he had connections in high places, for his "blood brother" in the Triad Society was Generalissimo Chiang Kai-shek, for whom he performed many valuable services.

Shanghai, city of prosperity, was also Shanghai, city of poverty, home to hordes of genuine beggars and ingenious false ones who fabricated purulent wounds from mud and the blood of pigs and collected dead babies which they held in their arms as they wailed, in order to encourage larger handouts. This latter category of beggars were used by Tu Yüeh-sheng in his various operations; they made superb informers and observers.

During his first year of marriage, Chow Hui-i left the house each morning to travel to the university by streetcar.

Chow Hui-i knew his city by heart—Jessfield Park, where concerts were held, the Whangpoo, jammed with boats, the gardens edging the river, closed to Chinese with signs that read "No Dogs or Chinese Allowed."

While Chow Hui-i attended the university, his young wife, Chung-ai, led a far more restricted life. As expected of all good Chinese wives, she had in effect become her in-laws' slave. Her day began at five in the morning, when she had to empty the family barrel of waste into a cart that passed by every morning. Then mother would return to the house and clean it from top to bottom, as would a servant—which is indeed what she was considered.

Chung-ai also cooked and served breakfast, but before doing so she had to fill the washbasins of Chow Tso-hung and Li Hsing-lan. In poor homes, these basins were made of wood; in more affluent homes, they were porcelain. Side by side were placed a bowl of warm water for brushing the teeth and a tongue-raker.

In addition, Chung-ai was also required to work in the store. Chow Tso-hung had certainly got his money's worth when he paid Aunt Ma her marriage broker's fee.

Some months after they were married, Chung-ai became pregnant; this made no difference in her work schedule, however, until the end of her eighth month, when her belly became so swollen and heavy that she was unable to bend over or run up and down stairs.

The baby that was delivered was, happily, a boy. My brother, the firstborn, was named Chow (our surname), Ching (denoting the generation, a name all of us siblings share), and Chung (his first name)—thus, Chow Ching-chung.

Despite having borne a son and heir, Chung-ai continued to be treated as a servant. When she became pregnant with her second child, her work load remained the same as before, with one exception—Chow Ching-chung was strapped to her back; thus her second child was born prematurely and died after lingering for only three days. Since the child was a girl, there were no mourners except, perhaps, Chung-ai.

When Chow Ching-chung turned four, my mother became pregnant for a third time. Relegated to an attic room by her mother-in-law, Chung-ai bore her third child, again a daughter, during the summer in the inferno of a room covered only by a zinc roof. If this treatment of Chung-ai seems cruel (as it was), it was no different from that meted out to many other women under the same circumstances in Old China.

The baby died, of course, after only one week. Chung-ai herself was seriously ill, and since she was suffering from what appeared to be a contagious rash, her mother-in-law refused to let her leave the attic, fearing she might contaminate the rest of the family.

Chung-ai, certain that she was about to die, insisted that she be allowed to see her own mother, who, when she reached

Shanghai, had no doubt that her only daughter was at death's door. A fervent Buddhist, Chung-ai's mother prayed night and day, especially to the Goddess of Mercy, Kuan Yin.

One evening, Chung-ai's mother had a dream. A godlike character appeared, dressed in a costume reminiscent of a Chinese opera, sporting a red beard—the symbol of happiness. Leaning forward, this bearded creature smiled at both Chung-ai and her mother, and then disappeared.

The next morning, on hearing her mother's story, Chung-ai confessed to having had the same vision. For both, the message was clear: Chung-ai must become a Buddhist, which she did. Two days later the rash had disappeared and she was in perfect health.

The near-death of Chung-ai and the cruel fate of her two little daughters seemed to soften Li Hsing-lan's heart toward her daughter-in-law. Thus, when my mother became pregnant for a fourth time, she was permitted to stop working and was given a healthy diet, including "white tiger soup," which is actually the juice of the watermelon, representing *ying* and *yang*.

Since it was I with whom mother was pregnant, I am fortunate that destiny smiled upon me by timing Chung-ai's pregnancy with a more magnanimous attitude on the part of her mother-in-law. But I am certain that I owe much more—the fact that I was not only born, but *lived*—to my mother's conversion to Buddhism.

In the final months of her confinement, Chung-ai prayed daily for a daughter. Hadn't she just lost two, one right after the other? And if the baby were a boy, he would belong to his father and his father's family. A daughter, on the other hand, would belong to her; no one would want to lay claim to a girl. Such a child could be a source of joy and consolation for the miserable life Chung-ai had spent under the domination of an implacable mother-in-law, with a husband too weak to protest or demonstrate any tenderness toward his wife, or who perhaps didn't care.

Chung-ai prayed fervently for a girl to the Goddess of Mercy, Kuan Yin.

In August, 1936, just a few weeks before my birth, my grandmother's behavior toward her daughter-in-law became not only tolerant, but positively generous. She did all sorts of little favors for her, even going so far as to visit my mother in her apartment at my father's school.

By this time Chow Hui-i had completed his studies. His father, Chow Tso-hung, had envisioned his son entering business, but was not displeased to learn that Chow Hui-i was actually something of a scholar, and dreamed of building a secondary school. Under Old China's social stratum, the top level was that of the scholar class; in the old days that meant competing against other scholars in a series of excruciatingly difficult exams each lasting several days; and if it did not require profound knowledge, it did require an excellence in calligraphy, a disciplined literary style, and a command of Confucian literature and philosophy. Those who passed were shown singular respect and were able to enter the higher levels of government.

All of this had, of course, changed by the time my father graduated from St. John's—but not the respect and honor accorded a scholar. Pleased by the status his son would receive, but more interested in the potential profit of the project, Chow Tso-hung consented to give his son the necessary money—painfully accumulated over a lifetime of hard work and penny-pinching—to build the school. The sum involved was considerably larger than anyone had imagined.

The secondary school was constructed in the suburbs of Shanghai. In addition to the classrooms, it also included apartments for the teachers and for my parents, an athletic field, and large gardens, some of which were given over to the growing of vegetables.

Thus my mother was happily ensconced with Chow Hui-i in rooms of their own at the school, well away from Chung-ai's in-laws, particularly Li Hsing-lan.

Li Hsing-lan, however, became increasingly kind and solicitous toward Chung-ai. As it turned out, all this care and affection had less to do with the expectant mother than with the expected child. For there was not the slightest doubt in my grandmother's mind that the baby would be a boy.

To Li Hsing-lan, this had been forecast by the deaths, practically at birth, of the two infant girls, and grandmother carried with her at all times two circular wooden discs that fitted into the hand—key elements in a popular method of prophecy. Each disc had one smooth side, the other painted or engraved with a motif of flowers. Both discs were tossed into the air, and if both fell with the same side up, the wish was granted. Thus, on the morning of August 26, 1936, when both discs fell with their flower side up, my grandmother concluded that the birth of a boy was imminent, and rushed to the school where in fact my mother's labor pains were just beginning.

The baby was born at eleven in the morning. A *girl!* Li Hsing-lan, who had brought only boys into the world, ran speechless and unforgiving from the room.

According to all accounts, I was a pretty little baby, with pale, smooth skin, the result of the "white tiger soup" Chung-ai had consumed during her pregnancy. Because my mother thought I was pretty, she named me Chow Ching-li—Li meaning "altogether beautiful."

Unlike his mother, Chow Hui-i was delighted when he saw the new baby girl. My father's warm and wonderful love for me was born at that moment, a love that would surround and sustain me through the difficult days that would follow much later in my life.

In July, 1937, slightly less than a year after my birth, the Second Sino-Japanese War was launched near Peking, the first having been fought in 1894. Ill-equipped and weak against the well-armed and disciplined Japanese, the Nationalists realized that they had no hope of winning, and that any defense of Peking might also mean the destruction and loss to the world of all its priceless art objects, historic relics, and architectural treasures. Thus the Nationalist forces evacuated Peking on July 28, abandoning the city to the Japanese; a few days later Tientsin also fell.

Like other foreigners who had been bleeding China for a century, the Japanese had caused untold pain and tragedy through the years; now, however, this latest assault finally awakened China's national consciousness, and the desire to set aside petty internal strife and unite in the face of the enemy was so strong that such hitherto implacable enemies as the Nationalists and the Chinese Communists declared a tentative truce and joined forces to fight against the invader.

In August, 1937, on my first birthday, the Chinese attacked the Japanese garrison in the Japanese Concession in Shanghai. The Japanese rushed in reinforcements and counterattacked.

This time the Nationalists were prepared. Chiang Kai-shek defended the city with his best-trained troops, successfully keeping the Japanese at bay for three months, until nearly the end of the year.

During this crucial and frightening period my mother, whose pregnancies tended to follow swiftly one upon the other, had yet another child, also a girl. My little sister was named Chow Ching-ling (Ling meaning "skillful" or "clever").

Another daughter! Li Hsing-lan was outraged; clearly bad luck would follow. And it did.

Our neighborhood in the Chinese quarter was on its way to being destroyed by constant bombardment, and people were being killed daily in the streets. It soon became clear that we would have to leave, and immediately.

The foreign concessions were the only areas that remained relatively undamaged, and thousands of Chinese sought refuge there. Thus, my grandparents found a sinister-looking but spacious house in an English neighborhood in the International Settlement. Its owners were eager to depart quickly and, for a ridiculously low price, we took possession.

I, of course, was still a toddler when we moved, but the minute I was carried into our new home I began to scream and cry without ceasing—not even to sleep. Since it was late September and unseasonably hot, all the windows throughout the neighborhood remained open, and my incessant screaming kept the whole neighborhood awake. The complaints became quite rude.

My grandmother tried every tonic and balm she could think of to calm me, but nothing worked. Finally a neighbor paid us a visit, saying she thought she might have the answer to my hysterics.

The house, she said simply, was haunted. *Haunted?*

She explained to my grandmother and mother that a woman

14

had committed suicide there, just before the previous owners had purchased the house. "Why do you think they left so quickly and sold so cheaply? Not because of the war, I guarantee." She then went on to explain that the woman who killed herself had done so because of an unhappy love affair, that the house was cursed and the woman returned regularly to haunt the place, adding, "If your baby cries so much, it's because she sees the ghost." The neighbor then suggested that we move as soon as possible.

Grandmother, who had listened expressionless throughout, thanked the neighbor and, turning to my mother, exploded at her.

"Nonsense! What a pack of lies! That woman is just trying to get us to move. If Ching-li cries, it's *your* fault, Chung-ai. You've brought nothing but bad luck by bearing a daughter. As if the war isn't enough we have to put up with her screaming. I don't care how you do it, but I suggest you keep her quiet—otherwise you can *both* leave. But *we* stay here!"

Mother finally quieted me down by sitting up in a chair and holding me close to her every night.

A sudden chill occurred one day. My grandfather, Chow Tso-hung, came home very late that evening. The door was opened by his eldest living son, my father's older brother, Hui-lin, who, with his wife, was living with us at the time. Incredibly, in that brief moment when he let his father in, Hui-lin caught a chill and was seized with violent stomach pains, turning white as a sheet. My grandfather immediately called an ambulance and Chow Hui-lin was quickly hospitalized. Three days later he died.

With Chow Hui-lin's strange and sudden death, my crying came to an abrupt end. Our superstitious neighbors (and who is to say they were wrong?) had a unanimous explanation: Unlike my parents, uncle Chow Hui-lin and his wife had been an extremely close and loving couple, and their happiness had obviously outraged the ghost, who took revenge by causing my uncle's untimely death.

Chow Hui-lin's death had a profound effect on our family, particularly on my father, and that, coupled with the constant bombardment of the city and growing apprehension that the

Nationalists would soon lose to the Japanese, made my grand-parents decide to move.

We next moved to a fashionable neighborhood in the French Concession, where my grandparents purchased a large, sunny, modern three-story house that could accommodate all of us comfortably, and we were quite happy.

And then catastrophe struck again.

The grounds surrounding Chow Hui-i's school had grown green and lush, and horses from neighboring areas were given to occasional grazing there. One day, the pilot of one of the little Japanese planes that were forever flying back and forth over Shanghai spotted the horses. Certain the school was a barracks for a cavalry troop, the pilot circled around, flew over the school, and dropped his load of bombs. In a few seconds the school buildings and most of the grounds were completely destroyed.

Fortunately, school was not in session, and no one was killed, but the school's destruction completely wiped out Chow Hui-i financially. Instead of comforting his son, Chow Tso-hung took to blaming Hui-i for his misfortune and the loss of Chow Tso-hung's money. Trapped at home, poor Hui-i was obliged to endure his father's sarcasm and lamentations day after day. Finally tiring of inveighing against his son, Chow Tso-hung began to rail at my mother, claiming that because she had borne four girls in a row (two of whom had died at birth), Chung-ai had brought nothing but bad luck and misfortune to the house of Chow. If he could, Chow Tso-hung would even have blamed the war on both his son and daughter-in-law.

Then one day late in November, as my father was crossing the French Concession, he noticed a sudden stillness. The guns had ceased firing. It was much too quiet. He continued walking, but apprehensively, and soon a policeman halted him. The road ahead was closed. What was now left of Chiang's army, those who had so courageously defended Shanghai for three terrible months, were withdrawing.

Chow Hui-i wept. Shanghai had fallen.

The whole city was soon flooded with Japanese soldiers. The occupiers were barbaric in their treatment of the Chinese, and rumors circulated freely of wholesale executions, of bayonet drills carried out on prisoners for amusement. Our fear and hatred of the Japanese grew even stronger after the fall of Nanking in December, when 100,000 civilians were indiscriminately slaughtered, but not before terrible atrocities had been committed against the victims, many of them, women and children. In fact, the infamous "Rape of Nanking" was so shameful, even to the Japanese, that the Japanese military successfully concealed the true facts from their own people until after the war.

For the now Japanese-controlled sections of Shanghai, the worst period was only just beginning. Not only were people being harassed, tortured, and killed daily, but those who survived were starving. There are always some, of course, who manage to take advantage of almost any situation, and a thriving black market developed.

A month's hard-earned salary was often not enough to buy a week's worth of food. Wet weather had ruined the rice, but the fact that it was riddled with worms and vermin did not keep speculators from selling it. Indeed, storekeepers who hoarded rice while waiting for the price to rise were called "rice vermin."

It was the puppet government, however, that set the example in speculation. They clandestinely speculated on everything from food to opium. But the rich had no monopoly on this sort of traffic; countless people were forced into such unsavory dealings by circumstance. Inflation and deprivation were rampant. Salaried employees watched the value of their money decline until it became clear to many that only those who trafficked in the black market could survive.

Even the occupying army suffered from food shortages and restrictions. At one point, it is said, the Japanese descended upon the Shanghai dog-racing track and made off with several hundred of the best greyhounds, which expired subsequently in the regimental kitchens.

My grandfather, who still unreasonably reproached his son for the loss of the school, even tried to convince Chow Hui-i to try his hand in opium traffic! But Chow Tso-hung's efforts were in vain.

Instead, my father continued to pursue his dream of opening a second school. Grandfather, of course, refused to offer any financial aid, but Chow Hui-i rented a small building in the International Settlement, which he used as a school and named Hsin-min. Thus armed with newfound hope, my father decided to bring back mother, my brother, Ching-chung, my younger sister, Ching-ling, and me from Chao-chou, where he had sent us earlier following an ugly period in Shanghai, and where he thought we might be safer.

For although the city of Canton had fallen to the enemy in October, 1938, Japanese penetration of the province of Kwangtung was not as deep as elsewhere in China, and there were pockets in Kwangtung still being held by the Nationalists, including the town of Chao-chou.

Apart from the conditions in Shanghai, Chow Hui-i's decision to send us all to Chao-chou was due to the birth of a boy (at last!) to Chung-ai, which greatly pleased both Chow Tso-hung and Li Hsing-lan. Thus my grandparents not only decided to accompany us all to Chao-chou, but Chow Tso-hung shocked my parents by offering to pay our boat fares, albeit fourth class, which put us on the deck. And although he could afford it, he himself refused to travel first class, and instead booked third class.

Thus in December, 1940, during the coldest month of the year, Chow Chung-ai and her four children set sail from Shanghai for Kwangtung, packed together on the deck in the middle of a noisy mob of demoralized, frightened refugees fleeing to—what? No one knew.

As night fell, the sea became rougher and rougher. The boat began to pitch and roll, and sheets of icy sea water cascaded over the passengers jammed on deck. All around us people were spitting and vomiting; the air was fetid with urine and excrement. Pushed and shoved by the crowd, we were pinned to the rail; my mother clutched my two-month-old baby brother tightly while the rest of us huddled against her.

As the waves rose higher and higher, striking the boat with increasing force, Chow Chung-ai screamed. My younger sister, Ching-ling, had slipped and almost fallen overboard. Mother dropped the baby and grabbed Ching-ling, snatching

18

up the baby again just as he too was about to be washed over-board.

After that terrible scene, we were moved by a sympathetic crowd into the middle of the throng, where, prostrate, we all began to sob hysterically, terrified of whatever else the future might bring.

Fortunately, certain passengers on deck knew our family and went off to seek my grandfather. Finding Chow Tso-hung in third class, they scolded him roundly for having the heart-lessness to leave his daughter-in-law and four grandchildren exposed to the elements on the open deck of fourth class.

Shamed, my grandfather not only made up the difference and purchased third-class tickets for all of us, he also de-manded that we receive berths, albeit only two, which we shared between us.

The trip lasted a week. Although we were more comfortable in third class, it was so cold that my poor baby brother, who had been frail since birth, caught pneumonia and died just as we were pulling into port. My mother never ever quite recovered from the loss of that little boy whose birth, because of my grandparents' attitude, meant so much to her.

We returned to Shanghai early in 1941. During this time the Japanese had occupied all of the eastern half of China, taking over the major cities (except foreign concessions) and all supply and communication lines, while the hapless Chinese army could only withdraw, burning everything behind them. Their only strength manifested itself in the guerrilla warfare they waged in the countryside, although even there they seemed to be fighting a losing battle.

All of this was of course far from my mind; indeed, at the age of five, I was completely unaware of what was going on. It was not only my tender years that kept me ignorant; it was also healthier for any citizen in Shanghai, regardless of age, to ap-pear indifferent.

We continued to live in the French Concession, which the Japanese, by virtue of the Axis alliance, had allowed to remain under Vichy French control following the German occupation of France in 1940. We were forced, however, to move into a smaller house because my grandfather, obsessed with the fear that he might have to finance my father's school again, decided to move in with his youngest son, Hui-ying, who did no work, but also spent no money.

Unfortunately, my father's school, Hsin-min, did not prosper, and Chow Hui-i was finally forced to realize that life in inflationary Shanghai could not continue without some better means of a livelihood; otherwise, the financial disasters that had befallen so many others would eventually crush him as well. It was then that Chow Hui-i remembered his childhood friend, Yao Chu-lo, who now lived in Chungking, in the province of Szechwan.

Yao had left Shanghai long before its occupation, because of pecuniary difficulties. Knowing that his friend's financial situation was bleak, Chow Hui-i had paid for Yao's entire family's return to Chungking, where Yao was now prospering as the owner of a large bookstore and publishing house. Chow Hui-i had followed his friend's career closely, and since there was no help forthcoming from Chow Tso-hung, the only recourse was for Chow Hui-i to turn to his old friend, Yao Chu-lo.

Thus Chow Hui-i decided to go to Chungking.

My mother, again pregnant, was so filled with anxiety about the proposed trip that she miscarried. The fact was that Szechwan, where Chungking was located, was still under Nationalist command; however, to reach Szechwan, one had to hazard passing through the Japanese Occupation Zone.

Fully aware of the dangers of such a journey, and the possibility he might not survive, Chow Hui-i took great pains to provide for his family's security before he left. Taking the few shares of stock he owned, he turned them over to a trusted friend, Chang Yao-lun, specifying that Chang pass the interest earned to Chung-ai when it became due. Chang readily agreed, assuring my father that he had nothing to worry about.

I have never forgotten the day of my father's departure. He had been everything to me, and I to him. He had protected me both against my grandmother, who had never forgiven my birth, and against my mother, from whom I felt an increasing alienation. He spoiled me. As far as Chow Hui-i was concerned, I could do no wrong, so I clung to him, taking such advantage of his love that my own mother became resentful.

20

I was eight years old when father left for Chungking. He would be gone only four months, but I felt abandoned. I cried silently during the day, and openly at night under the covers. Daily I waited for a letter from him, which never came.

Weakened by her miscarriage, my mother fell ill. Grandfather, who had become increasingly difficult and hardened over the years, never came to see his daughter-in-law, although grandmother visited us secretly, bringing something delectable to eat from time to time. Whereas she had once been cold as ice to her daughter-in-law, she was now clearly anxious to be close to us. She was as upset as we by her son's absence and, unified by a common worry, her attitude toward us changed.

At the same time, the man to whom Chow Hui-i had entrusted his stocks, and whom he had thought of as his friend, turned out to be a scoundrel. When so much time passed, and my father still had not returned, Chang assumed he had been killed. Chang's visits grew increasingly rare, and finally ceased altogether. Mother tried to see him at least a dozen times, but to no avail. Fortunately, another friend of my father's, a Korean, came to visit one day, and immediately saw that we were in financial difficulty. He succeeded in locating Chang, and, menacing him with all sorts of threats, forced Chang to turn over the small amount of money due us. There is an old Chinese proverb which says: There are two sorts of friends, one who gives you coal when it snows and the other who adds a single blossom to a flower bed. Such was the difference between my father's two friends.

My mother had become ill, and I had to take care of both her and my young sister. I tried with all my strength to keep the house going, to act like a little wife. And every day all of us offered up ardent prayers for the safe return of Chow Hui-i.

Across the street there lived a fortune-teller, a fervent Buddhist about whom I had heard a great deal. At this time, I was obsessed with two fears: the death of my mother and the death of my father. But whom could I confide in? Certainly not my grandparents, nor my simpleminded uncle. I had no friends; finally, unable to bear my anxiety any longer, I made up my mind to go see this fortune-teller and ask her the two questions which so tormented me: Would mother get well?

Would my father return? But I needed money to pay her and secretly I began putting aside small amounts until at last I managed to collect the necessary coins.

I went to see the woman immediately after school one day. Entering cautiously, petrified that my little nest egg would not be enough for such an eminent fortune-teller, I cautiously stole through a long hallway until I reached a tiny room with the door half-open. The fortune-teller was deep in prayer, surrounded by statues of Buddha. I lost my footing and fell to the floor. Startled by the noise, the old woman turned around. The smile on her face immediately calmed my anxiety and convinced me not to take to my heels and run.

"What are you doing there, little one?" she said. "Come in, come in. Don't be frightened."

I edged closer. She continued to smile. In the face of such kindness, I burst into tears and sobbed as if my heart would break.

"But what is the matter, my child?" the good woman asked.

"When will I see my father again?" I choked through my tears. "And is my mother going to die?" Then I poured out my whole story to her.

She asked me my birthdate, and told me to kneel before the goddess Kuan Yin, and there I repeated my two questions. After several minutes of silence, the fortune-teller spoke.

"My daughter," she said, "return home and be reassured. Your mother will get well very soon. You must watch the moon every night, all night, now, while it is full. When it is shrunk to half its size, you will see your papa again."

Then she began to talk about me. She told me I was very intelligent, that heaven had blessed me with many talents, and that I must always worship the goddess Kuan Yin.

"One day," she went on, "you will be a famous person. It is written in the stars. You must learn an art in which something with wood and metal is used."

Flattered by what she told me, and grateful for her kindness, I reached for my money.

"Do not pay me," she said, catching my hand. "When you are grown and begin to work, give your money to the poor."

With these words, she fell silent.

22

Her image remains engraved in my mind and in my heart for all time. Later, when I became a young woman, I tried in vain to find her. I never saw her again.

When I reached home, I was so overcome with happiness that I had to share my secret. I poured everything out to my mother. Chung-ai only half-believed me. I was so young; I had surely invented the whole story. But I didn't care. From that time on, I spent every night staring at the moon. Full and round at first, it gradually began to shrink, and soon the crescent I had been waiting for appeared.

Early one morning, as my brother and I were getting ready for school, the sky darkened and rain mixed with fog fell over the city. Suddenly the telephone rang. My father, my beloved father, rang to say that he had just arrived at the railroad station. Sobbing with joy, I screamed, "Papa! Papa! Papa!" into the receiver.

Ten minutes later, my father, wet from the rain, was home at last! And because it reminds me of the joy and love I felt on seeing my father, I have ever since that day loved the rain.

2

Chow Hui-i had been gone four months. But in fact he had spent most of this time simply trying to get into and out of Szechwan. On finally reaching Chungking, over two months after leaving Shanghai, he quickly found his friend, Yao, whose success had made him well known. Father's faith in Yao was not misplaced; on hearing my father's story of bad times, Yao without hesitation gave my father a sufficient number of small gold bars to start anew. After a short stay with Yao, father started the long and dangerous journey back to Shanghai, hiding the gold in the lining of his clothes and the soles of his shoes, which, since he had to walk most of the way, made his return trip as uncomfortable as it was dangerous. He would joke later that he didn't know which was worse, the thought of facing poverty (by removing the gold from his shoes), or capture by the Japanese or by bandits.

It was a difficult decision for Chow Hui-i to reach, but because times were so hard, father decided to forsake teaching, which he loved above all else. He resolved instead to try and make his way in the money market and began by buying into a brokerage house, convinced that he couldn't do any worse as a

24

broker than as a teacher, and that he might even do somewhat better.

In fact, father did surprisingly well. The commissions he earned managed to keep us more or less apace with rising prices, and slowly, as his commissions multiplied, we began to live more and more comfortably at home.

In changing his profession, however, my father had also changed his way of life. Now he had to make contacts and keep up a social life, often arriving home late, long after we children were already in bed. And with every passing day I felt him slipping away from me. Luckily, though, there were still Sundays, and Sunday was my day with father. As the favored child, I was taken by my father on long walks, often to Jessfield Park, with its beautiful flower beds and a wonderful small zoo, where we fed peanuts to the monkeys and laughed together at their antics.

Those were marvelous Sundays, ending all too soon. And then the interminable week began. Every evening, as the sun set, I would sit in our doorway, waiting for my father to return. I knew he wouldn't arrive until well after dark, but waiting for him was a ritual I enjoyed. It seemed to bring me closer to him, and he also looked forward to being greeted by me.

If father returned home later than usual, however, it was a source of terrible worry for both mother and me. With each day under Japanese Occupation, Chinese collaborators seemed to multiply—or at least the Japanese led us to believe so—implying that they were spying everywhere, eavesdropping on conversations and reporting everything. Just a few ill-chosen words and the Japanese "Gestapo" would appear, dragging the offender away to their headquarters at 76 Yü Yuan Road, in the old International Settlement, where prisoners were frequently tortured and executed.

My second love was my older brother, Ching-chung. Six years older than I, protective and vigilant, he was in my eyes a man. He supervised my schooling and checked my homework nightly; but most of all I loved the stories he told me.

The Chinese language is a poetic one, and conversation—even among peasants—is often indirect and metaphorical, reflecting a philosophical turn of mind intrinsic to the

Chinese. Thus the teachings of Confucius or Buddha, codes of behavior, morality, and the like are often taught through the retelling, generation after generation, of the exploits of legendary heroes and heroines and stories exemplifying the Chinese ideals.

Since both my parents were so preoccupied—father with his business, and mother again pregnant—Ching-chung took it upon himself to be my teacher. Each day I would wait impatiently for another story to begin. They always involved supreme sacrifice: the loyal servant ever ready to die for his master; the peasant equally willing to sacrifice himself for his emperor and country; the good son eager to bring honor to his family. But always stressed were filial piety, ancestral worship, reward for the good, and punishment for the bad.

As I was a girl, my brother would tell me of many heroines who sacrificed themselves for their fathers, brothers, or husbands, always practicing the virtues of humility, modesty, and servitude. My favorite heroine was one Mu-lan, or "Wild Orchid." She was an only child when war broke out (the story took place centuries earlier) and her father was obliged to fight. Being fifty years old, a sanctified age at that time, he was far too old for battle. Because she loves her father and is imbued with the Chinese spirit of sacrifice, she dresses herself as a man and takes her father's place in battle. Throughout the fierce fighting no one realizes she is female; and when the Emperor, in recognition of her achievements, offers her a distinguished wife, Mu-lan is forced to reveal her true sex. She then has to avoid becoming an imperial concubine by taking command of another punitive expedition against marauding barbarians.

These daily stories, exemplifying basic Chinese obligations and principles, made an enormous impression on me, and would affect my attitude and personal philosophy throughout my life.

But my brother had his tyrannical side as well. He went through a period during which he forced me to memorize the Four Chinese Classics—*The Analects of Confucius, The Great Learning, The Doctrine of the Mean,* and *The Works of Mencius*—none of which I understood. He also made me memorize and copy out in careful calligraphy such maxims as: Render filial piety to parents; show respect to seniors by the generation-age order; remain in harmony with clan members and the community; teach and discipline sons and grandsons; attend to one's vocation properly; and do not commit what the law forbids.

From Ching-chung, I learned that sons were to be filial to their fathers, wives dutiful to their husbands, and brothers affectionate to each other; that laziness, extravagance, violence, and gambling were the most offensive conduct. And he insisted that I copy out each and every maxim. After holding the brush for hours on end, my fingers became cramped and useless. One day I simply burst into tears and, thoroughly exhausted, sat down on the floor and refused to get up. Fortunately my father intervened, and my brother's tyranny came to an abrupt and permanent end.

My reading was not confined exclusively to Chinese literature, however. Although my father continued to make us all read and recite the tenets of certain Mandarin sages, by this time my adolescent, pre-teen tastes tended toward romantic European novels, many of them translated into Chinese. As I was attending an American school, however, I preferred to read the English translations of books like *The Three Musketeers* and *The Count of Monte Cristo*. It was this latter title that made the deepest impression on me. I knew whole passages by heart, and even took the trouble to reread the book in Chinese, the title of which translates as *The Vengeance and the Gratitude of the Count of Monte Cristo*, reflecting a more Chinese concept in its translation.

In either version, I loved this strong and willful character who was so undeserving of all the misfortune that befell him. I suffered far more from his unhappiness than I delighted in his revenge; and like him, I felt I should always be grateful to those people who had been kind to me.

Throughout Shanghai, the authorities had set up barbed-wire fences separating one neighborhood from the next. One of our favorite games consisted of trying to get through the barbed wire, a feat we were always able to manage, but not without tearing our coveralls and occasionally receiving a good knock on the head by our outraged parents.

My parents were particularly upset with me for going about

27

in pants, since, under the rules of propriety and elegance in the French Concession, little girls wore dresses, not trousers. Mother would always shake her head and predict, "You'll never get married, you'll wind up a hoodlum!" My father only laughed.

Mercifully, my mother did not know something worse—that my brother Ching-chung had taught me how to defend myself by "monkey boxing." My lessons in this peculiarly Chinese sport, which involves a lot of jumping around, took place early mornings in Jessfield Park, where we had ostensibly gone for a walk.

Sunday mornings, however, were special days, reserved exclusively for my father and me. One Sunday, though, he stunned me by refusing to take me out.

"Mei-mei," he said, using the diminutive, "I have an important meeting to attend, and this time I can't take you along."

I began to cry—partly out of disappointment, but also because I had already learned the power of feminine tears. My father succumbed, of course, and taking me by the hand, he took me with him.

After what seemed a long walk, we arrived at a lovely home, also in the French Concession. The door was opened by a beautiful young woman, elegantly dressed. She greeted both of us with a warm and welcoming smile, but her eyes shone when she looked at my father.

The three of us went out to Jessfield Park. Young though I was, I immediately became aware of a specialness in the relationship between this mysterious woman and my father. They rarely spoke and, as was proper between Chinese, they never touched. But their eyes were so fixed upon one another, and with such intensity, that they might as well have been in a public embrace.

I had never witnessed such an exchange between my father and mother.

My mouth went dry and my heart began to beat furiously. I understood.

Overwhelmed with ambivalent feelings, I didn't know what to do or say. Until now, my father's love had been reserved exclusively for me; and now this stranger had stolen him away.

28

Sensing my distress, she turned her attention to me, flattering and caressing me until she won me over.

It was dusk when we returned to her home. Announcing she had a surprise, she brought out an elegantly carved teakwood box and asked me to open it. It was filled with jewels, and to my astonishment, she selected a beautiful little gold brooch set with a jade butterfly and handed it to me saying, "Take this, Mei-mei, it's for you!"

As a child who had never before seen such jewelry, I was in a daze and desperately wanted to accept the gift. But I thought of my mother, and could not bring myself to accept the brooch.

The lady seemed to understand, and returned the brooch to its box.

"We must go now," my father declared. "It's getting very late."

Father was silent as we walked homeward; but just as we arrived, he said, "Please be a good little girl, Mei-mei, and don't mention our meeting with the lady. When you are grown up, Papa will explain everything to you."

I said nothing to anyone.

Nevertheless, mother must have sensed that something was wrong, for I could hear crying in the privacy of her own room. On occasion, I heard my parents arguing.

Then my father began to come home later and later. I no longer waited for him at the doorstep, and my mother's weeping became more frequent and less private. If, after an argument and as a gesture of good will, my father came home for dinner, the telephone never failed to ring. It was the lady. My father invariably gave in, and would stay only for dinner, leaving immediately afterward.

Unable to stand it any longer, and receiving no help or solace from her in-laws, mother finally decided to leave my father, taking me with her. Knowing how much my father loved me, and how relatively indifferent he was to his other children, Chung-ai thought this would be the best way to get him back.

Thus when I returned home from school one afternoon, mother had already packed both our bags and had a taxi waiting. We drove to father's office, arriving at the exact time mother knew the lady would be there.

The elegant lady was indeed in Chow Hui-i's office when we entered. Seeing me, she immediately realized she was being confronted by Hui-i's wife.

For what seemed an eternity, the three looked at one another in silence. I saw pain in the lady's eyes, and the suffering on both my parents' faces. I loved them both and felt utterly helpless. What would happen if they became enemies? Whose side would I choose? Tears formed in my eyes.

Mother broke the silence. "Why are you taking my husband? There are many other men everywhere! Why do you want to destroy a whole family? Have you no conscience?"

"I love Hui-i," the lady replied. "I have no intention of leaving him, even if I must remain as his mistress."

This was a courageous declaration, for in China, more so than elsewhere, mistresses are the object of considerable scorn, and their position is that of a pariah.

"That may well be, but I refuse to share him!" Chung-ai cried, launching into a description of the hardships of her early married life, of the babies she had borne, three of whom had died, of the cruel treatment she had received from her in-laws, and of how she had stuck by her husband through bad times. And now that their life had grown easier, and their troubles overcome, was it fair to make her suffer anew?

"Either you give up this woman, or you lose both me *and* Ching-li! We are ready to leave for Chao-chou now. Forever."

"Is this true, Mei-mei?" my father asked.

It was unfair of both parents to use me that way. I was much too young to make any decisions, and I loved them both. I couldn't bear to see either parent suffer this way and, for some strange reason, I even felt pity for the pretty lady, who I knew loved my father, as he loved her.

But even if my mother and father had never experienced love—how could they, betrothed as they were as children, with such different backgrounds?—mother had always been the perfect wife, and didn't deserve to suffer now.

I took my mother's side, and told my father—tears streaming down my face—that I was indeed leaving with my mother, and would never see him again.

Apart from any sense of guilt he may have felt about his

30

wife, the thought of being forever parted from his favorite, his little Mei-mei, was too much for Hui-i to bear. And so on that day my father offered me the ultimate proof of his love. He left the pretty lady he so adored.

Since kindergarten I had been attending the MacIntyre School, an establishment founded, as were most Western schools in China, by an American church group for young girls of good family. Referred to by the Chinese as the Sino-Occidental School, it was the best girls' preparatory school in Shanghai. It carried courses in foreign languages as well as in Chinese, and was generally accepted as *the* school from which one could receive a proper Western education.

The school was divided into three sections: kindergarten, primary, and secondary. Whereas the kindergarten was isolated from the rest of the school, the primary students participated in many joint activities with the secondary school. Among other things, both schools attended the same concerts and plays.

When I was eight, a concert was given by the girls in the secondary school. Those of us from the primary school crossed the big garden with its luxurious green grass and magnificent trees on our way to the auditorium. Ordinarily this marvelous garden formed a kind of barrier between the younger and older children. No one was permitted to cross it without permission and without being accompanied by a teacher.

32

All of us children felt a sense of excitement as we were led into a theater which, with its red plush seats arranged in semi-circular tiers and its stage hidden by a mysterious velvet curtain, appeared to me to be a setting right out of a fairy tale. We all took our seats and at last the curtain rose.

A hundred older girls appeared in full-length white *cheong-sams*, the traditional Chinese high-collared fitted dress that falls straight to the floor and is slit at the sides from the ankle to the knee. Each dress had a pink carnation pinned to the front of the stiff collar. I thought they were all breathtakingly beautiful, and I wished I were one of them.

The girls formed part of a choral group, and when they sang I thought their voices were absolutely celestial. I was transfixed, and disappointed when they concluded and the curtain fell. But my disappointment was short-lived, for when the curtain rose again, to my delight and wonder, the stage was bare except for a piece of furniture, whose name and function were totally unknown to me.

This strange, shining black object stood in the center of the stage. Wide-eyed, I craned my neck in order to see it better. Then a graceful young girl appeared, bowed to the audience, and seated herself on a bench facing the object. A moment's silence passed as she seemed to stretch her fingers; suddenly her hands flew over the keyboard like enchanted birds, and the sound that was emitted from that strange black object was more beautiful than anything I had ever heard.

I had to be nudged out of my seat when the concert was over, so transfixed was I, the sounds of the piano concerto still ringing in my ears.

As soon as we were dismissed from school I raced home; long before reaching our front door I was panting and shouting excitedly, "Mama! Mama!" Chung-ai was busy tending to my new baby brother, Ching-chang, as I burst into the room.

Startled, Chung-ai tried to make sense out of my excitement. She had no idea what a piano was either, and all I succeeded in doing was to disturb and confuse her. Finally she ordered me to calm down and be quiet, suggesting that I had best discuss with my father whatever it was that bothered me.

When Hui-i returned I immediately launched into what I

had seen and heard at the concert, begging him to allow me to take piano lessons. To quiet me, and also because I was his favorite, he agreed. Having gotten him to agree to the lessons, I went further and demanded that he also purchase the instrument. I was amazed and overjoyed when he quickly agreed to that as well.

Several days later a crate arrived. Its size seemed much smaller than the piano I remembered, but considering that I had seen the instrument only once, and then from afar, I thought I might have been mistaken. When the crate was opened, however, I had a great deal of difficulty recognizing my lordly piano. The crate contained a harmonium, a small reed organ in which a bellows forces air through free metallic reeds. Not only did it not resemble my precious piano, it was also far less expensive, which is why my father had acquiesced so easily to my pleading.

My disappointment was painful; but it was hardly my father's fault. My confused description of the piano, interrupted by my equally breathless interjections about its sound, had led my father to believe I was talking about a harmonium. Once he realized I had been talking about a piano, he became more reluctant about its purchase, and instead told me to be patient, he would take care of everything in due course.

In the meantime I started on my piano lessons. My teacher, Miss Winfield, was British but both spoke and was knowledgeable in Chinese—highly unusual for a foreigner, particularly the English-speaking ones, who prided themselves on speaking no Chinese (even after as long a stay as twenty-five years) except for that which was necessary to address the servants. It was Miss Winfield who not only transliterated my name from Chow Ching-li (in Chinese our last name rhymes with "show") to the more European "Julie" ("show-li"), which became my Western name and would stay with me for the rest of my life, but she also convinced me that if I intended to study seriously, I had better have a piano at home on which to practice constantly.

I wasted no time in repeating Miss Winfield's advice to my father. Unfortunately, I picked the day when grandmother was visiting. When I told father what Miss Winfield had said, he immediately called a music shop to ask if there were any pianos available. Yes, of course, the shopkeeper replied, adding that the price was ten times higher than that of the harmonium. Stunned, my father repeated the price to grandmother. She, of course, admonished Hui-i for even thinking of so great an extravagance. After all, I was only a child, not even the eldest, and a daughter at that! It was unthinkable.

Father kept silent. I assumed all was lost and wept bitterly.

But father came up with a solution: we would *rent* a piano! This did little to assuage grandmother's contention that I was being spoiled rotten, and in retrospect, she was probably right. In any event, she took every opportunity she could to remind my family of that fact; these occasions irritated me tremendously, but they also inspired me to prove to her and my family that I hadn't been wasting either father's money or my time.

Spurred additionally by the memory of the white-haired fortune-teller's prophesy that I would succeed in life and become famous through an instrument "made of wood and metal," I practiced religiously for at least two hours a day.

My playing, however, was hardly comparable to that of the pretty girl I had seen on stage, and I was often discouraged. My dreams were such it never occurred to me that she was several years' practice ahead of me.

A few months later my little sister, Ching-ling, joined me at the piano. My father, always fair-minded, thought she should have the same opportunities as I. Now that there were two little girls practicing the piano, both my mother and grandmother were delighted; after all, four hands on a rented piano were cheaper than two.

Unlike me, however, Ching-ling initially showed no enthusiasm for the piano and clearly preferred to be outside playing with her friends, whose voices she could hear while banging away in agony at her scales.

I myself had long since graduated from the scale stage and was now playing rather complicated pieces. By studying and practicing exhaustively, I had managed to make considerable progress by the end of my first year.

At the same time that I was discovering the delight and torment of music, I was also exposed for the first time to the reality of death. One day after school, my mother met me at the door of the house and warned me to stay close to home. It seemed that my aunt had just died and we would be going to the morgue almost immediately.

This aunt was the wife of my simpleminded uncle Hui-ying. Mother took us to the morgue. I had never seen such an establishment before, with its tiers of coffins, hundreds of heavy wooden boxes covered with black lacquer and stacked one on top of the other. In China, coffins can be kept for years in perfect condition before they are put into the ground, which is a godsend for the poor. The rich, of course, are buried immediately, for all the arrangements have been made long in advance. Although he could have had his daughter-in-law buried right away, my grandfather, Chow Tso-hung, had no intention of laying out money for the funeral of the wife of a son who had never done a day's work in his life.

In China, the body is first exposed in an open coffin in a room draped in white, the color of mourning in China. The portrait of the deceased, also draped in white, stands in front of the coffin on a table covered with a long, white cloth. Little dishes of fruit, vegetables, and meat, meant to accompany the dead on their journey, are placed in front of the portrait, while candles stand at either side. A thick carpet is unrolled in front of the table for the benefit of those who come to kneel and pay their last respects. After a ceremony in the presence of the entire family, a sack of lime is sprinkled over the body. Only then is the coffin closed and the nails driven in. It is customary at that moment to cry and sob dramatically with great passion to prove to all how much the dead was loved. People sobbed noisily, cried out, and even spoke to the corpse. "How could you leave us?" they would wail. "How we are suffering!" All this was simultaneously sung and spoken, as in a Chinese opera.

Terrified by the racket, I was filled with horror at the idea of anyone being shut up in a box. At last all the mourners collected themselves, my aunt's coffin was placed on one of the many shelves, and the ceremony came to an end.

That same year saw both the end of the war and the birth of my youngest sister. Both events took place in August, 1945.

36

On August 6, the Americans had dropped the atomic bomb on Hiroshima, frightening the Japanese into capitulation. And while the official surrender did not take place until September 2, on board the U.S.S. *Missouri* in Tokyo Bay, for all intents and purposes the Japanese admitted defeat on August 14, with the issuance by Hirohito of an imperial edict ending the war.

All Shanghai went wild with joy. In my little-girl view, I thought that the whole city was celebrating the birth of my new sister, named Ching-ching, or "Celebration," in honor of the occasion.

The war might be over and the Japanese crushed, but the eight-year struggle had left its toll: China was devastated, and the Chinese people exhausted almost beyond endurance. Peasants were starving and restless, while inflation, caused by the continual increase of note issues, ruined many lives, reducing all but the corrupt and very rich to a state of destitution. Weary and impatient after having waited so many years for peace and recovery, the people, with some justification, blamed everything on the party in power, the Kuomintang.

My own family, however, like so many others in Shanghai, were far more concerned with the daily struggle for existence than with the conflict being waged between the Nationalists, led by Chiang Kai-shek, and the Communists, led by Mao Tse-tung.

While a whole world was being transformed in the northwest, Chow Hui-i's brokerage house was in fact flourishing. My father became sufficiently affluent so that my mother, with her five children, was able to hire a servant.

One evening, our new servant was standing in the doorway with my littlest sister in her arms, gossiping with one of the neighbor's servants. The neighbor's daughter was there as well, a rather chunky girl a year or so older than I and whom I knew slightly. Unnoticed, I was standing a few yards away. Suddenly their conversation made my ears prick up.

"I sometimes wonder," the neighbor's servant was saying, "just how you manage to eat so well in your house. Your master must earn a lot of money."

Since our servant had been with us only a short while, she said nothing.

The neighbor's daughter answered for her.

"Everybody knows what he does," she said. "He makes his money from opium."

My blood froze.

"That's a lie!" I screamed, rushing over. "My father is not an opium dealer! And he'll never be one!"

I knew from various conversations I had overheard that my grandfather had tried to push my father into the opium trade when times had been bad, but my father had always refused.

Looking at me insolently, the girl repeated that my father was a dealer. Overwhelmed with rage, I threw myself at her, even though she was bigger than I. Grabbing her around the neck, I said, "Repeat that my father is an honorable man! Say it! Say it!"

She refused, taking hold of my braids and yanking so violently that in my agony, I involuntarily bit her hand. She let go immediately. Suddenly I remembered the monkey boxing my brother had taught me, and my fists hit out almost without my realizing it. To this day, I have no idea what really happened. Suddenly the girl was lying on the ground. I threw myself on her, and began pummeling her face with my fists, smashing that ugly mouth that had tarnished my father's reputation.

The two terrified servants, each with a baby in her arms, rushed into their respective houses seeking our mothers.

"What have you done, you horrid child!" mother cried when she saw the girl lying on the ground. "Ask her to forgive you!" mother shrieked at me.

Panting, I refused. The girl got to her feet, covered with blood. Her mother appeared and her servant blurted out the true story. Ordering her own daughter into the house, our neighbor took up my defense and apologized for her daughter.

When my brother came home, he was immediately informed of what the neighbor's girl had said, and of the beating I had given her.

"Little sister," he said, turning to me and smiling, "I am very proud of you. You have defended our honor. That is good." And the next day he brought me a box of candy.

Ching-chung, then sixteen years old, was already considered a man in China. I was ten, considered almost a young woman. Indeed, it was because of my age that Chung-ai reprimanded me severely.

"What will become of you?" she wailed, taking up a refrain I had heard many times already. "A girl who spends her time playing in the streets, a girl who fights! You run around like a boy! You laugh like a boy! You'll never, never get married . . ."

From childhood, Chinese girls are required to be reserved and never express feelings. Condemned to playing the humblest of roles, they are forbidden to show joy or sadness. A girl could only suggest a smile, walk softly, and take small, mincing steps. I was the exact opposite.

But my father defended me, which infuriated mother. In China, the father should be severe, the mother indulgent. With us, however, it was the reverse. Father continued to spoil me while my mother futilely attempted to discipline me.

Shortly after this incident, Chung-ai suffered one of the most painful experiences of her life. Coming home from school one afternoon, I found mother in tears—she had just learned that her own mother had died.

I hardly knew my maternal grandmother. I vaguely remember having seen her in Chao-chou when we made that sad trip from Shanghai to Kwangtung. That I had not known her was not unusual, however. In China, once a man and a woman marry, it is the husband's parents who take command. The young couple normally move in with the husband's family, while the wife's parents are kept at a distance. In fact, the inferior position of the wife's parents is reflected in the language. In Chinese, they are called "the outside grandparents." My maternal grandmother was not exempt from this custom. She had had long experience with solitude, for her husband had died before my mother was born. Only the woman fortunate enough to have a son could be assured of support in her old age, for even if this son married, she would still be surrounded and sustained by his family. A daughter could never provide such consolation. That is why this woman, embittered by a life without a man, had been so harsh toward my mother when Chung-ai was small. "Why weren't you born a boy!" she used to shout at her, striking her.

Although my grandmother was widowed very young, she never remarried because of an old Chinese sanction decreeing that a widow's moral obligation is to remain a widow. Remarriage was equivalent to dishonor; it brought disgrace upon her and upon her family.

And so my grandmother ended her days as a vegetarian in a shack in Chao-chou. My father sent her money, not out of duty, but because of his kind and generous nature. But it came too late for her to take advantage of it. Death earned her the right to be placed among the saints in the ancestral temple of Chao-chou, an example of ideal Chinese womanhood.

During the winter that followed the departure of the Japanese, our family life underwent a radical transformation. Yao, my father's close friend from Chungking who had financed father, left his home in Szechwan and came to settle in Shanghai. Yao and my father thought of each other as brothers; thus, they decided that both families should live under the same roof.

Yao, a big man of thirty-eight, was the same age as my father. He had two wives, a privilege still permitted in China. Curiously, the wives were sisters. Having married the oldest and ugliest first, he subsequently met the younger, as she often came to their home to visit her sister. In fact, her visits became so frequent that one day she found herself pregnant. Thus, Yao married her as well. In China, the second wife is referred to as the "little wife," a more or less pejorative term. When he arrived in Shanghai, Yao had two sons and two daughters by his first wife and two daughters by his "little wife." As there were five children in our family, that made a total of ten children and nine adults, including Yao's oldest son and his wife and two servants. We were going to need a great deal of space if we were all going to live together.

After a long and arduous search, we finally found a suitable house. It was huge, with three floors (entirely furnished), and belonged to a widowed Englishwoman who wanted to return to her country. On the ground floor, large doors opened onto a garden carpeted with thick, green grass and enclosed by a high wrought-iron grillwork fence. A paved alley on one side led to the garage. There was room for everyone to be more than comfortable, and the decision to buy was unanimous.

Because his friend Yao was heavy, and therefore quickly became short of breath, my father generously turned over the second floor to him. Fortunately, this floor contained a sufficient number of rooms for each of his wives to have separate quarters. Our family occupied the third floor, where, as on Yao's floor, there were four bedrooms: one for my parents, one for my older brother, one for me and my next youngest sister, and another for the two little ones.

The Englishwoman had already reserved passage on a boat for England, but she was not leaving for another week. Consequently, we had decided to move in in two stages: first our family, then Yao's. Everything would have been fine had it not been for the Englishwoman's enormous dog. Chinese are not accustomed to seeing dogs in houses, and this one made a particularly disagreeable impression on us. Its mistress had assured us that it had the sweetest disposition on earth and we had absolutely no cause to be frightened. The fact is we were terrified of the dog, which probably explains the disaster that followed. When Ching-chung first laid eyes on the creature, my elder brother took to his heels. The dog raced after him, managing to bite his hand. My mother took the Englishwoman to account.

"Madam," she declared, "I have five children. I do not intend to sit by and watch your dog bite them one after the other. Would you please be so kind as to do something to keep this animal out of the way?"

The woman was disconsolate because she was unable to take the dog with her and had hoped to leave it with us. Fortunately for the dog, she managed to find another home for it; unfortunately for me, however, this encounter inspired in me a lifelong aversion to dogs of all kinds.

42

As soon as the woman left for England, Yao installed his family on the second floor. Or, more accurately, he installed himself throughout the house, imposing his family on all of us. To begin with, his second wife was furious because her room was not as nicely furnished as that of her elder sister. Although Yao clearly preferred his second wife to his plain, dull-witted first, he was obligated by tradition to make certain that the first wife be given preferential treatment, and she therefore occupied the better of the two quarters. However, the second wife was not only stubborn, but a born troublemaker as well; no one was going to tell *her* what to do! On the very first night we were treated to a concert of shouts, arguments, and slammed doors beneath us. The second wife's obstinacy had finally driven Yao wild with rage, and from the sound of it, he had decided to beat her up. Thus we passed our first night together in the new house.

The days that followed did nothing to change our impression of Yao as a bad-tempered character who could behave abominably toward both his wives and his children. Had we not seen him slap his twenty-year-old son across the face in the presence of the son's wife, because of some minor infraction, we would not have believed it. All the children in the house scurried away at his approach, like mice before a cat.

Well aware of the situation, Chung-ai constantly reminded us that Yao had saved our father, and that without him, we would all have been reduced to begging. It was therefore our duty to show our utmost respect for "Uncle" Yao. I did my best, but it wasn't easy.

In fact, Yao was simply behaving like a typical old-fashioned tyrannical Chinese father of the peasant sort. I therefore appreciated all the more the love and affection that reigned in our own family, and I was especially grateful for my father's gentleness. Hui-i never lost his temper, although it is difficult to say whether his goodness was the result of a more modern code of behavior, or simply because of his own good nature. Whichever it was, the comparison with Yao only endeared my father to me all the more.

Hui-i and Yao had not only decided to live together, but to

become business associates as well. Together they established a company that imported textiles from Europe, particularly materials such as velvet and wallpaper from France. Our home was filled with samples of velvet and one room was even covered with French wallpaper. The company had a warehouse in Shanghai and three cars, two Fords and a Buick, which were parked in our garage. Thus began a period of prosperity, if not to say luxury. This transformation in our lives was due in part to Uncle Yao's taste for the extravagant. Legend had it that people from Hangchow spared no expense when it came to creature comfort, and Uncle Yao had been born there. Indeed, it seemed, the natives of Hangchow were the exact opposite of those from Chao-chou.

The two partners ran their business at full speed. Not only did they work with feverish intensity, but they were obliged to cultivate a vast network of social acquaintances as well. Thus they also frequented the best restaurants in Shanghai, and gave many parties. The house was often turned upside down by the preparations for their various receptions. Yao had hired a cook, two maids, and a gardener. We were living in the lap of luxury.

Chung-ai, whose one maid was sorely overworked by keeping track of five children, wanted to hire a second *amah*. After all, our standard of living had risen spectacularly. But my grandmother, who was regularly consulted even though she no longer lived with us, was firmly opposed to such an extravagance. There matters stood, a stalemate, until my grandmother herself came up with a brilliant idea. Instead of "hiring" the services of a maid, why not simply buy two girls from Chao-chou?

This sale of little girls was still commonplace in the 1940s. People flocked to the village to buy pairs of girls as if they were purchasing a couple of goats. The children, forced onto the market by the poverty of their families, were usually eight or nine years old and were never told the truth. Their suspicions were allayed by various stories—such as that they were going on a sightseeing trip with some nice people—and they were brutally awakened only upon arrival at their destination. Their training began immediately, and whatever was left of

44

the child in them was quickly eradicated. Individual fates were of course subject to the character of their masters; some girls were bought by decent people and were well treated.

Others, however, suffered terribly and were powerless to protest. All of us had heard our fair share of ghastly stories, and so my grandmother's proposal was met with great hostility. We all felt that the purchase of little girls was barbaric and we cited the case of one of my father's cousins, who had bought a nine-year-old girl and could barely contain himself until she was old enough to be seduced. When the girl found herself pregnant, the cousin's wife, who had four children herself, grew insanely jealous. Terrified of her husband, she dared not beat her "rival," but she became obsessed with the idea of killing her. She managed to turn her children against the servant and when the right occasion presented itself, she ordered them to surround the girl and kick her in the stomach. The children fulfilled their task so well that the girl had a miscarriage. Bleeding profusely, she was forced to take to her bed where her seducer's wife calmly watched her die.

In spite of all this, however, we were finally compelled to carry out my grandmother's decision. To disobey your parents is to annul a hundred good deeds, the Chinese proverb goes. And so my father, in order not to void any good deeds, consented to a bad one. One of my grandmother's friends was commissioned to buy two little girls. It was understood that we would take one, and my grandmother the other.

The two little girls in question were eight and nine. The one we took was called Tso-fei. She was very sweet and was received by us as if she were one of the children. The second, Wo-li, went to my grandmother's, where she suffered a different fate. In order to calm her fears, she had been told that she was going on a lovely trip to visit Shanghai. When she found herself alone with an old shrew who put her to work immediately, Wo-li threw a colossal temper tantrum. Possessing neither understanding nor compassion, my grandmother began to beat her. The child was desperate. Hearing what had happened, my mother was so shocked that she proposed an exchange at once; she would take the "impossible" little servant and we would give the gentle Tso-fei to my grandmother.

45

And so we found ourselves with a rebellious child-slave. It took her a while to learn to accept us, and when she finally did so, it was only because of the kind treatment she received from my mother, who did everything possible to help her forget her unhappy situation. Our own situation, on the other hand, became rather more difficult. Not used to shoes, Wo-li insisted upon walking barefoot in the house. Since we had no central heating, the house was usually quite cold. Wo-li's nose ran constantly, but, refusing to use the handkerchief we had given her, she wiped her nose on her sleeve. Consequently, the sleeves of her cotton shirt served both as cleaning rag and handkerchief. She was filthy.

Still believing that she had been brought to Shanghai as a simple tourist, she now began to demand to be sent home. We had never told her the truth; finally, after ten days, she disappeared. My mother combed the neighborhood without success. What became of her no one knows.

Tso-fei, her little friend, had better luck, even though she had to put up with my grandparents. My mother, Chung-ai, kept a sharp eye out for her well-being. My family gave money to my grandmother for Tso-fei's education. A maid by day, she attended school at night, receiving a good education. Some years later she left grandmother to marry a man of her own choice. Settling in Hong Kong, she had three children, and ran a small factory that made beaded purses and, as far as I know, is still prospering.

After the disappearance of Wo-li, my mother refused to hear any more proposals about the purchase of little girls. Instead, she hired an older woman from Shanghai. Now she had two full-time maids, who relieved her of a great many domestic duties.

My father's import-export business continued to flourish. At home, however, the differences in behavior and morality between Yao's family and our own became increasingly troublesome.

Indeed, the essential difference between Yao and my father was one of education. As far as Chinese customs were concerned, Yao represented the worst, my father the best. In China, at this time, there were two kinds of schools and two kinds of instruction. The secondary school that my father had first attended was completely Chinese. Later on, however, he attended St. John's University, one of the numerous establishments founded by missionaries. It was there that he came in contact with the books, language, and thought of the Western world.

My father never wore anything other than Western-style dress. Shanghai offered a wide variety of European and Asian clothing, just as American cars mingled in the streets with coolie-pulled rickshaws or more modern motorized ones. Chinese dressed in Western style for important dinners at lavish restaurants such as the Park Hotel, which, with twenty-four floors and a view of the racetrack, was the tallest and most fashionable building in Shanghai.

Yao, however, was always dressed in the traditional Chinese costume worn by both men and women. It was not that Yao was more Chinese than my father—only his lack of education had made him less open to change.

On the other hand, my father cultivated an easygoing and affectionate manner with his children that had something of the American in it. He went out with us, played with us, never scolded us, and knew how to create and maintain a warm family atmosphere.

Yao was exactly the opposite; he beat his children and spent hours playing mahjong with his male friends. My father would never play mahjong in front of his children, for fear of their developing a taste for it. But as gentle and indulgent as he was with us, his own father was a strict disciplinarian who displayed no warmth or emotion whatsoever.

At the MacIntyre secondary school, to which I progressed in 1946 at the age of ten, two subjects became especially important to me: English and music, particularly music. My progress on the piano had been rapid, and I was in a fever of excitement when I saw my name on the list of girls selected to perform in the annual concert. I shall never forget the first piece I played in public, *The Lark,* by the nineteenth-century Russian composer Glinka. Here I was at last, alone on the brightly lit stage, like the beautiful girls I had marveled at years ago. To say that I was moved would be an understatement. Somehow, I managed to play my piece through to the end, when applause broke out and sounds of praise were heard throughout the school.

A few days after the concert, my parents were summoned by the headmistress.

"You have an extremely talented daughter," she told them, in the presence of my piano teacher. "We must begin to encourage her in this direction at once."

At this time, it was necessary to have completed six years of secondary school in order to enter the university, but only three were required for the conservatory. The headmistress felt that I should go there, but first I would have to find another piano teacher. Not that my school did not have excellent ones, but they were concerned with teaching music as a complement to a general education, whereas for me it was now a question of a career. Thus, I needed a teacher from the conservatory itself.

The following day, clutching a recommendation from my headmistress and accompanied by my little sister Ching-ling, I took the bus to the home of a Miss Ling, who had agreed to take me on as a pupil. She was indeed far more demanding than my piano teacher at school, for she taught me not only technique but gave me exercises to make my fingers stronger and more dextrous. The price was higher, too, the more so since in my mother's eyes the lessons were a total waste of time and money. The first month went by peacefully enough, but she balked at the second. Not daring to stop everything, she nonetheless decided that my younger sister would take no more lessons. All I had to do was pass on to her what Miss Ling taught me and thus we would get two lessons for the price of one. Unfortunately for Ching-ling, I was of course unable to teach her as well as I was taught, and in the end, Miss Ling took pity on her and allowed her to continue, teaching both of us for the price of a single lesson. Needless to say, Miss Ling rose several notches in my mother's esteem.

I was almost eleven, my brother Ching-chung going on seventeen. He was a handsome boy, tall and athletic, a good soccer player. And although he had begun to study law, he continued to watch over me. He had always been my favorite of all my brothers and sisters and I looked on him as my protector, as a sort of second father, which is why the secret he confided to me in 1947 was so shattering.

It all began after dinner one evening. My father asked Chung-ai and the children to leave the room; he wanted to talk to his son in private. Everyone went downstairs, but I lagged behind, piqued by both curiosity and a strange uneasiness. When I knelt and peered through the keyhole, I realized that Ching-chung was in for a scolding. In China, respect for one's children requires that such confrontations take place without witnesses. Ching-chung stood while my father sat on the sofa, and as the sofa was near the door, I overheard everything.

"I have just seen your grades," my father was saying gravely. "They are extremely poor. And in addition, your behavior these last few months has been most peculiar. I would like to ask you two questions. Why is your work going so badly? And why do you come home so late at night? I am well aware that you play soccer, but surely not in the dark?"

Troubled and embarrassed, my brother did not reply. Hui-i repeated his questions. Still no reply.

"Have you decided not to answer me?" Hui-i's tone of voice rose in anger.

I had never in my entire life seen my father angry; I had never seen him raise his voice or his hand to any of his children. But now, for the first time, I saw his face suffused with rage. Ching-chung had gone white as a sheet. Unable to bear the sight of my brother's misery, I began to cry, at the same time keeping my eye at the keyhole. As Hui-i's shouts grew louder, my brother continued to maintain silence. I began to sob audibly. My father stopped in mid-sentence and, striding to the door, wrenched it open.

"What are you doing here, Mei-mei?" he said, using the diminutive.

"You are being mean to my brother," I blurted out, rushing to Ching-chung's side as if to protect him.

"I am *not* being mean to your brother," my father replied. "And in any case, none of this is any concern of yours!"

"It is, too! I love my brother!"

My father relented and, thanks to me, the inquisition ended. I was very happy. Hui-i turned one last time toward his son.

"I demand that you return home at a more reasonable hour," he said in conclusion, calmly but severely. "And I also hope that you will now begin to work more diligently."

Alas, his words fell upon deaf ears. Chung's work during the second trimester was even worse than during the first. In fact, it was so bad that the faculty suspended him from classes for an entire trimester.

My father was stupefied. Ching-chung seemed unruffled. As for me, given the high opinion I had of my brother's intelligence, I found such a punishment inconceivable. Every time my father scolded him, I could not help crying. What saddened me the most, however, was that I could not understand what had happened. What could have possibly brought about the disgrace of a brother whom I considered a hero? Could he have changed so drastically? There *was* something strange about his behavior. When Ching-chung realized how troubled I was, he made an effort to explain.

"Don't cry, little sister. Your brother will never be a hooligan. On the contrary, I am following the way of the true Chinese spirit. I am working for the good of the people and the state. I will never bring disgrace upon our family. You must trust me." I nodded in agreement, but I didn't understand.

Three months later, Ching-chung went back to the university, but his behavior remained unchanged. I continued to find him strange and withdrawn, but since I believed in him, I stopped interrogating him for a month or two. Then one day at school, I ran into a friend. She seemed so upset that I insisted upon knowing why.

"My brother's been arrested by Chiang Kai-shek's police," she told me. "We don't know where he is. We haven't had any news from him for a week. They must be torturing him . . ."

She went on to tell me what she'd heard about people being picked up on the street or at home for interrogation; about how they were tied to chairs and had their nails torn out with pincers.

50

"But why has your brother been arrested?" I asked. "What has he done?"

"Because he's a Communist revolutionary," she replied.

I didn't quite know what she meant, but I felt an awful fear for my brother. Could it be that Ching-chung was one of them? Could he too be a Communist? And then I suddenly remembered his words: *What I am doing is for the good of the people and the state.*

I broke into a cold sweat; if my brother was mixed up in all this, he too might be arrested and tortured. I was terrified.

Anxiety-stricken, I waited all day on our front steps for Ching-chung's return, my eyes fixed on the gate at the end of the garden. I felt I was living through a second great tragedy, the first being my father's departure for Chungking, when it seemed as if he had abandoned me. And now I might lose Ching-chung.

As the sun reddened the horizon and evening came at last, I prayed to God to protect Ching-chung. It was becoming chilly, but I continued to sit there, staring at the gate, imagining the worst. Suddenly he was in front of me, his books under his arm, wearing his usual open-collared shirt and navy pullover. He looked strong and handsome. Visions of his arrest and torture fled as I rushed to him, my face streaming with tears of joy.

"Whatever is the matter, little sister?" he exclaimed, surprised by my distress. "Why are you crying?"

His hand was on the back of my neck, an old gesture of his I remembered from my earliest childhood. I clutched his other hand tightly. My whole day had been filled with the agony of anxiety and now tears of relief coursed down my cheeks. I pulled Ching-chung into my room and closed the door carefully. Whispering so as not to be overheard by the other children or the servants, I asked the question that had been tormenting me.

"Are you a Communist?"

"What are you talking about?" Ching-chung exclaimed, looking wide-eyed. "Where did you get such nonsense?"

"If you love me, you must tell me the truth," I insisted, refusing to be put off. "I can't stand not knowing what you're doing! You must tell me everything."

"Little sister," Ching-chung replied gravely, "I will tell you a secret. But you must promise that it will remain between us, because I do not want to worry our parents. Will you swear never to tell a soul?"

"I swear!"

"All right. Now first of all, you must stop crying."

And then Ching-chung told me the whole story. It was true; he was a Communist.

"If you talk," he added, "I will be arrested."

"I won't talk."

But I thought: *My brother could be arrested, tortured—killed even—at any minute!*

"You're crazy," I cried. "Why? Why?"

I thought of the many ugly stories I had heard about the Communists, and here was my brother, sacrificing himself for people who were being called outlaws and rapists! I repeated these stories to him.

"Nationalist slander!" he replied angrily. "You live in a beautiful house, little sister, and you eat every day, and you have nice clothes and go to school. But do you realize how many starving peasants there are in our country, who sleep in holes, with only some straw for blankets? You're lucky to be able to go to school, but this is a country of illiterates because China is corrupt and has been a slave to foreigners who have been allowed to exploit us, insult us. Do you remember, before the war, in the parks in the foreign concessions the signs on the grass that said 'No Dogs or Chinese Allowed'? China has disgraced herself in the past; the Nationalists disgrace us now, enlisting foreign help, exploiting the peasants, robbing the cities, and diverting public funds into private accounts. Why, little sister, do you realize that Chiang Kai-shek preferred to lose China to the Japanese rather than let the Communists, *Chinese* Communists mind you, 'gain' any territory!

"The Kuomintang is rotten to the core and destroying China. I cannot live with this. But the Communists under Mao Tse-tung's leadership can heal China. We are in the middle of a civil war, and it would be dishonorable not to participate, to join on the side of Mao. And if you are courageous and really love me, you will encourage me . . ."

Fired by his own rhetoric, Ching-chung continued talking about the class struggle, the protest against foreign elements in China, the Confucian traditions that were holding China back, the necessity of changing society, of acting, not reacting, to events. Over and over again the name of Mao Tse-tung cropped up. Ching-chung spoke about him reverentially, as if he were a messiah.

Even now when I close my eyes I can hear my brother's voice—fired with enthusiasm and heroic resolve as he spoke of Mao, of the struggle for a new China.

I was only eleven, and hardly understood what he was talking about, or what events were taking place in China. I only knew that my beloved brother was dedicated to something I didn't comprehend but which might cost him his life. I began to cry.

Bending down, Ching-chung put his arms around me.

"Little sister," he said, smiling, "if everyone were afraid of arrest or torture, who would help China to become great and strong? Cowardice is unforgivable. Instead of crying, you should be proud of me."

He handed me his handkerchief. I dried my eyes and willed myself to stop crying. I had always loved and respected my brother; but now my respect had grown a thousandfold. Everything he said rang with such heroism, such conviction. If he was willing to risk everything—perhaps even his life—for his cause, I knew I must, too.

In 1948, during Easter, my school organized two trips for its pupils. We all talked of nothing else for weeks; going on a trip seemed the most exciting event in the entire world. We were to visit Suchow and Hangchow, two famous old cities which contained some of the most sumptuous treasures in all of China. An old Chinese saying goes: In heaven there is paradise, but on earth there are Suchow and Hangchow.

The first trip was short, for Suchow was only an hour and a half by train northwest of Shanghai. We were to leave in the morning and be back home again by nightfall. Even so, I had to have my father's permission, which he gave, but only on the condition that my brother accompany me as a combination chaperon and bodyguard. He was not to lose sight of me for an instant; he was entirely responsible for my precious person. Poor Ching-chung! Not only was he the only boy in a group of fifteen girls, but he was required to remain a certain distance away and had to travel alone, bored and embarrassed, keeping his eye on me from afar.

In this manner, led by a teacher, we visited Suchow, the Hill of the Tiger, and the seven pagodas. In this elegant city—which had once been a fashionable meeting place for the idle rich, the sensual intellectuals, and the women with the smallest waists and feet in China—a certain number of famous gardens remained intact, marvelously landscaped, like the parks of the Forest of the Lion with its belvederes and fountains, haunted by the meditations of countless generations of monks and mandarins. I was still too young to appreciate all this; in fact, I was not even interested in the bonbons we bought at a candy shop, for I had never had a sweet tooth. And so I returned home with no particular memories.

My second trip however, was more memorable and took place in the fall. The excursion to Hangchow was to last for three days and it seemed highly unlikely that my father would consent. How could he imagine his little Mei-mei absent from home for three days! When I wanted something, however, my father was rarely able to resist. This time he behaved as if I were leaving for the North Pole. He ordered money sewn into each article of my clothing—if I were lost I would always be able to get back home. My pockets were filled with little pieces of paper on which my address had been clearly written. Given the fact that my brother was forced to accompany me once again, the likelihood of my becoming lost was minimal, to say the least!

The unfortunate Ching-chung had to spend three days in almost total solitude, sleeping at a hotel while all the girls slept in a school, always watching me from a distance. In spite of his absurd situation, he never once complained; in fact, he seemed perfectly content just to fulfill his obligations. As for me, although I had not appreciated the beauty of Suchow, Hangchow impressed me enormously. We went to West Lake, the mosque, the statue of the Giant Laughing Buddha, Yellow Dragon Cave, Dragon Well Spring, the Grotto of the Purple Clouds, where people came for a bit of fresh, cool air in summer, the Pagoda of the Six Harmonies, and countless other monuments and tombs which have delighted thousands of tourists. I remember, too, that the food was exquisite. There were exotic salted dishes, lots of shellfish and lobster, and the famous Hangchow tea, the best in all of China.

On the third day, our little group took the train back to Shanghai. It was one o'clock in the morning when we pulled into the station and the buses had stopped running. Our teacher decided there were too many of us to take taxis and that, in any case, it would be too expensive. Suddenly she remembered that one of the girls lived quite close to the railroad station and suggested that all of us should spend the rest of the night at her house. And so we went, my brother following at his customary distance. We spent the whole night chattering and listening to records instead of sleeping. Then, as soon as the sun rose, my brother took me by the hand and led me home.

We found my mother alone in the living room. When she saw us, she jumped to her feet.

"Why are you so late?" she cried. "Where have you been! You were supposed to be home last night!"

Pale and exhausted with worry, she had waited up for us all night long. When we managed to explain what had happened, she scolded us severely for not having telephoned. Indeed, we hadn't thought of it.

"Your father's been waiting for you at the station since eleven o'clock last night," she cried, suddenly remembering. "He's still there . . ."

Apparently, we had missed each other because my group did not leave the station by the main exit. Tormented by guilt but also furious, I rushed back to the station with my brother. From far off, I could see Hui-i pacing up and down on the platform. I rushed up and threw myself into his arms, showering him with kisses. It was highly improper for a child my age to kiss a parent in public, but that morning I didn't give a fig for convention! Instead of scolding us, as another father might have done, Hui-i instead smiled with relief, and we all returned to the house.

From this time on, my brother went with me on each of my excursions. But whereas these first two were unimportant, the third, alas, was to have grave consequences for Ching-chung.

But that was far off in the future. Meanwhile, Hui-i's business ran smoothly and we were becoming more and more prosperous. As for my mother, now that she had two servants at her beck and call, she had a great deal more time to spend on herself. Her first project was to install an altar in the house with a statue of the goddess Kuan Yin. Morning and evening, after preparing the three sticks of incense, the cup of tea, and lighting the wick in the small bowl of oil, Chung-ai knelt before the statue to pray. Like all good Buddhists, she abstained from meat and fish on the first and the fifteenth of each month, but she also spread another ten days of abstinence through the month. On these days, the orthodox eat neither meat nor fish nor even eggs, confining themselves exclusively to fruit and vegetables.

Chung-ai's religious faith was born while she was carrying me, and all the sufferings of her early years—her poverty, the cruelty of her mother-in-law, the children she had lost—inspired her, now that her life had changed so dramatically, to give thanks to Buddha. In the face of such sincere piety, even my grandfather Tso-hung was moved; he began to visit us more frequently and he even began to pray, although he loved eating meat too much to become a vegetarian. On the Buddha's birthday, my mother went to a small temple near the house, which was presided over by a nun. Unlike many of her colleagues who had joined the order for financial gain, the chief nun was not only a fervent believer but a very wise woman. She could read their destinies simply by looking in the faces of her congregation. Chung-ai consulted the nun frequently. She thought of her as a mother, and because she hoped her daughters' fate would be more fortunate than her own, she always repeated to us what the priestess had told her.

In fact, my mother gave us a good Buddhist education. We all knew that people had several lives, that our terrestrial existence was meant to be one of suffering, that reincarnation was a result of one's sins, and that everything we did, be it good or bad, would determine the course of our next life—unless, of course, we deserved to go to Paradise, which was located to the west of Heaven and which sheltered all the buddhas. Those who reached Paradise would remain there forever and would never have to return to earth. In the here and now, however, no one was immune from the mechanisms of cause and effect. Those who, in a previous existence, had killed many animals would live out their next incarnation in disease and suffering; those who had snatched baby animals from their mothers would suffer painful separations from their own families. As for those who are deaf and dumb, the reason is simply that they had spread malicious rumors about others in a previous existence. Those who stole from the poor would, in turn, know poverty. A happy or unhappy marriage was dependent upon the quality of love or hatred in a former incarnation; there was always a reason for being reincarnated as a daughter, a mother, a son, or a father. We enter this world with four great trials before us: birth, illness, old age, and death. And we must pray not only for a better life, but for the current life to be the last.

Generally speaking, these Buddhist teachings formed the bases of my mother's philosophy. All of this might have been simple enough had we not also begun receiving a Christian education at school, one which was wholly centered around Jesus Christ.

One day in the auditorium, where all the girls were assembled, a man of about fifty, dressed in Western clothes although he was Chinese, waited for us on the stage. He was a Protestant clergyman, a pastor. He told us a long story, much like a fairy tale, in which he described the life of Jesus: his birth, his childhood, the miracles he had performed, and how he had died on the cross in order to save the world. I was filled with indescribable emotions. Although I had no way of knowing for sure, it seemed to me that the others were also greatly moved. The pastor fell silent a moment, then his voice rose once again.

"My dear children," he intoned, "who among you desires to become a Christian? Raise your hands, please."

Without stopping to think, I raised my hand. When she saw me, my sister Ching-ling did the same. The candidates were called together and told that in order to become Christians, we would have to participate in a ceremony called a baptism, which had something to do with water. As far as we could tell, we were to be baptized by immersion on the first of December in a church near the school.

Once outside, I immediately realized that my new religion was bound to create certain difficulties in my family. But since I was basically an obedient child, I never dreamed of concealing my decision from my mother. When Chung-ai learned that both my sister and I intended to become Christians, she was, to say the least, more than a little displeased. Frowning, she tried to dissuade us.

"A Chinese must follow the Buddhist religion," she explained to us. "If he doesn't, he will have nothing but misfortune.

"In addition," she went on, "Chinese custom dictates that every year children must celebrate the anniversary of their parents' deaths. Not only must they pray before photographs of the dead, but they must have a banquet. If they do not, their parents will die a second death, but this time one of starvation."

The first argument may have been directed toward our well-being, but the second, a non sequitur, was obviously calculated to instill a sense of guilt.

"Do you want me to become a starving phantom when I die?" mother lamented.

"But Mama," I replied, my new religion providing me with a perfectly logical response, "you won't be hungry once you're dead because if you become a Protestant, you'll go to Paradise. All Christians go to Paradise."

My argument failed to impress her. Chung-ai forbade us to be baptized, threatening that if ever we did such a thing, we would be expelled from the family.

"You will no longer be my daughters," she threatened.

For several days, I continued to hope she would change her mind. But each time I broached the subject, she flew into a rage. The only thing we had not told her was the upcoming

58

date of our baptism. The first of December grew nearer and nearer. What should we do? Cancel the ceremony? Impossible. Both my father and brother had taught us that a promise made is a promise kept. The most troubling thing about the whole affair was that, if the pastor was to be believed, those who renounced Paradise went directly to Hell—and that included not only my sister and me, but the whole family as well. Protestants simply did not treat such things lightly. If I became a Protestant, I would be the salvation of my entire family. But what would become of *me* if my mother kicked me out of the house?

By November 30, I was in a torment of confusion, while my sister did not seem the least bit concerned. A year younger than I, Ching-ling was nevertheless more determined. She had prepared all the things for baptism in a little bag: two big towels and clothes to change into after the ceremony. On the fatal morning, she woke up early and asked me if I was ready.

"It's impossible," I murmured, "impossible. We'll be thrown out of the house!"

"What a fool you are!" she exclaimed, looking at me with scorn. "Do you actually think I plan to tell Mama that we're going to be baptized? And even if she does find out about it, do you really think she'll kick us out? Mama throwing us into the streets—you and me? Really!"

My fears vanished in the face of such logic. In any case, Ching-ling gave me no time to think about it. Before I knew what was happening, I found myself in the little Protestant church, immersed and baptized, a proper Christian.

Once home, Ching-ling gave our wet clothes to a servant she knew would not betray us. And thus, without my mother's knowledge, we became Christians. Indeed, there was no reason for her to be suspicious; at school we may have been busy with Jesus, but at home we were always proper Buddhists. Only my brother knew of our conversion, but since he was preoccupied with Communism, he was completely indifferent to the state of our religious beliefs. As far as my father was concerned, his principal preoccupation was making money and he had little time to concern himself with the spiritual life of his daughters.

When I was in my second year of secondary school, I took part in a piano competition in which all the schools of Shanghai were represented. Two girls were selected to represent the MacIntyre School—an older girl, in her last year of high school, and me. The contest took place in the Municipal Auditorium in the presence of a great many spectators, including certain Shanghai music critics. The jury was made up of professors from the Shanghai Conservatory. It was a great triumph for the MacIntyre School, for my comrade won the first prize and I the second, with the *Impromptu* by Chopin and Beethoven's *Moonlight Sonata*. Several critics remarked that if I had not won first prize, it was because I was only eleven, whereas my comrade was seventeen. In any case, they added, I was clearly a "pianist with a future." My teacher, Miss Ling, continued encouraging me to enter the conservatory.

I knew I would have to work much harder the following year if I hoped to pursue my career at the conservatory. There would be an entrance examination and, assuming I were to be accepted, my life would change dramatically, for the conservatory was a considerable distance from Shanghai and its students were therefore obliged to board. Indeed, all conservatory students were boarders, returning home only on Sundays. When I mentioned this to my mother, she was firmly against the idea. In fact, she demanded how I could possibly have imagined for a minute going to live at the conservatory, which everyone knew was filled with wild and crazy boys, long-haired artists, and so forth. I didn't understand what any of this had to do with my education, but mother made herself perfectly clear.

"A fine thing!" she exclaimed. "A pretty girl like you in the middle of all those disreputable, shifty boys! The first thing that will happen is that someone will try to seduce you. I know you—you like all those flowery phrases, you won't be able to resist!"

This was the first time my mother had spoken to me of my sensitivity to "flowery phrases," but she had recently been exhibiting a strange anxiety about me and had in fact been watching me closely for some time. Her sharp maternal eyes had spotted the first signs of my emerging femininity and

60

from then on she became afraid of misadventures, of possible misfortune leading to poverty, her chief obsession. Perhaps she had too strong an imagination, but the deprivations of her own childhood had made a lasting impression on her.

Deeply disappointed, I knew I would not be able to attend the conservatory without her consent. I still had not resigned myself to her decision when a year later my mother and I came upon Ching-ling in our room one morning, tying a knot in a large bundle that was sitting on her bed.

"As you can see," Ching-ling replied simply to our questioning gaze, "I'm leaving. Leaving home."

We had no idea what she was talking about.

"Have you gone crazy?" my mother cried. "Are you serious? Where do you think you're going?"

"To the conservatory. I took the entrance exam and was accepted. All I have to do now is go."

Ching-ling had accomplished all of this without anyone knowing of it. Both mother and I were stunned speechless.

"Why didn't you tell me?" mother finally asked.

"Why should I have told you?" my sister replied. "So that you could repeat the scene you created last year for Ching-li? So you could keep me from going too?"

My mother could think of nothing to say other than to enumerate all the possible pitfalls of the trip. But in the end she asked my father to allow Ching-ling to be driven to the conservatory in one of our chauffeured cars. Faced with this reversal of attitude and the ease with which my sister got her way, I could not help but be stunned and outraged.

"How could you?" I blurted my indignation. "Is this fair? Is this justice? My sister hides what she does from you and there she goes, without a struggle. I'm obedient, I do as you wish, I tell you everything. And what happens? I'm punished. I'm denied the right to go to the conservatory!"

Incredibly, my father and mother joined forces against me.

"You are too innocent," they said, "too gullible. The conservatory is too dangerous for you. Your sister may be younger, but she's more mature; she has her feet on the ground. You're a dreamer. You still need us."

They were not entirely wrong. My sister and I were exact opposites, and she was by nature more sophisticated and aggressive than I. Nevertheless, I smarted at the injustice.

If 1948 was for me a year of hurt, anger, and frustration, it was for my brother Ching-chung—and his Revolution—a year of triumph. Although the Nationalists had made some stunning gains during the first part of 1947, including the capture of the Communist capital of Yenan, Chiang's propensity for poor strategy and bad timing caused the tide to turn in favor of the Communist forces, who were soon winning battle after battle throughout the balance of 1947 and well into 1948.

By September, 1948, the Communist army under General Chen Yi had conquered Shantung, continuing to push onward toward Nanking, then the Nationalist capital. Again Chiang's unerring nose for wrong military decisions, coupled with his usual bad luck (his armies became immobilized in a downpour of rain, sleet, and snow), cost him the loss of all his advantages. Two divisions of well-equipped but demoralized troops defected to the Communists in October, exposing portions of the defense of Hsuchow, the gateway to Nanking. By mid-December, Hsuchow had fallen. The last defenses at Nanking fell five months later.

But for me, aged twelve, the civil war seemed remote and far away. I had much more important things to think about: movies and—a new phenomenon—boys.

Given my tender years, I did not go to the movies very often. The first time my father took me to see an American film, he had the chauffeur drop us at the entrance to the Roxy Theater (all movie theaters in Shanghai had American names). I was particularly impressed by two things: the Metro-Goldwyn-Mayer lion that roared at the beginning of the movie, and the odd behavior of the foreign actors. There were several scenes when the star and her partner exchanged long, intense looks, their faces moving closer and closer, their mouths coming together like leeches. Never in my life had I seen people kiss on the mouth, and I was shocked.

The Americans, who continued to support the Nationalists, not only influenced us with their movies, but also inundated us in a postwar tidal wave of cigarettes, nylon stockings, and vitamins. I did not wear nylons as yet, but as far as the vitamins were concerned, I seriously doubt that anyone else swallowed as many as I. Hui-i always worried about my delicate health and had laid in a gigantic stock of vitamins practically through the alphabet! Not a single one was missing. I had to take each and every one throughout the day, my father pushing them into my mouth as if he were feeding a bird. Perhaps it was because of this that I suddenly began to grow by leaps and bounds until I was the tallest girl in my class and looked older than twelve, and when the boys saw me riding by on my bicycle in jeans and a pullover, with my pale complexion and my black hair in two long braids, they began following me. When one of them got close enough, I would cast a ferocious look in his direction and refuse to speak, just as I had seen done in the American movies, a strategy as consistent with my training as with my natural instincts.

In China, an expression of sentimentality is exalted while one of sexuality must be discreet. Therefore, love songs sung by Bing Crosby and Frank Sinatra were extremely popular. Love-struck boys telephoned the radio station with requests dedicated to their sweethearts. In fact, I received my first declaration by radio—"From John Wang to Julie Chow, *I love you truly* . . ."—a message I heard one evening from a boy to whom I had never spoken but who had somehow managed to find out my name.

At the same time, I began to receive my first love letters, a development directly related to my having become a secret Christian. I often accompanied the hymn singing at the church, and I was noticed one day by the older brother of a girl in my class. He sent me a delirious letter that said: "You are so beautiful that I haven't slept a wink since I first saw you. Night and day, your image pursues me. From the moment the sun appears, I think of you . . ." I remember this note quite well simply because the envelope was addressed to me at home and my mother, of course, opened it. There was a terrific scene. She forced me to read the letter aloud and then demanded an explanation. I swore by all the gods I could muster that I did not know the boy in question, which was the absolute truth. It was only later that I realized he was my friend's brother. My mother refused to let the matter drop.

"I'm warning you," she said menacingly, "if you see any boy at all without telling me about it, I will punish you."

I understood absolutely nothing of all this. I felt as if the letter I had just read had been addressed to someone else. Even when love songs on the radio were dedicated to me, I listened with only half an ear. I may have been approaching thirteen, but I knew no more of what my mother was talking about than an infant in its cradle.

In spite of my colossal naïveté, I too finally realized boys were noticing me more and more. Very soon, it wasn't only a question of boys. Lao Li, a hideous old marriage broker with a pockmarked face, who had arranged a disastrous second marriage for my uncle Hui-ying, began coming to the house regularly under the pretext of chatting with my mother. Already her professional eye was sizing me up greedily; already she was counting her chickens.

"How gorgeous she is!" exclaimed Lao Li from the doorstep one day as I arrived home from school on my bicycle, my cheeks rosy from the wind. "Oh! The little jewel! Her skin is so tender one hesitates to even touch her! Just look at her; she's lovelier than the Four Beauties!"

Lao Li was referring to the four famous beauties from old Chinese dynasties. The old witch smiled toothlessly and continued mumbling to herself.

"Your eyes are as large as the phoenix bird's . . . you have an adorable little upturned nose . . . when you smile, your mouth is a marvelous arc . . . you are tall . . . your skin is as soft as silk, as sweet-smelling as a flower. Yes, yes, you will be a great lady. I must find you a good husband."

Indeed, she lost no time in beginning her search. In just a few weeks, this frightful harridan managed to unearth some extraordinarily rich people from Chao-chou who were now living in Shanghai. They were none other than the family of the notorious Ko, the opium dealer who had made such a fortune during the war. Lao Li told my parents that Ko had enough money to keep all four of his children in luxury until the end of their days, even if they were to live a hundred years. This was

64

an understatement, for Ko had built a sumptuous mansion in the middle of a vast park in Shanghai, surrounding it with an iron grillwork fence complete with a set of double steel doors so that the gate closely resembled a huge safe. His children did not go to school because Ko was afraid of kidnappers, a fear not entirely unjustified, as the snatching of rich children for ransom was a widespread practice in Shanghai. And so the whole family lived sealed off from the rest of the world behind these walls.

Ko's two sons were eighteen and twenty. Lao Li thought the elder would be an unwise choice as a fiancé, apparently because he was both fat and stupid. The younger brother was only stupid. Naturally, I knew nothing of these negotiations, but ever since my mother had noticed boys running after me, she was terrified that I would be seduced by "flowery phrases" and that my seducer would be a poor young man who would lead me into a life of suffering and slavery.

"That a girl like you should become enslaved to her husband and her children," she lectured one day, "and that you should live a life of constant torment over money, that would be too unjust! But if you had the luck to marry a Ko! You have no idea how rich . . ."

My brother and I thought mother had lost her mind. In the first place, I wasn't even certain what marriage actually meant. All I thought it meant was leaving home and going to live somewhere else, where I would eat and sleep for the rest of my life, and never again see the outside world. I remembered our neighbor's daughter and the fight we had had because she accused my father of trafficking in opium. And now they wanted me to marry one of the biggest opium dealers in the city! My only protector was Ching-chung, and he rose to my defense.

Patiently but firmly, my brother besieged Chung-ai. His arguments finally succeeded in convincing her that I was still too young to marry. The matter was dropped as suddenly as it had arisen, and the horrid Lao Li shown the door.

I'd had a narrow escape, but the respite would prove to be short-lived.

5

In January, 1949, two significant events took place: Peking capitulated to the Communists, and Chiang Kai-shek was forced by his own party to resign, temporarily turning over the reigns of government to Vice President Li Tsung-jen. Nothing could stop Mao now. On April 21, Mao Tse-tung crossed the Yangtze and three days later was in Nanking, seat of the Kuomintang; the Nationalists fled to Canton.

Shanghai could no longer ignore what was going on. Panic set in; the Communists, it was said, would soon take everything away. There would be no such thing as private property, and the Confucian precepts—family loyalty, filial piety, the Three Bonds (between ruler and subject, father and son, husband and wife) and Five Relations (between brothers and between friends)—already heavily eroded by Western influences, would be done away with completely, destroying all family and social structure.

As the clandestine member of the Communist Party, my brother, Ching-chung, lived the most feverish hours of his life. Over a period of time he had quietly revealed his secret, for he was anxious to keep our parents informed while not frightening them. He was frequently absent from home, and would return with news we hardly comprehended.

Before its final defeat the Nationalist government in Shanghai began making massive arrests, terrifying all its citizens to no avail. By October we soon heard the news that the Nationalist government had fled from Canton to Chungking. Uncle Yao was in panic. Chungking had been Yao's native city, and since he had had a few too many friends among the supporters of Chiang Kai-shek both there and in Shanghai, he was fearful of coming face to face with the Communists, and he wanted to get to Hong Kong if he could.

My father, on the other hand, was not the slightest bit uneasy. Even though he belonged to the upper middle class, he refused to entertain the idea of leaving. I was too young at the time to understand the issues and thus I cannot describe with certainty his state of mind. But I think he was convinced, either by my brother or by the declarations of the Communists in the liberated territories, that the new government had no intention of acting precipitously or seizing private property. As for me, ever under my brother's influence, I was on the side of the Red Army, which was expected daily. And so, like many others, we waited quietly. There was no special excitement at home, and children went to school as usual.

This was the prevailing climate when on the evening of May 25, the radio announced, "Our Army of Liberation has entered Shanghai."

The streets remained calm and although some combat was reported in the suburbs, most of the Nationalist troops had already fled.

The city may have seemed outwardly quiet, but inwardly it was tense. No one slept, and everyone was now eager for the slightest bit of news. Like many others, my family gathered around the radio, where, from time to time, the music was interrupted by bulletins. One in particular was frequently repeated: "Have no fear, people of Shanghai.... Beware of rumors and slander. The People's Liberation Army will take nothing from you, not even a pin. The Red Army is your family..."

Suddenly, we could see the troops of the Red Army with our own eyes. They were on our street, advancing cautiously in single file, their rifles fixed with bayonets. They looked nothing like the soldiers of Chiang Kai-shek; for one thing, they were far less elegantly dressed. But the simplicity of their padded uniforms, of their caps and their cotton shoes, made them seem less frightening.

I remember, too, Ching-chung's eyes filling with tears at the sight of these soldiers. He even launched into a long, sincere, and enthusiastic speech on the unity of the peasants, the workers, and the soldiers, and on the new future beginning for China.

Since it was only a question of time before the Nationalists would be completely routed, Mao impatiently proclaimed on October 1 the establishment of the People's Republic of China. Finally, on December 8, 1949, the Nationalist government quit Chungking for Taiwan. After twenty-eight years of sacrifice and struggle, the Communists had won.

Despite this extraordinary event, surprisingly little changed in our daily lives. Apart from the fact that my brother could now be open about his politics and frequently bored us with his rhetoric, very little else happened to alter our way of life. My father continued to prosper in his business, mother continued to make my life miserable, and I continued to attend Miss MacIntyre's.

And then, suddenly, our home became the theater for a family drama that would alter the course of my own life forever. On the day in question, I had to stay later than usual at school. The Christian students had an extra hour of catechism and Bible study after classes, but since returning home late was not the sort of thing tolerated by my mother, I jumped onto my bicycle and raced home as fast as I could, pedaling furiously.

I arrived, panting and drenched with sweat, only to see a strange man at our gate, his finger poised just above the bell. There was nothing particularly remarkable about him; he seemed to be about the same age as my father and was dressed in Western-style clothes. He started a bit as I skidded to a stop a few inches from him.

"Don't bother ringing, sir," I called. "I have the key."

As I rummaged in my bag, I asked who he was.

"I am a friend of Mr. Yao," he replied. "And you, I presume, are the daughter of Chow Hui-i. You must be Ching-li."

I replied in the affirmative, still searching for my keys. Sud-

68

denly I realized that this stranger was studying me with unusual attention. Smiling, he looked me up and down, from head to toe and back again. I finally found the keys, opened the gate, and led him across the garden, leaving him in front of the door to the part of the house occupied by the Yaos. Propping my bicycle up next to the other door, I entered our part of the house and soon forgot about the strange man.

Two or three weeks later, I arrived home from school and found my mother waiting for me in the room I shared with Ching-ling.

"There are things I must talk to you about, Mei-mei," she declared in a voice charged with emotion, which surprised me. "You're a young lady now. These childish braids must go. I'm going to take you to the hairdresser for a permanent."

Bewildered and delighted, I could not believe my ears. For a long time now, I had been envious of other girls my age who had their hair fashionably styled and waved in the European manner, the last word in chic. I had begged many times for a permanent, but had always been refused. It was my brother who put up the strongest resistance.

"A girl ought to be simple, clean, and modest," he would say. "Worry about your studies and leave your hair alone."

Since anything my brother said was gospel for me, I stopped talking about it. Who would have believed that one day, out of the clear blue sky, my mother would *order* me to the hairdresser to have my braids cut off? This time my brother could not object. Mama's word was law.

And so one morning, Chung-ai took me to a hairdresser. It was the first time in my life I had seen such a place. A long line of mirrors faced a row of shining armchairs and in these mirrors were reflected lights and faces, a battalion of women rushing about in white coats giving manicures, shampoos, sets. I was dazzled.

"Give her a permanent," my mother ordered.

I sat down in an armchair which seemed to me a throne; the hairdresser drew an enormous white cloth around me and picked up the scissors. Until this moment, I had been in a state of euphoria. But suddenly, when I saw he was going to cut the long black hair that hung all the way down my back and that had been with me for so many years, I grabbed my braids and jerked away.

"Don't be afraid, miss," the hairdresser smiled unctuously. "As beautiful as you are, all you can do is become more so. Once your hair is waved, you'll look like a real European!"

Then he turned to my mother.

"Madame," he murmured obsequiously, "how is it possible to have such a charming child?"

And, having lulled me into resignation with his beautiful phrases, he took one of my braids. One can't have everything, I comforted myself. I heard the snip, snip! of his shears. The braid fell to the floor. Snip, snip! There went the second. I felt different immediately, lighter. Reverently, mother picked up the braids and put them into her purse. Her own hair was rather sparse, and she planned to use them as a chignon.

Then the big operation began. My head was bent back over a basin that cut into my neck and was tossed from side to side as it was lathered and rinsed, and I learned all at once that to be beautiful was to suffer. Despite his politeness, the hairdresser was a brute. A mysterious liquid smelling of ammonia was poured over my head and, lock by lock, my hair was rolled into curlers. A strange apparatus rose around my head as I stared into the mirror; then an enormous helmet equipped with wires and clips was attached to each paper-covered roller. Strange vapors drifted up around me; I heard sizzling and crackling. My hair was being electrified, and I was paralyzed. With a professorial air, the hairdresser watched the paper around the rollers; when it started to burn, the plug had to be pulled immediately. My mother never took her eyes off me, following the stages of the operation with the solemnity befitting a magical and religious rite. What a relief when it was over and they took the helmet off! My head was covered with little black curls. But we were far from done; I had to have a set first, with different rollers, followed by a baking under a hair dryer.

At the end of two long hours, I stared at myself in the mirror. The child's head was gone and I was unrecognizable, but did I really like what I saw? I had been fond of my braids; now I looked bizarre. It was true that I resembled a European, and since that was considered the ultimate in style, I had no choice but to be happy. My face was now that of a young woman. People would look at me differently, and Chung-ai would grow even more concerned and vigilant. But after all, this is what she had wanted.

A few days later I arrived home from school early, around three o'clock. Ordinarily, when this happened, I would spend the rest of the afternoon at the piano and leave my schoolwork for the evening. This time, however, I had barely sat down when my mother ordered me upstairs to change my clothes. She seemed nervous.

"You'll have to make yourself presentable," she replied to my questioning glance. "We are going out to drink tea with some very important people."

"Now?"

"Yes, now."

Normally I would have been thrilled by such an invitation to "drink tea," the idiom for a very special type of meal served throughout the afternoon. The meal starts with a fragrant selected tea, and is accompanied by many delicious varieties of dishes, served on tiny platters placed simultaneously in the center of the table, from which each guest would take a bit of this and a bit of that, much like a smorgasbord. It was easy to make a pig of myself, and I usually did.

Today, however, I had enough work to do, and this unexpected excursion only made me cranky. I grumbled that I had a lot of homework to do, didn't see that anyone else was going to do it for me, and begged off.

"I understand," my mother replied. "But I promised these people that we would come and a promise is a promise. So hurry up and get dressed. I've put everything out on your bed. Your father's already waiting for us."

Furious, and unable to understand what possible connection I might have with this nonsense, I went upstairs grudgingly. The sight of the clothes my mother had laid out for me brought me up short. There was a Chinese dress I had never seen before, a gorgeous thing of white silk slit up one side, with huge red flowers at the throat, a high collar, and a tightly fitted waist. A pair of nylon stockings lay next to it, along with the most incredible object of them all—a *brassiere*! A European invention emphasizing the breast, the brassiere went contrary to Chinese taste and tradition; mother was obviously attempting to make me look older than thirteen.

"But this is impossible!" I cried. "I can't wear a thing like that!"

"Be quiet," mother snapped, "and get dressed. Had you planned to go out looking like a tomboy? Don't forget that you're a young lady from a good family. You must be elegant. Especially today, given the importance of the people."

As far as elegance was concerned, nothing was missing. The whole panoply was present—dress, underwear, a pair of white pumps, and a matching purse, the perfect color for summertime. My peasant mother had apparently asked a well-brought-up cousin of hers to advise her in the selection of my sumptuous new wardrobe. Mother helped me to dress. Indeed, I needed all the help I could get. Everything was tight, the brassiere, the Chinese dress with its suffocatingly stiff collar, the shoes. When I looked at myself in the mirror, I could hardly believe my eyes. Suddenly I had become a tall, slender girl, seductively arrayed in a spectacular outfit, who looked like someone else altogether, particularly when my mother began applying lipstick.

"Hurry up!" she cried. "It's time to go!"

Hurry up indeed. Easier said than done, I thought, hampered as I was by the dress. But I did my best.

"Slowly, slowly," my mother cried in alarm.

Already she envisioned me splitting the seams with my usual long stride. My handbag swung back and forth idiotically from one arm; I had no idea what to do with it. Once out on the landing, however, Chung-ai gave me a few last pieces of advice, her mouth tightly pursed.

"You are going to spend two hours in public," she lectured. "You must pay very close attention to the way you walk, your gestures, the way you carry your bag. Your father's reputation is in your hands. I trust you understand." I didn't.

"Thank God my brother can't see me now," I thought. "He would say I looked like one of those fancy women who lie around all day eating chocolates."

72

I eased my way downstairs carefully, taking precaution that no sudden movement would split the dress. The entire Yao family, along with their servants, were waiting at the bottom. When I came into view, a chorus of cries and compliments rose up beneath me. Yao examined me carefully. The chauffeur was waiting for us in front of the garage with my father beside him. Hui-i had never seen me dressed up before, and he was speechless with admiration. Then we all got into the car and started off for the famous tea.

The event was to take place in downtown Shanghai. We were to meet in a well-known restaurant called the Green Pavilion of Yangchow, named after a city in the Nanking region. At four o'clock, we entered the restaurant and saw ten people seated around a table. At the sight of me, they stared and began whispering excitedly among themselves without embarrassment. Was there something wrong with my dress, I wondered? Or with my hair? Fortunately, I had no time to worry about it.

"Mr. Liu is expecting us," my father told the headwaiter.

"Please go right up, sir," the man replied, motioning toward the stairs.

"Watch your dress," mother hissed in my ear. "Don't forget to hold your purse carefully."

As far as my dress was concerned, I had been doing little else but looking it over, particularly after all the stares and whispers. I felt eyes burning into my back as I climbed the stairs. Once on the second floor, I saw a small group of people at a table. One of them got up and rushed over to greet us. I recognized him immediately; it was the mysterious stranger I had run into that evening in front of our house. As it turned out, his name was Yuan. Bubbling with pleasure, Mr. Yuan led us to the table, where a most imposing couple sat, a man and a woman about fifty years old, and next to them, a young man. The introductions began.

"Mr. and Madame Chow, and their daughter."

"Mr. and Madame Liu, and their son."

The family was dressed in traditional Chinese clothing. Mr. Liu wore a long, beige silk tunic; his wife, a traditional dress like mine, only simple and of dark color. Her feet were squeezed into small embroidered shoes. As for the young man, he seemed to be about twenty-six or twenty-seven. He wore a jacket buttoned up to the neck and wide trousers. There was a sickly air about him; his face was waxy yellow and a pair of spectacles perched precariously on his nose. It wasn't that he was unattractive, but he looked as if he had just risen from a sickbed, and appeared frail enough to be knocked flat by the slightest gust of wind. The Liu family rose to their feet, and once the introductions were over, Mr. Liu turned to my father.

"That is my *little puppy*," Liu exclaimed, pointing to his son.

I had never actually heard the expression used before but I knew it was the traditional way of introducing one's man-child in Old China. It was de rigueur never to refer directly to "my son," but rather to "my little puppy," a term that was not meant to be pejorative, but was intended more as an expression of modesty on the part of the proud father.

There was no doubt that the Liu family was far from modern.

After these formalities were exchanged, one other remained before we could all be seated. In China, the tables in restaurants are usually round and the place of honor is designated by a seat facing southward. Mr. Liu, of course, insisted that my father take this seat; my father, of course, refused, saying that it should be occupied by the more worthy Mr. Liu, who declined on the ground that my father was much more worthy than he. This seesawing continued for another full minute until my father, still expressing his unworthiness, finally sat down in the place of honor, as expected.

I was starving. At last the meal began with the waiter bringing a large teapot of *lung ching*, or dragon-well tea, steaming and fragrant, followed by a huge platter of long fried dumplings having the texture of a doughnut, which we dipped in a soybean soup. This was followed by a seemingly unending flow of dishes—several varieties of steamed and fried dumplings and thin, many-layered pancakes imbedded with chopped scallions, tiny, crisp spring rolls, large, round steamed buns, filled with succulent, sweet diced pork or chopped green vegetables, boiled dumplings, encasing a meaty soup which spurted deliciously into the mouth when

74

pierced, and accompanied by a dip of thinly sliced ginger and rice vinegar. And, finally, my very favorite, steamed noodles with chicken, a specialty of the house.

Apart from the fact that I was hungry, the conversation around me seemed extremely boring, and I therefore buried my nose in my plate, devouring dish after dish, paying little attention to anyone except between courses.

Mother began eyeing me with increasing disapproval. Such conduct was highly unbecoming and ill-mannered. Young ladies were supposed to eat sparingly, taking only a little here and a little there, and *never* focusing on a single favorite dish. I, of course, had gobbled up most of the steamed noodles and, much to my mother's chagrin, a second platter had to be ordered.

Madame Liu, on the other hand, seemed enormously pleased with my display of appetite, as it indicated to her that I was a simple, unspoiled girl who tolerated no waste, a quality greatly admired in Chinese women.

Since some of the dishes were very hot, or had to be replenished, I was forced to pause from time to time. In those brief moments I grumpily glanced around me, examining the other guests. Mr. Liu was first. The palms of his hands were extraordinarily red and his forehead gleamed with reflected light. Aside from his Chinese clothes, there was something curiously impressive about him. His wife, too, interested me; her eyes exhibited the kind of strength I considered the mark of a great lady. As for the son, he seemed a nonentity, a marionette whose strings were pulled by his mother, and he kept glancing at me surreptitiously out of the corner of his eye.

Unfortunately, my father stood up to leave at a most inopportune moment, just as I was about to attack the second platter of exquisite noodles and chicken. I had to abandon my bowl and say goodbye. The Liu family accompanied us to the top of the stairs along with Mr. Yuan and we all exchanged bows in the old-fashioned manner. This was the first time I saw my father in such a posture and I imitated him as best I could—or rather, as far as my dress would permit.

The oglers were still there when we reached the ground

floor, and the stares and whispers began all over again. I was outraged and hastened out the door; it was not until much later that I learned exactly who they were.

The chauffeur was waiting for us, and only when I was safely ensconced in the back seat did I begin to wonder about this odd tea party, about the other guests, and particularly about the imposing Mr. Liu, with his red palms and shining forehead. I had never seen a more profoundly "Chinese" family; their Confucian manners were even more pronounced than those of the Yaos. But I was especially curious about my father's connection with such strange individuals and I had no suspicion whatsoever that the event might in any way concern *me*.

I asked my parents about the Lius.

"Mr. Liu is a well-known and highly successful business-man," my father replied. "In fact, he's one of the ten wealthiest men in the city. He owns property in Shanghai, in Hangchow, and in Ningpo, where he was born. And he owns banks and factories as well. No one knows how much he's worth, but he's not only a millionaire—he's a philanthropist. He's as generous as he is rich; he gives money to orphans and widows and hospitals ..."

What really intrigued me, however, were the red palms and the glittering forehead.

"Those are two very special, very rare signs," my mother explained. "They are the marks of great wealth and of omnipotence."

With that, Mr. Liu ceased to interest me and by the time we reached home, I had already forgotten him.

For me, something far more interesting occurred shortly thereafter. It was a Saturday afternoon, and one of my classmates had invited me, along with a few other friends, to have tea at her house. We had been listening to records for a while—exclusively European music, of course, love songs and Viennese waltzes—when the doorbell rang. My friend went to open the door and came back with a young man who so resembled my brother that at first glance I actually thought it was Ching-chung. He was the same size, had a similar face, and he even wore a navy blue pullover and jeans like my brother's. I was stupefied by the likeness and could not take my eyes off him. To be sure, he noticed my stare right away, smiled, and came over to where I was sitting.

"You look so much like my brother that I thought you were..." I hastened to explain, embarrassed and confused.

"If I had a sister like you," he replied without a pause, "I would be the happiest boy in the world."

Something in his voice bewildered and delighted me. A Strauss waltz was playing and he asked me to dance. I had always been a good dancer, and had even studied classical ballet. He was good, too, and we danced every dance together. Like so many other young people at the time, he had both an American and a Chinese name. He was called Louis Ho. As we danced, my embarrassment and astonishment gradually gave way to the feeling that I had known Louis Ho for a very long time indeed. The waltzes succeeded one another, and the time flew by until suddenly I realized it was six o'clock! I would have to leave right away, for I had promised my mother not to return later than six. Everyone, particularly Louis Ho, begged me to stay a while longer, but it was out of the question. Then Louis Ho offered to accompany me, and since I did not live far away, we walked.

When we reached the house, he asked for my telephone number so that he could call and invite me to the movies. I replied that although I loved the movies, I would have to get my mother's permission before going with him.

"I didn't realize," he smiled, surprised, "that you were still such a baby..."

In fact, I was almost thirteen at that time, and in Shanghai many parents gave their children a good deal of freedom. Louis had no way of knowing what a tight rein my overprotective mother kept on me.

Louis telephoned the following Saturday afternoon and asked if I could go out with him. The phone was on the ground floor and at that moment, my mother was on the second.

"Mama!" I shouted, putting the receiver down for an instant, "can I go to the movies?"

I have no idea what my mother heard, or even if she understood my question. In any case, she leaned over the banister and shouted down, "Yes!"

Unable to believe my ears, terrified that she would come down and ask for details, or that she would suddenly change her mind, I tore out of the house, across the garden, and into the street.

Just before hanging up, I hurriedly told Louis that I would meet him in front of the American Church opposite my house. Five minutes later he arrived, and off we went. Other than that the film was American, I have forgotten everything else about it. Indeed, nothing could have been less important, for I was having my first date, my first rendezvous with a boy! Both of us were extremely decorous. Our hands never so much as brushed. Holding hands in public, even between engaged couples, was frowned upon.

When we emerged from the theater, I was seized with panic at the thought of what I would say to my mother. I told Louis that I would have to return immediately, and he was considerate enough to let me go without protest. It was not a scolding I feared as much as the idea of hurting mother or, especially, worrying my father.

I went directly to my room the minute I got home, desperately hoping to escape interrogation. But all I succeeded in doing was to provoke it.

"Where have you been?" mother demanded.

I might easily have said that I had gone out with a girlfriend, but I couldn't. My upbringing prevented me from lying.

"I went to the movies with Louis Ho," I admitted.

Mother went through the roof. First I was besieged with questions about Louis Ho. Who was his father? Who was his mother? I would be obliged to go back three generations, but the trouble was I knew absolutely nothing about Louis, except that he was a friend of one of my classmates and that I had met him at her house.

"What!" Mother exclaimed. "Do you think you can go out with a boy when you know nothing about his background? What if you'd been kidnapped? What if you'd been sold?"

Such things were not uncommon at that time. Young girls

were frequently spirited away, sold, and turned into prostitutes. Nevertheless, mother's reaction appeared excessive under the circumstances. Her tirade went on for a long time, coming to a halt only after she had completely exhausted herself. But it was only temporary. The following morning Louis phoned to say hello. With incredible naïveté, I could think of nothing better to do than ask him all the questions my mother had flung at me. I could sense that he was both embarrassed and perplexed.

"Louis," I said, "if you want me to be able to go out with you again, you'll have to answer. Put yourself in mother's place. How can I answer her questions unless you tell me what to say?"

And so he quietly told me everything I wanted to know. It seemed his mother had one day discovered that his father had a mistress; they were divorced and each of them remarried. Soon afterward, both abandoned Louis, who had gone to live with an uncle.

Later, when I repeated this to mother, she was horrified. Divorce was scandalous.

"I forbid you to see that boy ever again!" Chung-ai said categorically. "And I don't advise you to try to disobey, or to hide anything from me. I never want to hear another word about this Louis as long as I live!"

A few days later, Louis telephoned again. I told him what my mother had said.

"Louis," I announced, "you can call me on the phone but I can't go out with you anymore."

He insisted. That we could not see each other at all was unthinkable, he said. He went to St. John's, the American university, which was not far from the MacIntyre School. Could he not come to meet me from time to time after school? Why not, indeed, I replied, without thinking that for the first time in my life I was going to hide something from my parents.

Louis Ho came to pick me up several times after school and accompanied me as far as the American Church. When we parted, I would rush home and from the window of my bedroom, which had a good view of the church, I would wave to him. Only then would he start for home. This soon became a ritual and when he was too busy to meet me, or if for some reason we missed one another, he would telephone.

Then one evening after dinner, mother called me back into the dining room.

"We must have a serious talk," she declared.

My sister Ching-ling was there, as well as my brother Ching-chung. Mama motioned to them to stay.

"For some time now," she said, turning to me, "there have been far too many boys running after you. I am being torn apart with anxiety. I can't sleep."

And so the litany began all over again: I was too susceptible to flowery phrases, I would be seduced by a poverty-stricken boy, I would end up a slave to my children, a prisoner of my kitchen . . .

"And how will you endure such a hell? You who are as fragile as a flower."

This time, however, the familiar lament was only a prelude to something more serious to be said. Indeed, it was that very evening that I learned about the event that would alter my life forever.

"I see only one way out," she continued. "I must find you some in-laws. Only then will my anxieties and fears be calmed."

In China, the expression "finding in-laws" is unambiguous. Marrying a man means marrying his family.

"Mama," I replied, "please, let's talk about this when I'm older."

I was barely thirteen. In three years I would be sixteen, which was considered an appropriate age to marry. I wanted to finish school.

"You can finish married or unmarried. Anyway, that's something we'll have to work out with them."

"*Them?*" I felt a cold sweat. "*Who* are you talking about, Mama?"

"I'm talking about the Liu family. Don't you remember Mr. Liu and his son? The people Mr. Yuan introduced us to?"

"What Liu?"

"*What* Liu?" my mother repeated angrily. "The Lius we had tea with at the Green Pavilion!"

Two months had passed since that famous tea, and I had completely forgotten it. Suddenly everything fell into place. The image of the "little puppy," Mr. Liu's skinny, yellow-tinged son, rose before me, the one I imagined could easily be blown over by a gust of wind. Was *he* the one they wanted me to marry? Surely Mama couldn't seriously be considering marrying me off to *him!* No, it was too ridiculous. It was a joke. It was some kind of a game cooked up to frighten me.

Turning to my brother and sister, I launched into an unattractive description of young Liu, ridiculing him and bursting into laughter at appropriate points.

"Stop!" my mother cried. "Do you know how many families have proposed their daughter to the Liu boy since he turned seventeen? Dozens, that's how many! Yes, dozens! And he's refused every one. Not one of them appealed to him. And some of them belonged to the best and richest families! Mr. Liu has been in a terrible state; the boy's twenty-six now and he's the oldest son. When Mr. Yuan talked about you to him and insisted that the two families should meet, I can tell you Mr. Liu was not at all enthusiastic. He was afraid his son would refuse again, that there would be another failure. But Mr. Yuan insisted; he swore that this time he would introduce the son to a girl who would please him. So Mr. Liu agreed and things went perfectly, exactly as Mr. Yuan had predicted. For the first time, young Liu Yu-huang agreed, he liked the girl at first sight. And do you know who that girl was? You! Now do you understand?"

I was speechless, frozen to my chair.

"And now you listen to me," my mother went on, "Liu Yu-huang wants to marry you. He wants you, whatever the price. His mother and father are ecstatic. Mr. Yuan came right away to ask for your hand on behalf of Mr. Liu. In fact, he comes every day to talk to your father. And why does he have to come so often? Because your father has not given his consent. He says you're still too young. And how, I ask you, do you expect a man like Mr. Liu to understand your father's hesitation when all the girls in Shanghai are clamoring to marry into that family? Even Uncle Yao is hurt; he's richer than we are, he has a daughter, but still Mr. Yuan never asked to introduce her to Mr. Liu. It is at Mr. Liu's request that Mr. Yuan comes to see your father every day, to urge him to consent. And now your Uncle Yao has put aside his own disappointment and criticizes your father. He can't imagine how he dares hesitate to give his daughter to a family like the Lius, a family which is not only rich but honorable and virtuous . . ."

Now it was all out in the open. I was the victim of an elaborate conspiracy. At last I understood all those astonishing things that had happened to me recently: the haircut, the permanent, the beautiful dress, the shoes, the bag, the meal at the Green Pavilion, even the oglers downstairs, for obviously they were either friends or relatives of the Lius who had come to observe the curious little creature everyone said was so pretty.

My mother had never been more serious.

"Mama, did you really look at Liu Yu-huang?" I cried. "He's as yellow as a pear! He's skinny and sickly. Ching-chung could toss him around like a rubber ball. *Mama, I don't like him.* Did you see how he was dressed? He hasn't had any education at all and he's as out of date as a fossil!"

"You don't know what you're talking about!" my mother retaliated. "Your father and I have already asked about his health. If Liu Yu-huang looked pale, it's only because he had just gotten over a case of typhoid fever. That's why he was so yellow and thin. And as far as his studies are concerned, I'll tell you why he couldn't go on with them. His father is involved in so many important businesses that he needed his son to help him. As soon as he finished high school, he started work in one of his father's banks. And there you have the whole truth!"

It was not, of course, the whole truth; in fact, it was a tissue of lies fabricated by Mr. Yuan. He had done his work shamelessly and well. And since my parents were good people, they had believed him; they suspected nothing. When we all finally found out the real truth, it was too late to do anything about it.

"And in any case," my mother went on, "why should a rich man like Liu Yu-huang have to study forever? Take Mr. Yuan, or Uncle Yao. Neither of them has had as much schooling as your father. And who's the poorest of the three? Your father, that's who. And this in spite of all those long years of school!"

Ching-chung, who hadn't opened his mouth during the whole scene, interrupted at last.

"Mama," he said, "I think you're wrong. Education is a very important thing. Mr. Yuan and Uncle Yao belong to another generation, to the past. But times are changing."

Once again, my brother had come to my rescue.

"A boy like Liu Yu-huang," my brother continued, "is like a spoiled child who has not been prepared for life. When things change, he'll be lost, finished. As rich as he is, he may not even be able to feed himself or Mei-mei."

"This Mr. Yuan," Ching-ling interrupted in turn, "he ought to be thrown out the door the next time he comes bothering father! As if we need a marriage broker! All he wants is to ingratiate himself with the Lius and be paid for it! And as if we need the Lius when we have someone as beautiful and as intelligent as Ching-li! There are hundreds of boys who would give their right arm to marry her, who are far more worthy of her than that ridiculous . . ."

"That's precisely the point!" Mother agreed sarcastically. "It's because of boys like Louis Ho that I don't sleep at night! I know someone poor will wind up seducing her! But if she's engaged then all of us can sleep in peace!"

We had been talking for over an hour. The air was charged with tension; both sides refused to give in. There was a long silence. It was clear that enough had been said for one evening, and all of us went to bed.

Mr. Yuan continued coming to the house every day and my father continued to put off his reply. The Liu family began to show signs of impatience. To try and break through my father's resistance, they chose a new intermediary, someone far more important than Mr. Yuan, a Mr. Chen, who was a personal friend of the Lius. And so each day, the two men laid siege to my father until, at last, he gave in.

It is difficult to know what Hui-i's real feelings were, but I think I know. There is no doubt that he felt I was too young, and that he detested the idea of giving me to the Liu family. Perhaps he also felt in his heart that it was too soon to lose the daughter he loved so much. But when all is said and done, the prospect of an alliance with such a rich and important family must have flattered him. And this was a once-in-a-lifetime opportunity for me, he thought. The days flew by with Hui-i still unable to make up his mind.

Autumn arrived, the season of those big freshwater crabs the Chinese love so dearly. My grandfather, Tso-hung, was particularly fond of them. One day, my mother bought a large quantity despite their cost, and when they were cooked, she sent the chauffeur to fetch my grandparents. Knowing how much they adored crabs, Mother had invited them to come and stay with us for a few days. Those crabs, however, would cost me dearly.

For two months, Mr. Yuan had been harassing my father without success. My grandfather's arrival seemed to offer him a ray of hope. Mr. Yuan consulted with Mr. Chen and they decided to change the target of their attack. Recognizing a good thing when they saw it, they presented the problem to Tso-hung, and this time their efforts bore fruit.

No one had breathed a word to Tso-hung about the meeting at the Green Pavilion or about the plans drawn up for me. Messrs. Yuan and Chen were the first to do so. When my grandfather heard the name Liu—one well known to everyone in Shanghai—and when he learned that this family sought an alliance with ours and that I was the one who had been elected, his feet literally left the ground. Such an alliance surpassed even *his* most extravagant dreams. And when Messrs. Yuan and Chen informed him that his son, Hui-i, had not as yet given his consent to the marriage, Tso-hung went through the roof.

"What did you say?" my grandfather roared. "Has my son lost his mind?"

At first he was furious. Then he merely sat and shook his head. It was clear that Hui-i's opinion was irrelevant. He ordered him to appear at once and with a single wave of the hand swept aside all his objections. There was absolutely no point in discussing the matter any further. Hui-i had always been an obedient son and, in any case, the weeks of uncertainty and inner turmoil had taken their toll. He was exhausted, and abandoned the whole project to Tso-hung. As far as my grandfather was concerned, the case was closed. He announced his decision the following day: I would become the wife of Liu Yu-huang. Tso-hung begged Messrs. Yuan and Chen to ask the Liu family to set a date for the engagement ceremony.

I knew nothing of this decision, of course. A few days later, my brother, sister, and I were doing our homework when my mother entered the room, her face beaming with pleasure.

"My children," she announced, "I have a wonderful piece of news for you. Grandfather has decided that Mei-mei will be engaged. The Lius have chosen the twenty-eighth of October."

It was already September 20.

My mother had barely finished her declaration when Ching-chung smashed his fist down on the table.

"You are all mad!" he shouted.

At this sudden demonstration of violence by my normally calm brother, I went numb.

"You have no right to destroy Mei-mei's life!" My brother's voice rose.

My sister, Ching-ling, interrupted.

"Don't get hysterical," she said. "Since it's grandfather who's made this decision, let's tell *him* to marry the Liu family! As for us, we'll keep our sister!"

Mother's face crumbled. She looked so unhappy that I took pity on her.

"Mama," I said softly, determined at any cost not to cause her pain, "we'll discuss it another time. Let us finish our homework now."

Mother left the room without another word. As soon as the door closed behind her, Ching-ling turned to my brother and me.

"We'll have to act," she declared. "We can't let such a thing happen. It's monstrous!"

"Yes," Ching-chung replied. "We may love our parents, but we must save Ching-li from this terrible wrong."

My brother's words reverberated like a declaration of war. But if he was a revolutionary in the outside world, at home he remained a most obedient son. And in any case, how effective could an alliance be between my nineteen-year-old hero and two young girls of thirteen and twelve against the invincible authority formed by my parents and grandfather? What could the three of us possibly do? The two younger children, my brother Ching-chang and my little sister Ching-ching, were still in their cradles and so no help to us at all.

Clearly, our best weapon was silence. In the past, we had never failed to greet our mother when we got up and to bid her goodbye when we left for school. But on the day following this painful scene, none of us wished her good morning and none of us greeted her on our return home in the afternoon. In fact, we stopped speaking to her altogether!

By evening, we were extremely proud of ourselves. That night, Ching-chung remained a long while in the bedroom I shared with Ching-ling, for the two of them were planning a second line of attack.

"You're going to have to see a lot more of Louis Ho," Ching-ling told me. "You'll have to go out with him. All the better that he's such a likable boy."

For my part, I would have liked nothing better than to continue seeing him, but unfortunately I had had no news of him for some three weeks. He'd stopped coming to meet me after school and he hadn't telephoned.

It did not take my mother long to realize what was going on. The house rang with her anger, but each time my brother and sister replied:

"You can't sell our sister! You have no right!"

These violent exchanges were invariably followed by long periods of tense and icy silence. Thus had the climate changed in a household which had previously known only warmth and affection, even in times of misfortune. We were all miserable over it, my mother most of all, for our defiance humiliated her terribly. Finally, she could stand it no longer and complained to our father. What happened afterward still makes me tremble.

On the morning in question, my sister, brother, and I were just about to leave for school when Hui-i appeared on the landing, his face a rigid mask, his eyes smoldering with suppressed anger. He called my brother and sister into his room, where my mother was already waiting, and ordered me to remain outside. As the door closed behind them, I was filled with a terrible premonition. And so, just as on the day when my father had berated Ching-chung, I knelt down at the keyhole.

What I saw made the hair stand up on my neck. His face distorted with fury, my father had quietly removed his belt and was advancing on my brother and sister.

"I demand an explanation! Why do you refuse to talk to your mother?" he shouted at them.

I almost fainted when I heard my little sister answer him back, and in as loud and angry a tone.

"As if you didn't know!" Ching-ling retorted. "As if you didn't know that Mama is forcing sister to marry the Liu boy!"

My father brandished his belt over Ching-ling's head.

"How dare you speak to me like that!" he shouted. "Your mother loves all of us, and your sister most of all. And you know it! She's given her whole life to bringing you up, all five of you children! She's given you everything, and now that you're grown up, you turn against her! Do you have any idea at all what you're talking about? Do you have any idea why your mother wants Ching-li to marry? I'll tell you why, because your mother loves her! That's the only reason! And instead of trying to understand, all you do is insult her. You deserve to be beaten, both of you! You can still stop me on the condition that you speak to your mother immediately!"

Of the two, my big brother Ching-chung had the gentlest nature. I saw right away how ashamed and guilty he felt.

"Mama," he whispered, turning toward Chung-ai.

"And now you!" my father ordered Ching-ling.

"No!" Ching-ling replied firmly, opening her eyes wide and looking first at my father, then my mother. "As long as Mama tries to force my sister to marry, I refuse to speak to her! When she agrees to give up the project, then I'll . . ."

It was inconceivable that a Chinese child should speak that way to a parent. Ching-ling had overstepped all bounds and my father raised his belt against the daughter he no longer recognized. I wrenched open the door and rushed to defend her. Too late! The belt fell cruelly on my sister, and although her eyes filled with tears, Ching-ling remained silent, refusing to cry, staring with hatred at my mother. Never had I suffered so greatly as I did then. My father, the gentlest of men, had actually struck his daughter! And all because of me. My sister didn't deserve that; I was the guilty one, not Ching-ling.

"You're here just in time!" my father said hoarsely when he noticed I'd entered the room. "I was about to call you. I order you to speak to your mother immediately!"

At this, he raised his arm, threatening me with the same treatment.

"Papa!" I sobbed. "Hit me if you want, but leave my brother and sister alone, I beg you!"

My father stared at me. In the face of such grief, he sighed deeply. His arm fell back to his side.

"I've no wish to harm any of you," he said gently. "But you have behaved badly and you deserved a lesson . . ."

Ching-ling was just about to open her mouth and continue the argument when my brother interrupted.

"It's time now for school. We'd better go."

And so we left the house. Throughout the day, in the middle

of my classes, that terrible scene kept passing through my mind. I scarcely heard what my teachers were saying. But there was one person in particular whose image continued to appear before me: Mr. Yuan, the man I had almost run into on my bicycle one afternoon in front of the house, the man whose bold look had sealed my destiny. He was the one responsible for our misery. I hated him.

The atmosphere at home grew heavier and more tense with every passing day. If we now said good morning to my mother, it was simply to avoid another confrontation. But all joy was gone, and we hardly spoke to one another.

The date proposed by Mr. Liu for the celebration of our engagement was the twenty-eighth of October. But Hui-i had still not given his consent to the marriage. He still hesitated because of us. My grandfather assailed him every day.

"My son's an imbecile!" he told the persistent Mr. Yuan. "He's so weak he takes what his children say into account, which just proves how much authority he has over his own family!"

I heard grandfather's many outbursts and knew how much my father suffered over them. I remembered father's perilous trip to Chungking. Hadn't he risked his life for us then? Hadn't he crossed the Japanese lines just for our sake? And hadn't he abandoned the woman he loved for my sake? As I recalled these incidents, and more, I began to feel a tremendous sense of guilt. My father had sacrificed so much for me, and all I had done in return was to make him unhappy. But the thought of marrying young Liu was so abhorrent to me, I said nothing.

And then one day I heard a terrible story. All the newspapers had carried it some years earlier—I don't know how many—and it now came to my attention through some neighborhood gossip.

It seemed that a rich Szechwanese family's youngest daughter had fallen in love with a poor boy. The girl's father, however, wanted her to marry the son of one of the city's wealthiest families. In desperation the girl and her lover eloped. Furious, her father called in the police, who finally found the young couple, throwing the boy in jail and returning the girl to her family.

Nevertheless, she continued to defy her parents. Since her father had already agreed to the marriage with the other family, there was no way for the engagement to be broken without a great loss of face. And so, unable to extricate himself with honor, he announced to the world that his daughter had died suddenly of an illness. Then, to prove her dead, he went through with the funeral. While carrying the coffin, the bearers suddenly felt something move within; they even heard feeble cries, but everyone pretended things were as they should be. In the presence of the entire family the coffin was lowered into the ground as if nothing at all were wrong.

Everyone in the province of Szechwan knew this story, and it had appeared in all the Shanghai papers, but the father was never arrested. Apart from his wealth and influence, as a father whose daughter had defied him, he had everyone's sympathy. All he had done was punish his daughter's disobedience, and who could reproach him for that? Everyone knew that as a last resort it was better to kill your own child than lose face.

I didn't know if the story was true or not, but the power of the family towered over me, and any laws to the contrary seemed feeble and remote.

I shuddered in horror.

Today it could not have happened. Had that poor girl (or I, for that matter) been born just a few years later in a China purged of its cruel and archaic customs, she would have lived to marry the boy she loved. And I might not have been facing this terrible dilemma.

The only difference I could see between the girl from Szechwan and me was that she was dead and I was alive, with my father allowing me to bargain for my life.

I became so obsessed with the story of the girl from Szechwan that for nights on end I would imagine every detail of that coffin and think of myself being nailed into it—particularly since I still had vivid memories of my own aunt's funeral. I had terrible nightmares in which the morgue, with its quicklime, blended into that meal at the Green Pavilion, with the abominable Mr. Yuan serving both as waiter and procurer.

When I would wake, all I could think was *What can I do, what can I do, what can I do?*

I finally came to the conclusion that the only thing left was for me to submit to my destiny. I had no right to prolong my family's anguish—particularly my father's. I would have to do what was expected of me. I would have to agree to the marriage.

At the same time I thought of several avenues of escape. After all, Mr. Liu had said that although the engagement would take place immediately, the marriage might be postponed for three years because of my extreme youth. I was only thirteen, still a baby! And a lot could happen in three years! Although my parents could never annul the engagement, it was still possible for me to explain things to young Liu in private. He seemed reasonable enough and surely wouldn't force me to marry him, especially if I explained to him that there was simply no affinity between us. He might then ask his family to release me from our promise, and if Mr. Liu agreed, I would be saved!

There was also one last argument. Ching-chung had often tried to dissuade my mother by telling her that in Mao's New China, the future of the capitalist was more than a little uncertain. Wouldn't it be absurd, he argued, to force Ching-li to marry a man because of his money, when he might actually lose all of it and be unable to earn a living for his family? Of course, mother never let herself be swayed, but I clung to the idea that a lot could happen in the three years to ruin a family like the Lius. After all, my brother was usually right.

Since my birth, Hui-i had the habit of coming into my room to say goodnight. It was a kind of ritual with him; he could not imagine going to sleep without first looking in on his daughter. In the summer, when we slept uncovered, he would bring a coverlet with him and place it over me. In the winter, when we all used heavy cotton quilts, Hui-i would spread a coat on top of my blankets. I was the only one of his five children for whom he performed this ritual.

When he came into my room on the evening I reached my decision, I had a heavy blanket over me, for although it was only October it was already cold in Shanghai. The lights were out. Very gently, so as not to awaken me, Hui-i placed his coat on top of the blanket. But I wasn't asleep.

"Mei-mei," he whispered, "why are you still awake?"

"I'm thinking, Papa."

"You must go to sleep now, it's late."

"Papa, listen to me. Listen, I accept. I agree to the marriage..."

Father was too overwhelmed to say anything. He simply caressed my cheek and hair a long moment, then left the room.

When I woke up the next morning, the news of my decision seemed to have spread through all of Shanghai. In addition to the Liu family, the entire neighborhood came over to congratulate me. "You were born under a lucky star. What a magnificent match! Yes, you must have been born under a lucky star!"

Ching-chung and Ching-ling reacted quite differently.

"You must have seen a ghost," they said. "How else could you have brought yourself to accept? Yes, a phantom must have frightened you out of your wits and made you lose your mind..."

But my decision was final, and neither my brother nor my sister could dissuade me.

A few days later, coming home from school late on an October afternoon, I looked through the window and saw the servants setting a magnificent table. They were using the organdy tablecloth and the sterling silver. In the kitchen, Mama was decapitating ducks and chickens one after the other, while a servant labored over a burning stove.

"Are we having a party?" I exclaimed, full of curiosity.

"A party?" my mother replied, her face beaming. "A party? I should say so! This is the first time your fiancé has been invited to our home!"

I fled upstairs in a panic and locked myself in my room.

At precisely seven o'clock, Liu Yu-huang rang the doorbell. He was alone. My father, mother, and grandparents began fluttering around him, wagging their heads and waving their arms, as if the young man was not just another young man, but the only son of some supreme god.

Even my brother and sister went downstairs to greet him. I had no choice but to follow.

At that moment, the servants brought out four platters of cold dishes, then four hot dishes, then four more platters containing chicken, duck, an entire fish, and a ham. Each dish was served as a separate course.

As yellow-complexioned as ever, Liu Yu-huang took the seat facing south, between my father and my grandfather. My brothers and sisters sat facing north, on the other side of the table.

The sole subject of conversation throughout the entire meal was food: the infinite varieties of bamboo one could eat in the spring, melons in summer, crabs in the fall, salmon and turtle in the winter.

My brother and sister opened their mouths only for eating. As far as I was concerned, the gastronomic talk so bored me that once the meal was over, I got up to leave the table. Liu Yu-huang suddenly noticed me.

"May I invite Miss Ching-li to accompany me to the movies next Saturday afternoon?" he inquired, looking at my mother.

"But of course," my mother replied, without so much as a glance in my direction. "Saturday afternoon will be perfect. Ching-li is always free on Saturdays because she doesn't go to school."

I was furious, but since my mother had agreed, I could scarcely refuse without risking a scandal. In any case, what was the use? Liu thanked my mother profusely; he was obviously delighted.

At three o'clock in the afternoon that following Saturday, I was practicing the piano on the third floor when Liu arrived. He came upstairs to get me, and without taking my eyes from the music, I told him quite simply that I couldn't interrupt my work, that I couldn't go to the movies, and that the only time I could go out with him was for dinner. Mother did her best to hide her anger; I could see her biting her lips. Liu, on the other hand, seemed not at all perturbed and retired to the next room with my mother, where he spent the rest of the afternoon playing with my little sister, Ching-ching, waiting patiently for the dinner hour. At six-thirty, I announced that I was ready.

This was the first time I had been alone with my fiancé. Walking beside him on the sidewalk, I noticed that he was only slightly taller than I. He suggested we go to the Green Pavilion, probably because it had pleasant memories for him. I was indifferent to both him and the succulent dishes he ordered for me. We had yet to exchange three words, and behind my frosty façade, I was bursting with impatience. Indeed, we had not even been served when I blurted out:

"My mother has told me that we're going to celebrate our engagement on October twenty-eighth. I just want you to know that I refuse this."

"But why?" Liu Yu-huang asked, thunderstruck.

"I've heard that when two people marry, they have to love each other. If they don't, their marriage is without foundation. Now as far as I know, there is no real love between us . . ."

Liu was silent for several moments.

"This is all right," he declared at last, turning to me. "Love, you know, is like a flower. You have to plant the seed and then it will grow."

I shook my head vigorously.

"I don't think that's the case between you and me. First of all, you're not my kind of man. I like boys who are learned and strong, like my brother. You look as if you'd fall over at the least bit of wind. Second, our families are too far apart. Even though my father's a businessman, we appreciate beautiful things in our family, we like music, we have taste, whereas all that counts in your family is money."

Despite the brutality of my words and the humiliation they should have provoked, Liu Yu-huang continued to speak calmly and evenly.

"That too is all right," he said, smiling. "If you like music, well, I'll go with you to concerts. I won't keep you from studying the piano. If you don't like the way I do things, I'll change. And if you don't like my family, we'll go live somewhere else. Why not try? Just try?"

"No, no, absolutely not," I answered. "When a marriage fails, all that's left is divorce. No, it's not something you *just try*, it's too important."

I could hardly have been firmer. I had told him everything and I felt such a tremendous relief that when the waiter

94

brought our dinner, I ate with relish. Liu was even paler than usual and had lost his appetite; he just sat and watched me eat. We had nothing left to say to one another. The same heavy silence of the early part of the evening now returned. Then once again we were outside the restaurant. I tried to start up the conversation again: I described to him what the atmosphere in our household had been like once, and what it had become because of him. I told him that I had said yes to my father only to restore peace in the family and to end the unbearable tension. And I told him that deep down inside myself, I had never really said yes. I had to make him understand that I was serious about breaking off, so I asked him never to come to our house again and to cancel our engagement festivities. Anxious, I forced myself to be insistent, adamant, knowing only that I had to make him promise on the spot. And in fact, I succeeded so well that finally, unable to counter me with any more arguments, his face drawn, he sighed deeply and replied:

"So be it. I promise."

He looked so miserable that I felt a genuine regret and as we had arrived at my gate, I wished him goodnight as warmly as I could. But when he'd gone, I rushed upstairs to tell my brother and sister. When I described what had happened, they clapped their hands and danced for joy.

We were all terribly young and sufficiently naïve to believe that my engagement was truly over and done with. For the first time in a long while, I slept soundly, and the following day, Sunday, went as smoothly as our Sundays always had. Hui-i went out in the evening; he had a business dinner in the city. Around ten o'clock, my sister and I were getting ready for bed in the room we shared when we heard the doorbell. We were more than a little surprised, particularly since no one ever came to visit us on the evenings my father went out, especially at such a late hour.

"Who could that be?" Ching-ling demanded.

"What difference does it make?" I replied. "As for me, I'm going to bed . . ."

We got into bed and spent the next fifteen minutes talking

quietly. Suddenly the bedroom door burst open and my mother appeared. Her jaw set, a severe look in her eye, she strode to the foot of my bed.

"What did you tell him last night?"

"Who?"

"Liu Yu-huang."

"Why?"

"Because he's here, downstairs."

The fool hasn't kept his word, I thought. *He came even though he promised not to.*

"How dare he come at such an hour?" I demanded.

"Because you rejected him yesterday," my mother replied. "You refused him. He didn't sleep a wink all night; he suffered atrociously. And now he has a fever and in spite of it, he hasn't stopped thinking about you, he couldn't help coming to see you. But you! You're a devil, a demon with no feeling whatsoever! The boy loves you and you think nothing of tearing him to pieces . . ."

I was in a rage and decided I had to unmask this impostor. He said he had a fever, did he? *Well,* I thought, *we'll just see about that.* I got out of bed, picked up a thermometer, and headed for the stairs. My mother grabbed my arm.

"Are you crazy?" she cried. "You can't go downstairs like that! You can't appear before a man in bare feet and a nightgown!"

All right, I thought, hastily pulling on a pair of trousers and slipping on my shoes. Descending the stairs, thermometer in hand and my mother at my side, all I wanted to do was show him up for the liar he was and shame him into fleeing. Only when I looked down, and saw the worry and the beseeching look on his face, did my anger begin to dissolve, although not my determination. I asked him nicely, but firmly, to please put the thermometer in his mouth. Docilely, like a child, he obeyed. Two minutes later I asked him for the thermometer; again he obeyed. It read 102 degrees. He did have a fever then! He hadn't lied after all. An icy north wind was blowing outside and in spite of that, sick as he was, Liu had come to see me! Suddenly, everything was different. The man had suffered for me. My rage vanished completely, replaced by compassion.

96

"You must go home at once," I told him. "You must go right to bed."

"Can I come tomorrow?" Liu Yu-huang murmured, delighted to see that my attitude had softened.

I didn't dare refuse him; it would only make him sicker. "You may come when you've no more temperature, and if you promise to take care of yourself first."

He happily bade us all goodbye, and went home whistling.

Three days later he was back again. And every day after that. While he was around I stayed in my room, and my mother and youngest sister, Ching-ching, who was four years old, would keep him company instead. He brought Ching-ching a present every time he came, and she grew very fond of him. When he was late, she would cry. As for me, I refused to give him a thought. What he did simply had nothing to do with me.

One day, as I arrived home from school, stiff with cold, I noticed part of the garden was lit by the light from the drawing room. What I saw on entering stopped me cold.

The room was filled with friends and relatives, who surrounded my parents and grandparents, all smiling and laughing. The center of the room was dominated by a huge square table, covered with a sumptuous red silk cloth, which fell to the floor, and I could read the words "Joy and Happiness," the Chinese characters embroidered in gold thread on the front of the cloth. Between two enormous red candles, four bowls were placed, each containing a special and significant dish: dates, representing a very early pregnancy after marriage; small sweet noodles, called *panpao*, which stood for many children; dried longans for a man-child who would become a Mandarin; and, finally, a bowl of peaches, signifying long life.

Around the rim of the table had been placed an incredible series of small elegant boxes decorated with red and green velvet flowers and containing rings, earrings, bracelets, brooches, and other pieces of ornate jewelry set in gold and jade. There was nothing inside these boxes that wasn't fashioned of precious metals and stones. This luxurious display was completed by piles of satin, silk, and velvet cloth, and by several fur coats, including mink and fox.

Now I understood. It was October 28, the date of my engagement. On the wedding day, the bride's family would offer the trousseau, but on the engagement day, the responsibility belonged to the groom's parents. All of this, then, was meant for me, the down payment on my acquisition. The Lius had scarcely been stingy.

The family circle opened to welcome—or devour—me.

"Well, Mei-mei—" my mother smiled—"I hope you're happy. Everything you see here has been sent by Mr. Liu. Isn't it a lovely party?"

Words failed me. I was neither happy nor unhappy, pleased nor displeased. I simply felt nothing at all.

Somehow I managed to get out of the drawing room and slowly, like a sleepwalker, climbed the two flights of stairs to my room. I tried to begin my homework but the vision of what was going on below kept coming into my mind, preventing me from concentrating. The sky had grown darker and the rain continued to fall. I leaned against the window and looked out. Nothing had changed. My eyes swept the street slowly. Across the way I could see the Protestant church, with its spire crowned by a cross. What should I do now, I wondered.

Suddenly the silhouette of a tall boy emerged from the darkness. It was Louis Ho, my first date, the boy with whom I had secretly gone to the movies. But how could that be? Louis Ho? I must be dreaming, I thought. It's just my imagination. The figure vanished into the darkness, melting back into obscurity as suddenly as it had appeared. I opened the window and breathed in the cold night air.

But there it was again, the same figure! This time, there was no doubt about it. It *was* Louis Ho. But what was he doing there? Had he seen me? I grabbed my coat, left the room, and crept down the stairs. Slipping outside, with no one the wiser, I crossed the street and headed straight for the church. Louis was standing there. He seemed a great deal thinner.

"Louis, have you been sick?"

"No," he replied. "I haven't. I've just lost some weight. And *you* know why . . ."

"What do you mean, *I* know why? How could I know why? You simply disappeared and I've heard nothing further from you!"

He remained silent.

"Why did you disappear like that, so suddenly?" I said impatiently. "Why didn't you send me news?"

"It's quite simple," he replied. "Three months ago, I called you. Your mother answered and forbade me to see you again, *ever*. She told me your engagement was going to be celebrated on October 28. It was a terrific shock. At first, I didn't want to believe it because you'd never even hinted at anything of the kind. Then, finally, I had to accept it. But even though I wasn't allowed to see you or speak to you, I could try writing to you. And I did. I wrote you a letter, then another one, then one after that, but I never got any answer. I was miserable, I was furious with you. I told myself that the least you could have done was to write me a farewell letter. . . . Every day I walk past the church, in memory of us. Today's no different from any other; I was walking by as usual, but since it's the twenty-eighth, I stayed a little longer. I just wanted to wish you happiness and good luck. I . . ."

"Listen to me, Louis," I interrupted. "I have absolutely no idea what you're talking about. No one ever told me that you'd phoned or written. On the contrary, I couldn't understand why you'd just disappeared like that. Are you sure you're telling me the truth?"

"If I'm not telling the truth, why would I be here now? How would I have known that this was your engagement day? But why didn't you yourself tell me the truth? Why didn't you tell me the last time we saw each other?"

"I didn't say anything because I never dreamed this engagement would actually take place . . ."

We paid no attention to the rain falling all around us. We just stood there together while I told him the whole story, how until the last minute I had naïvely believed that Liu himself would cancel our absurd betrothal.

"I think I understand," Louis said, once I had finished my tale. "But now you love your fiancé?"

"In the beginning," I replied, "he disgusted me. But now I think he's nice enough. No, what I really mean is that I feel sorry for him. Does that mean I love him?"

"I think I must do what your mother asked," Louis murmured, after a long pause. "I think I should leave you alone now and not bother you anymore. You must obey your mother and try to love your fiancé. I sincerely wish you all the happiness in the world. But before I go, I just want you to know that I love you, that I've loved you from the first time I saw you. My whole life changed suddenly when I met you. My parents live apart and I've been alone for so long, but when I met you, I was filled with hope. And even though I didn't see you every day, just the sound of your voice on the phone was enough for me. The day your mother told me you were getting married and that I couldn't see you anymore, I suffered terribly . . ."

His voice had dropped and he was unable to go on. I knew he was sincere and that he really was suffering, but I didn't know what to say.

"And now, run along home," he smiled, giving me a little push. "Or your mother will be angry . . ."

"I don't want you to suffer, Louis," I replied, not moving. "The minute I saw you, I loved you too, just as I love my brother."

"But I don't want you to love me like a brother . . ."

"There are very few men I shall ever love as much as I love my father and brother," I explained. "All that means is that I love you very much. Very much . . ."

"You are so young, Ching-li," Louis sighed. "You must understand that I don't love you as a sister. And neither does he . . ."

Louis pointed in the direction of my home.

I was moved and filled with tenderness. I was too young to understand the kind of love Louis was talking about. And Louis began to realize this, too.

"Go now," he said gently. "Go home. If you're happy, I shall accept my pain joyfully."

Louis stood there watching as I crossed the street. I turned around more than once to look at him before reaching the gate, then I ran inside and quickly upstairs so as to wave goodbye to him from my window, as I had so often done in the past.

Louis was still standing there, straight and tall in the rain. We stared at our distant figures for a long time. He seemed to

100

fade away and as I tried to pierce the blackness between us, I thought, *did I love him?*

I opened the window and the rain fell on my face. My cheeks were wet with raindrops. Or were they tears?

I was still standing in front of the open window when I heard a voice call.

"Miss! Miss! Madame wishes that you come down!"

I stared at the servant dumbly, walking past her like an automaton.

"What have you been doing up there?" Mother asked, meeting me at the bottom of the stairs. "How can you go off and hide on a day like this? This is your engagement party. Come down immediately!"

I didn't reply.

"Well?" my mother asked impatiently. "Are you coming?"

"Did Louis Ho phone here?" I blurted out, not moving.

"Once, yes."

"Did he write to me?"

"Yes, several times."

"Why didn't you tell me?"

"Because I had the right to forbid him to call you and to write to you. Because I didn't want him to upset you. Do you have anything further to say on the subject?"

She looked at me angrily, daring me to defy her, ready to fight it out if necessary.

"No," I answered meekly. Once again, I felt myself too defenseless to argue.

I entered the drawing room and was immediately surrounded by a sea of smiling faces, all paying me compliments. And then everyone was gone, and we all retired to bed.

Thus passed my engagement party.

7

My life as a recluse began. No more walks, no more playing with friends—not even with my brother and sisters. The rebel Ching-ling and even Ching-chung had stopped contesting my marriage. Not that they approved, of course, but since they were unable to prevent my being sold to the Lius, they, like me, were forced to accept the inevitable. In any case, what was the good of continuing the battle when I myself had surrendered? At least that was what I wanted everyone to believe. For I still hoped that I might have three years of respite, three years during which something was bound to happen. So I too stopped trying to think of ways to escape, and decided to bide my time.

My father, still preoccupied by his business, continued to come home late every night. Uncle Yao, on the other hand, had fulfilled his threat to leave for Hong Kong with his two wives, his children, and several gold bars. Busy with meetings and political discussions, Ching-chung was absent from home for longer and longer periods of time, reappearing only for brief periods. He had become a militant activist, and intended to participate fully in the great change that was taking place.

My daily life remained the same. School, piano, homework. With one significant exception—I began my apprenticeship as a wife. *Watch your tongue, don't laugh heartily, speak softly, take small steps.* Even before I was sold into this marriage, I had asked my mother to teach me how to sew and cook. To my surprise, Chung-ai had refused; her attitude remained unchanged now.

"I've done nothing but cook and sew, sew and cook, my whole life long," she said, "and I don't want to see you repeat my experience. You are going into a rich family. Of course, it would be good for you to know how to do certain things. But as a great lady, not a servant. The piano, for instance, that I approve of. That's something you should continue."

I was thrilled. The piano was all I really cared about, and now I devoted all my time to practicing. Mozart, Bach, Beethoven, Chopin became my daily companions. Progress was easy in an art that filled me with so much pleasure, and Miss Ling, my teacher, was delighted by both my seriousness and my enthusiasm.

Having taken on too many pupils, Miss Ling was one day unable to continue giving lessons to one of them, a seven-year-old girl. She asked me if I might not care to teach her, as the child lived quite close to our house. I was thrilled. Once a month, in order to make sure she was progressing properly, I took her to Miss Ling, who now looked on me as her assistant. I was very happy with my work, all the more so because the little girl came from a rich family who paid me very well indeed. Being only thirteen, I was so overwhelmed when I received my first hard-earned money that I rushed home immediately and gave all of it to my grandparents, who were then visiting us. It was particularly satisfying to be able to show the money to my grandmother, who had never stopped bemoaning the expense of my piano lessons. My earnings proved that I had not been wasting my time; for in her eyes, money was an unbeatable argument. Never again would I hear any complaint about music from her lips.

The only other events that broke into my quiet and uneventful life were the little concerts I gave from to time at school, and my weekly dates with my fiancé, Liu Yu-huang. Every Saturday now I went out to dinner or to the movies with young Liu. We always went unaccompanied, and gradually, as I came to know him better, our relationship began to change. In the beginning I had detested him and had taken no pains to hide it. But he was a very patient young man and he had a good heart. Finally, his attentiveness and his kindness made me more amiable. Although my friendliness was quite sincere, I had never, not for an instant, accepted the idea of marrying him. Despite our formal engagement, I had never given up the hope that something would happen to prevent the wedding. Something that would cause no one pain. I was counting on time; it was my only ally. And so I continued to play my game.

Two months went by peacefully enough, until one December evening, disaster struck. Chung-ai came into my room with a troubled expression on her face; she had just seen Mr. Yuan. Anticipating the worst, my heart began pounding furiously.

"Mr. Yuan has just given me some very bad news," my mother began. "It seems that Madame Liu is ill. She's in bed, with very high blood pressure. Everyone thinks it's going to get worse, and she's worried about her son, her eldest son . . ."

Her meaning, alas, was only too clear. Since she was the one responsible for organizing her son's marriage, Madame Liu's illness was all the more serious. According to tradition, only two events are considered good fortune: marriage and pregnancy. One of these happy occasions is said to be capable of wiping out three misfortunes, such as illness. And what indeed could cure Madame Liu's condition but the happy event of Liu Yu-huang's marriage—immediately.

I was heartsick.

A professional was consulted to read our horoscopes and determine the most opportune date: January 3, 1950.

The world fell to pieces around me, for all my dreams had crumbled. No glorious career as a pianist, no triumph after years of struggle and preparation. Terrifying visions that I had done my best to ignore flooded my mind. I would never escape from the Liu family.

Everything my girlfriends in school had whispered about the family came to me, all at once. The Lius were well known in Shanghai and my friends seemed to be quite well informed.

My fiancé had nine brothers and sisters; in addition, Madame Liu was from Ningpo, in the Chekiang region, and although it was common enough for mothers-in-law to be severe with their sons' wives, the custom in Ningpo dictated a particularly severe discipline, one that imposed upon the daughter-in-law a whole host of obligations toward *all* members of her new family. I had ignored such stories, believing I had three years in which to escape my fate. But now the certainty of my fate filled me with fear and despair. And even though it had been my own mother who had pushed me into this trap, I still clung to her. I couldn't believe that she wouldn't take pity on me and relent.

"Mama," I said, "do you think it's fair that I give up such a happy life? That I disappear into that family? Do you realize that I'll be the wife of the oldest son, and that I'll have to take over all my mother-in-law's chores and duties? That I'll have to become the mistress of the house and worry about salt and rice? I'll be a slave for life! And you, you who always said I would never have to live like that, you're turning me over to them! Mama, I'm not stupid and I'm not lazy, and I've had an education. And now you're destroying all of it!

"I don't want to get married!" I began sobbing. "You're always telling me I'm your favorite, but you've made me the unhappiest of all your children! I'll wind up like my poor aunt, sacrificing herself to Uncle Hui-ying! I don't want to marry! I beg you . . ."

Mother didn't know what to say. She thought I would calm down in time, and besides, I was already promised. There was nothing whatsoever to be done about it.

I couldn't sleep or eat and my hair began falling out in great clumps. This loss of hair terrified my father the most. He bought me a special lotion and I was supposed to massage my scalp with it every day, a pitiful remedy for my hysterical condition.

"Don't worry, dear one," he would say, "you're wrong to think your father and mother will be lost to you forever. We'll always protect you, even when you're married. You can go on with your studies, your piano, whatever you want. I promise you."

And so I lived through several days of tears and lamentation, the final throes of my defiance. Then I bowed before my destiny, this time without hope, praying only that my path would not be too difficult.

As my wedding day drew closer, Chung-ai grew increasingly nervous. I was, after all, the first of her five children to marry, and she felt completely at a loss as to how to cope. In China, the selection of the bride's trousseau is always a very complicated affair, putting one's honor to the test.

My mother counted on the proximity of the wedding date, and the haste with which the trousseau had to be assembled, to excuse its modesty. She intended to make do with the fewest possible items. Beginning with the blankets, which in China are quilted, she added a silk center, embroidered with a phoenix. Four such blankets were made, one for each season. Then four cotton pallets, used in China in place of mattresses, and two pairs of pillows with embroidered pillowcases. From the material offered by my future mother-in-law, Chung-ai had several dresses made for me. In addition, she gave me a gold medallion, two gold bracelets, a jade ring, and, for sentimental reasons, a small piece of green jade I had once swallowed when I was a baby, thinking it was candy, and which I had promptly thrown up. With these few pieces of linen and jewelry, Chung-ai considered my trousseau complete. She was counting on gifts from friends to supply me with whatever else might be needed. Then she took me to her favorite Buddhist temple.

I was taken there not only because I would soon be married, but because my mother hoped to meet other women who might be able to advise her. Chung-ai had few friends, and since leaving Chao-chou to marry my father, she had rarely gone out. When she announced to the chief nun that I was about to marry, the nun reacted with expected wisdom.

"What a pity," the nun replied. "It would have been better had she waited until at least twenty-five. She will suffer. But since your decision has been made, you must let God show you the way."

By coincidence, there was a group of women visiting the

temple that day who had come from Ningpo, Madame Liu's native city. My mother quickly consulted with them about the delicate matter of the trousseau. The advice she received was more than she had bargained for.

"In Ningpo," the first woman said, "the trousseau is a matter of the greatest importance. In fact, the richness of a trousseau determines the entire course of the marriage! If your daughter had an evil character, for example, a *good* trousseau would guarantee her a happy marriage."

"What would you call a 'good' trousseau?" my mother inquired anxiously.

"Well, you must take into consideration that the Liu family is large and powerful. The Lius have a great many relatives, you know. But what is most important is that their eldest son is marrying. Now, for this kind of marriage, in this kind of family, you need to start with at least fifty blankets. Then you should add two sets of dishes, one in porcelain for everyday, the other in silver for special occasions. And if you don't want the servants laughing at your daughter, you have to . . ."

She went on with her list, which included furniture, but my mother, who had gone chalk-white, was no longer listening. She was, in fact, on the verge of hysteria. Stingy she may have been, but the idea of losing face was unbearable. As the Chinese say: Both doors must be of the same wood; one cannot be of oak and the other of straw. It was clear that these women knew what they were talking about; yet how could she ever assemble such an expensive trousseau? Where would the money come from?

"Don't worry about the money," one of the other women said. "When the in-laws come for the trousseau, you have the right to demand money for what is called 'opening the door.' That way, you'll be reimbursed. After all, the Lius are very rich."

Since this custom existed only in Ningpo, my mother had never heard of it. She was, of course, delighted with the news, for it lessened the shock of the additional cost for a proper trousseau.

She was even more relieved when she verified the woman's statements with my fiancé. Since our engagement, Liu Yu-huang had become an even more frequent visitor than before. Chung-ai now showed him my trousseau—the four blankets, the few pieces of linen and jewelry, the glaring absence of furniture and dishes. Liu Yu-huang consulted with his own mother. Yes, she agreed, rather meager. After a great deal of discussion, the Liu family agreed to advise my mother, even though such an arrangement was unheard-of. They also reassured her, indirectly, that money was no problem. Accordingly, a "good" trousseau was begun.

Eight large trunks were ordered. Made by hand of lacquered red leather, they were from the city of Fukien. Once these containers arrived, they were filled with the following items: sixteen blankets, four per season (insufficient, perhaps, but since they were to be hand embroidered, there was no time to make more); two quilts, stuffed with goose feathers, which the daughter-in-law was obliged to offer personally to her in-laws in accordance with Ningpo custom; eight pairs of pillowcases; furniture consisting of several cupboards, beds, night tables, and chairs. Since a daughter-in-law was not permitted to live more luxuriously than her mother-in-law, my furniture was made of rosewood, which was cheaper than Madame Liu's ironwood. We would be living with the Lius, and as their house was an old one, it was against the law to modernize, and we therefore couldn't install a proper bathroom; we thus bought a wooden bathtub and five additional barrels for the bedroom and the bathroom. The first barrel was for bathing; the second, much shallower, was for washing the feet; the third, for the face; the fourth, which was very wide and sat upon three feet, was used for childbirth; and the fifth was a toilet. In families as wealthy as the Lius, these barrels were normally covered with gold; mine, however, were made of red-lacquered wood. We also received two sets of dishes, one in sterling silver for important dinners, the other, for daily use, in Kiangsi porcelain; each service contained 150 pieces.

Beside the traditional quilts for my mother-in-law, I had to offer to each of the women in the family a pair of embroidered silk shoes. We bought fifty pairs in a variety of sizes. We also purchased ginseng, an edible plant known as the "root of long life," swallows' nests, white mushrooms, and longans, for

108

these were ingredients for the dishes I would have to prepare for my in-laws during the long period devoted to the celebration of our marriage.

My room was soon filled with boxes and packages that finally spilled out over the whole house until it began to resemble a warehouse. My mother exhausted herself filling up the trunks. Terrified that some trunks might remain empty, she folded everything very carefully so that each article took up the maximum space. Unfortunately, when the trunks reached their final destination, their contents had collapsed like a soufflé.

Grandmother watched all the preparations with trepidation, moaning and groaning much as she had over my piano lessons. In vain, my mother reassured her that we would be reimbursed, that all this was the custom in Ningpo, but my grandmother remained skeptical. The increasing expense was making her ill with worry.

"It's unbelievable what you've cost your father since the day you were born," she reproached me. "The piano, the fancy private school, and *now* . . ."

This time, I felt she'd gone too far.

"I'm not the one who wanted to get married!" I snapped. "*You're* responsible for this. If you don't like it, then just say so and I'll be only too happy to break my engagement."

But nothing could make my grandmother cease her lamentations. When the trousseau was finally ready, my grandmother insisted on finding out from me exactly how much the Lius were going to pay for the privilege of "opening the door." Angry and humiliated, I strode to the telephone, threatening to call them. Chung-ai stopped me.

"That's enough!" she cried. "You're not going to call them!"

"And why not?" I asked defiantly. "There's no reason to be ashamed. Some people marry for love, don't they? But me, I'm being married off for money, am I not? So why shouldn't we all agree about the price? If they don't pay enough, then let's negotiate!"

I dialed the number. Liu Yu-huang answered.

"You're coming to get the trousseau in a few days," I told him. "I assume you realize that that's when you have to pay a certain sum?"

Chung-ai grabbed the receiver and hung up.

"You should be ashamed of yourself, talking to your fiancé like that!"

The poor woman! She didn't want to lose face, but she didn't want to lose the money either. My grandmother remained unusually silent during this discourse.

Barely half an hour had passed when my fiancé rang the doorbell. He wanted to know why we had hung up so abruptly. Both mother and grandmother greeted him with strained smiles. But I explained that all I had wanted to do was ask for the customary sum of money, and that it was my mother who had hung up the phone.

"Don't listen to her!" Chung-ai interrupted. "She's just a child, she has no idea of what she's saying!"

"I know perfectly well what I'm saying," I retorted. "I want to know what you're giving for me. If it's not enough, I won't marry you, that's all."

Mother was purple with embarrassment. She gestured frantically for me to be quiet, but my fiancé only smiled.

"I'll give whatever you wish."

"How much?" I asked. "I want a lot, you know."

"Stop it!" my mother gasped.

Upset by my mother's humiliation, Liu Yu-huang promised that everything would be satisfactorily settled, and then quickly changed the subject.

"Tomorrow," he went on, turning to me, "I'm taking you to be measured for your wedding dress."

"Tomorrow's a school day," I replied. "You can go without me."

"Don't listen to her," my mother interrupted. "Just come and get her at four o'clock."

And so Liu Yu-huang came the following afternoon, and I followed him docilely to the shop. He chose a beautiful wedding dress of muslin and raw silk, cut in the European style and finished with delicate Chinese embroidery.

That very evening, an incident occurred that demonstrates my colossal innocence. Liu Yu-huang had accompanied me home after our shopping expedition. The night was dark and cold and, once inside the gate, we had to cross the deserted garden. There was no light from the rooms on the ground floor. We were two steps away from the front door when my fiancé suddenly took my head in his hands and kissed me on the mouth. Shocked and surprised, I turned and ran. He ran after me.

"Aren't you ashamed!" I shrieked over my shoulder as I ran. "I'll tell my mother! You, you *hoodlum!*"

When he finally caught up with me I saw, by the light from the second-floor windows, that his face was pale and drenched with sweat. Gasping for breath, he begged me not to tell my mother, to swear not to say anything about it. I thought he was going to faint, and so I swore I would do as he wanted. Still, he was terrified. Since he knew I was a Christian, he begged me to swear by Jesus Christ, and to cross myself when I did so. I swore again, crossing myself. Only then did he let me go inside.

The next morning, Madame Liu came in person to take me on a shopping expedition for the more important purchases on Fourth Street, famous for its brothels *and* its embroideries. There was shop after shop of lingerie, linen, and shoes, all of them decorated with the famous embroidery of Suchow. All the windows, as well as the interiors of the shops, were piled high with merchandise in every color of the rainbow. It was a dazzling spectacle, crowded, and wholly Chinese.

Out of this wild and confusing mass of goods, Madame Liu was able to select just the right merchandise, for women from Ningpo were famous for their elegant taste.

For the first time in my life, I knew what the wardrobe of the rich consisted of. Even the selection of undergarments required meticulous attention—from the red-embroidered underpants which came down to mid-thigh, to the flattening breast bands we wore. The Chinese believe large-breasted women bring misfortune.

For major purchases, we went to one of the most fashionable shops on Fourth Street, where my mother-in-law chose a tunic embroidered in white silk, a rose-colored tunic with a Chinese collar, and finally a ceremonial tunic, also with a Chinese collar and full sleeves, sumptuously embroidered with phoenix birds and dragons in gold and silver threads and tiny beads. Then came the embroidered shoes, as well as a variety of other accoutrements. One outfit was composed of fourteen separate articles of clothing, an impressive figure that I still have not forgotten.

All that was left was my hair. I was given what can only be described as a Eurasian hairdo—curled in the European fashion, but pulled into an old-fashioned Chinese-style chignon. In my agony, I had lost a great deal of hair, but what was left was enough to cover up the thin patches. The chignon was caught in a pearl hairnet, two phoenix birds in seed pearls were placed above my temples, and two long earrings, which bobbed at every movement, were attached to my ears. The entire arrangement was called "the phoenix headdress." A stole made out of clusters of pearls in the shape of lotus flowers was draped across my shoulders, and there were hand-embroidered handkerchiefs for me to hold. I was the very image of elegance and wealth.

A professional horoscope reader was now consulted to determine the appropriate date for my in-laws to receive the trousseau. This was a very important occasion. The horoscope reader fixed the date one week before the wedding. By this time, there were not only the trunks, but a host of packages had collected as well, which my mother had tied in thin red and green silk ribbon—red being the color for the husband, green for the wife.

At nine o'clock on the morning of the appointed day, a car, followed by a small van, pulled up outside our gate. Two men got out, accompanied by the drivers and a flock of servants. And who should the two men be but the detested Mr. Yuan and Mr. Chen! According to tradition, in order to "open the door" the money had to be paid immediately, and as soon as our servant answered the bell, the two held out a small box wrapped in red silk. I was there when the box was presented to my father. It looked heavy.

"Papa!" I cried. "It's the money! Open it!"

But first Hui-i ordered the servant to bring in the two intermediaries.

Mr. Yuan and Mr. Chen entered the room, whereupon the

servants immediately began gathering up the trunks and packages we had prepared. A short comedy of manners ensued. My father pretended to give the box back to the intermediaries. The latter protested.

"No, no, no!" they chorused. "This is a sincere gift from Mr. Liu."

"No, no, no," my father replied.

"Yes, yes, yes," they repeated.

I knew it was only theater, but this didn't keep me from being a nervous wreck lest the box end up in the wrong hands. Finally, the concluding formula was pronounced:

"We hope you will accept this with a smile."

"To refuse would be improper," my father replied.

At last, the game was over. Now tea had to be given to the intermediaries and big tips to the servants who were loading the van. When everyone had finally left, we opened the red box. Inside, on a bed of silk, glittered ten small bars of solid gold.

I had been an expensive purchase.

I continued to live like any other schoolgirl, going to class every day and doing my homework every evening, but too quickly the day approached when I would have to leave home, a fact of which Chung-ai was only too well aware. She had begun to realize how alone and defenseless I would be within the Liu family, the family she had so ardently wanted me to enter. My mother and I had fought at first, and she had won. Now she was deeply troubled by her old maternal fears. Would I have everything I needed in that unfamiliar house where I would live? In the end, Chung-ai decided that her oldest and most trusted servant, Ah-san, would go with me to the Lius, for Ah-san knew all my needs and would protect me. Then, just a few days before the wedding, my mother asked that old harridan of a marriage broker, Lao Li, to come to the house in order to help with the final preparations. She knew a great deal, and would prove to be singularly useful.

The night before the wedding, Chung-ai called me into her room. All the grownups were there: my parents, my grandparents, the servants, and Lao Li. I was the only child present. My mother took me in her arms and began to sob. I too began to cry, my tears mingling with hers.

"Don't cry, Mama," I sobbed. "Please don't cry . . ."

But the more I begged her to stop, the more she wept.

"Tomorrow you'll be leaving us," she said, when she found her voice again. "Since the day you were born, I have always had you beside me. Now I am very sad. Yes . . . yes, I wanted you to marry. . . . But you are so young. . . . How can I let you go?"

Her words shocked me into finally realizing grim reality. *Tomorrow*, I would be gone. I would have to leave my house, my beloved parents, and go to live with strangers. *Tomorrow!* I broke down again and began to sob.

"Mama," I cried, turning toward her. "If it makes you suffer so, please don't make me leave you. I don't want to get married!"

"Listen to me, my child," Chung-ai replied, shaking her head slowly. "Listen to me and be good. You know why your mother has forced you to marry. You know it's because she has suffered so much from poverty. And you know why your father risked his life to go to Chungking. Because of the poverty that threatened his children. Just thinking about what we endured makes me shiver, and how could I think of you, so delicate, so fragile, like a flower, suffering from poverty? I couldn't stand the thought of it. That's why I pushed you into a rich family, for your own good, even though my heart was breaking. Tomorrow, your life as a woman will begin. You must obey the Three Bonds and the Five Relations. You must serve your in-laws with love, you must love and respect your husband, and you must have beautiful children and bring them up properly. And then your parents will be happy . . ."

I knew then that my time was up, that I would indeed have to go; that I would have to turn my attention exclusively to my new duties. Until the very last second, however, I could not believe that I really would be leaving. Until now, it seemed that I could somehow stay. Mother began to cry once more, but when I again urged her to stop, it was Lao Li who intervened.

"Let your mother cry," she said softly.

114

Lao Li knew all there was to know of ancient customs. According to her, the more a mother wept before her daughter's wedding, the happier the child's marriage would be. Such tears even had a name; they were called the Tears of the Flowered Palanquin because, in ancient times, tears were shed when the bride climbed into her flower-bedecked litter to be carried to her wedding. And so I let my mother cry; in fact, I joined her. Finally, my father took me in his arms, spoke soothingly, and sent me off to sleep.

He came into my room as I was getting ready for bed, pulled down the covers for me, and waited until I was settled comfortably. Then he left. But for a long time afterward I heard him pacing up and down in the hallway, only going into his own room when he was certain I had stopped crying. In the bed next to mine, Ching-ling turned and looked at me.

"You don't want to get married, then?"

I didn't reply.

"We've still one last chance," she went on. "If you want to run away, I'll help you."

I shook my head.

"Really, I don't understand you," my sister said, somewhat put out. "You're the unhappiest girl I know. Your hair is falling out, but still you do what you're told like some kind of trained dog. You let everyone walk all over you! Look, if you want to get married, then stop crying. Be happy and get ready for it!"

And with that, she turned over and pulled the covers up over her head, simultaneously pitying me and being angry at the same time.

I switched off the light. I could still hear the sound of father's footsteps in the hall, and I tried to stifle my sobs in my pillow. And so I finally drifted off to sleep on this very last night under my parents' roof.

8

My wedding day was also the first time I had ever missed school. When I opened my eyes, it occurred to me with childish pleasure that I could for once lie in bed all morning. But the faithful Ah-san, who was going to follow me into my new life, came in with breakfast at eight o'clock, and then rushed me off to the beauty salon. I'd only been to such places to have my hair done, but this time they would make up my face. And although the salon was Chinese, the makeup was thoroughly European. I was treated to plucked and redrawn eyebrows, eye shadow, and just the faintest bit of rouge on my cheeks, for my skin was pale as porcelain.

It was noon before we returned to the house. As on the evening of my engagement party, a large square table of ironwood, covered with a long, red silk cloth, sat in the middle of the living room. An incense-holder had been placed between the two red candles, and curlicues of smoke twisted up into the air above them. There were twelve different dishes on the table and my whole family was present for this initial ceremony, which was dedicated to our ancestors.

"Come here," Lao Li told me. "Kneel down and bid your ancestors farewell."

116

The old woman spoke to me in an odd, singsong voice, a chant peculiar to this occasion. She pushed me onto a red carpet that had been unrolled on the floor in front of the altar. I knelt down, touched the floor with my forehead, and felt the ache swell up into my throat at the thought of all these ancestors I'd never known, but would soon leave forever. Already Lao Li was pulling me to my feet, only to have me kneel a second time to thank my ancestors for having produced such a fine family lineage.

Standing again, I was then obliged to kneel a third time. And like a prompter in the theater, Lao Li whispered the words to me. This time, I prayed to my ancestors to protect me, to bless my marriage, and to give me a child as soon as possible, a perfect child. Then in her hoarse singsong voice, Lao Li ordered the servants to prepare the Feast of the Flowered Palanquin, the last meal I would eat as an unmarried girl, the last meal before climbing into the flowered palanquin—in this case an American car—that would take me to the wedding ceremony. The Palanquin of Joy, it was traditionally called. But for me, it was a palanquin of tears.

This meal was to be eaten alone. To this end, another, smaller table had been set up in the living room, and there I was ordered to sit once I had placed the required dishes where they belonged. But I didn't want to eat alone, stared at by everyone. I wanted all of us to eat together.

"No," Lao Li chanted. "You alone shall be carried in the flowered palanquin. And you alone shall eat the feast of the flowered palanquin."

And so I sat, surrounded by the tender and admiring faces of my entire family. My littlest sister Ching-ching, stared at me wide-eyed. Even my mother was impressed. If my family knew of the prayer to the ancestors, their origin was too modest to have known of this ritual in which the bride feasted alone, like an empress surrounded by her court.

The heaping bowl of rice Lao Li handed me was rounded off like a dome. I could not imagine how I might touch it with my chopsticks without spilling half the contents.

"This means you will possess everything in abundance your whole life long," intoned Lao Li.

Only then did I notice that all the dishes were filled to the brim, and only then did I begin to understand. Having finished her litany, Lao Li picked up the chopsticks and began to feed me like a baby. When the grains of rice fell to the table, she plucked up each one quickly in her fingers and restored it to the bowl. I was idly wondering how carefully she had washed her hands when she suddenly stuffed a round fish cake in my mouth and chanted once again, "May you know five generations issued from you before you die . . ." This fish cake is round and signifies the family, which will remain forever united.

Following the fish cake, a clam was popped into my mouth. "So that your life will be filled with gold coins . . ." recited Lao Li. In ancient China, pieces of gold or silver were minted in the shape of shellfish.

Then came a fried spring roll. "That you may have an abundance of gold bars . . ." The reference here was clearly to the contents of the strongbox that had been given to my father. And so, ignoring my appetite or ability to digest, Lao Li stuffed me like a goose. Finally deciding that I'd had enough, she called the servants and ordered them to escort me to my room, where I was to dress.

After I had donned the Chinese brocade dress with its red flowers, Ah-san arranged silk flowers in my hair. I was then helped into a pair of high-heeled shoes and wrapped in a mink coat. A terrific commotion arose from the stairway.

"Hurry up! Hurry up!" my family shouted.

My fiancé had arrived and it was unthinkable that he be kept waiting. Indeed, nothing was more important than the moment when the bridegroom arrived to meet his bride-to-be at her parents' home. We rushed down the two flights of stairs; Liu Yu-huang was waiting outside, an absurd figure in a long black Chinese tunic and an overcoat. Lao Li beckoned to him. He crossed the garden, and suddenly we both were kneeling in the center of the drawing room. This was the solemn moment in which the engaged couple, hitherto called the "new man" and the "new woman," thanked the bride's family and bade them goodbye. We both had to prostrate ourselves, foreheads touching the floor, before my grandparents, and then my parents.

"Hurry up!" someone cried as we were rising. "It's time for the picture..."

Everyone disappeared and I was seated in a limousine with Ah-san, holding the suitcase that contained my complete wardrobe for the ceremony. I would have to change clothes several times during the wedding. Rapidly, Ah-san gave me some last-minute advice: Take small steps, speak slowly, and whatever happens, never laugh. As if I could laugh, I thought. Five minutes later I was in one of Shanghai's largest photography studios. Liu Yu-huang appeared at my side, and we awkwardly posed together, stiff and formal. Then Ah-san and I were back in the car again, accompanied by a photographer from the studio who would follow us all day.

The wedding ceremony took place in a huge restaurant, The Apricot Flower, on Nanking Road. Its three floors had been reserved exclusively for the wedding guests, including not only relatives and intimate friends, but dignitaries and a host of executives and employees from the many banks, factories, and business enterprises owned by the Lius. All in all, there were 1,500 people present. Liu Pin-san was one of the ten richest men in all China—a fact in which the new government would soon express considerable interest.

The entire restaurant had been decorated with green-and-red silk ribbons and big balls of the same colors, with huge panels of red silk covered by inscriptions representing good wishes. Each of these inscriptions was followed by the name of the donor. The themes represented were the honeymoon, love, and eternal happiness.

When our arrival was announced, a vast throng of guests surged forward, enveloping me like a giant octopus. I could neither advance nor retreat, while my poor ears were bombarded with greetings and compliments from all sides.

"How lovely ... Look at those hands ... Like bamboo shoots in the spring ... Skin whiter than egg white ... Eyes like a phoenix ... Ah, what a rascal, that Liu ..."

When it comes to occasions of this sort, the Chinese are not stingy with compliments.

As I was being pushed and squeezed in the midst of the crowd, I heard a woman's voice behind me, a young woman.

"The Liu family is utterly unscrupulous," I heard her say distinctly. "This little flower will be crushed. What a pity . . ."

I tried to turn around and see who had spoken, but I couldn't move, and when I finally managed to disengage myself, the woman had disappeared.

The restaurant personnel elbowed their way through the crowd, forcing a passage for me to the second floor, where I was to change. Mother was waiting for me there, and, once the door was shut, I sighed with relief. But the words of the unidentified woman haunted me.

"Why would she say that?" I asked my mother, repeating what I'd heard.

"I'm sure she wasn't talking about you," mother hastened to reply. "How could you imagine such a thing? The Lius are good, virtuous people. And so is your husband. Please, don't always be jumping to conclusions. Anyway, now we've got to hurry."

There clearly was no time to discuss the matter further. I put on my wedding dress, the beautiful white European gown, with its tight waist and long train, that I had chosen with Liu Yu-huang. My mother and Ah-san rushed about like hens, each trying to outdo the other. My hair was taken down, the silk flowers replaced by fresh gardenias. High-heeled silver pumps were pushed onto my feet.

I looked at myself in the mirror. I was as pale as a ghost.

"The ceremony will now begin," a wedding official announced. The door to the room opened. Four small children, two boys and two girls, waited outside. They were dressed European-style, all in white, and each carried a small basket filled with flowers. My father entered and placed a white veil on my head, covering my face and shoulders. My eyes filled with tears.

It is you, Father, who place upon me the veil of slavery, I thought. *It is your arm which will give me to another man. And all this celebration only serves to separate us.* But before I could

120

speak, Lao Li, that old gnome with the pockmarked face, began bustling around me, hissing at me to hurry.

I moved forward slowly while flashbulbs sizzled and burst around me. Below, on the ground floor, the orchestra began to play Mendelssohn's *Wedding March*. I was led toward a huge room divided by an incredibly long and narrow red carpet. Holding my father's arm, I advanced with measured steps between the two ranks of well-wishers, preceded by the two little girls scattering flowers and followed by the two boys who were holding my train. Lao Li whispered to me to lower my head. From the first step in the ceremony, the bride had to assume that posture of humility which in fact symbolized her fate.

My fiancé was waiting at the far end. He too had changed his clothes. Now he wore a tuxedo, which made him no more appealing to me than before. At his end of the room, three steps led to a small podium and a table covered with red silk. Behind the table sat three men in Chinese dress: in the center, a very important person, the witness, whose name I have long forgotten; to his left, my future father-in-law, Liu Pin-san, and to his right, Tso-hung, my grandfather.

The music stopped just as I reached Liu Yu-huang.

"New Man," the wedding official intoned loudly, "take the veil from her face . . ."

This was the first of a series of rituals that would take place. Liu Yu-huang stepped forward, lifted my veil, and handed it to an attendant. A great murmur of approval arose, dying down only when the "witness" at the podium began his speech. This Shanghai dignitary, a close friend of Liu Pin-san, first praised the virtues of my future in-laws at great length, then those of my father, the eminent professor, and so on. These tributes were followed by advice to the new couple to avoid dispute, to respect one another—the list seemed to go on interminably. When he finished, he asked that the register containing the names and civil status of the couple be brought forward. Turning to my grandfather and to Mr. Liu, he asked for their consent to the marriage, stamping the register with a seal. Then the witness handed Liu Yu-huang a ring which he slid onto the third finger of my left hand, a gold ring into which was set an enormous solitaire. Including the speech, this part of the proceedings lasted some three quarters of an hour.

"The ceremony is over!" the official announced. "The newlyweds will rest!"

To be sure, this was only a figure of speech, for in fact, the ceremony had barely begun. The exit march was struck up, and amidst great noise and confusion, covered with confetti and paper streamers, I returned to the smaller room. My new husband Liu stood beside me as I sank, exhausted, into an armchair. I was no longer Chow Ching-li. From now on, I would be called *Liu* Chow Ching-li.

Now two longer ordeals awaited us. The first was a solemn occasion that inspired both respect and fear—that of prostration before the families. The second was lighthearted and utterly unbearable—the traditional ragging and teasing that started and stopped and started again throughout the day.

In any case, we had to change clothes once again before the next stage. Liu Yu-huang dressed again in his Chinese clothes, while I had to get into the fourteen-piece costume my mother-in-law had purchased for me on Fourth Street. I glittered from head to toe, encased in gold threads mingled with multicolored embroideries, my chignon enveloped in a hairnet of seed pearls and my head and ears covered with jewels. A long pendant, a gift from my mother-in-law, hung from my neck, its gold disc engraved with four words: *Beautiful Without, Intelligent Within.* Lao Li handed me the obligatory red silk handkerchief.

Once again, I studied myself in the mirror, a comforting distraction. I was still a child, and all the finery pleased me, thus helping me to forget myself. The image reflected was that of a girl from another century, of Old China, so strange when one considers that this ceremony was taking place while a new China was being born.

To my mother's dismay, I could not keep from bursting out laughing when Liu Yu-huang appeared, his narrow body all afloat in a long wedding robe. But Liu himself only smiled.

"I always dress this way," he apologized, "when paying homage to ancestors."

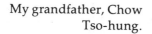
My paternal grandmother,
Li Hsing-lan.

My grandfather, Chow
Tso-hung.

Shanghai in the Twenties was the great cosmopolitan city of the
Far East. It was on the shore of the Whangpoo that my father
mixed with coolies and saw Europeans for the first time. (Photo by
Roger-Viollet.)

Engaged at four, married at sixteen, my mother Chung-ai was an educated peasant.

My brother, Chow Ching-chung, six years older than I, was my hero and protector. A secret revolutionary at sixteen, he was the first to pronounce before me the name of Mao Tse-tung.

My father, Chow Hui-i, educated at Shanghai's St. John's University, was a young bourgeois indoctrinated with Western ideas when he married at eighteen.

In Shanghai, under the Japanese occupation, the quarters were separated by barbed wire. As children, we amused ourselves by climbing over the obstacles, not without tearing our clothes! (Keystone photo.)

Red Army soldiers entering Shanghai less than a year
before my marriage.

January 3, 1950. In my white wedding gown.

Liu Yu-huang, my husband.

I am only fourteen, still a child myself, as I hold on my knees my first child, Paul, the "little prince" of my life.

In my ceremonial red wedding gown of fourteen pieces, with gold and silver thread woven into the embroidery.

The powerful Liu Pin-san, my father-in-law, one of the richest men in China, whose palms were red and whose forehead shone like a mirror.

His wife had sparkling eyes, the bearing of a queen, and a voice as imposing as her person.

In 1959 my husband, Liu Yu-huang, though ill,
took personal charge of arranging for the burial
place of his parents. At Ningpo he found a favorable spot according to the horoscopes, and
he acquired a hillside (shown above and at left).
He would be buried here before them.

My oldest, Paul, born with
the New China in the
year of the Tiger.

My second child,
Juliette, at the age of two.

The goddess Kwan Yin, to whom I have often
prayed.

With that, Lao Li hustled us out the door for the ceremonial prostration, which was to take place in the main room. As I was making my way there, walking slowly as required, a girl my own age suddenly burst out of the crowd and snatched my red silk handkerchief. I was terrified, but Lao Li reassured me.

"Don't worry," she said, handing me another one. "That's the custom. Everyone has the right to grab something from the bride's hand."

"You might have warned me," I pouted. "I was so scared . . ."

Two square ironwood armchairs with red cushions stood in the middle of the room. The wedding official began a litany, similar to the one chanted earlier by Lao Li, to announce our arrival.

"New Man and New Woman will now greet their families!"

Liu Pin-san and his wife were led up to the chairs, their faces wreathed in smiles.

"Let the married couple kneel!" intoned the official.

My husband and I knelt down side by side, touching our foreheads to the red carpets in deference and respect.

"You may rise!" We did so.

Immediately afterward, we were ordered to kneel, and then to rise again. Thus we would *kowtow* three times before each honored couple. My mother-in-law helped me up after the third time.

"You are doing beautifully," she murmured, "very well indeed."

Now Tso-hung and grandmother occupied the armchairs and received our *kowtows*, followed by my parents.

There remained, however, the entire Liu family—approximately fifty pairs of aunts, uncles, and cousins—before whom I had to prostrate myself three times per couple. I shall leave it to the reader to calculate the total number of movements accomplished!

During the prostrations, Lao Li stood next to me and as each *kowtow* was completed, I handed her the small red envelope which each couple offered us, containing bank notes or gold coins. This part of the ceremony lasted two hours, and at the end my husband's face had paled noticeably, the veins standing out in his neck and forehead. The fourteen pieces of my costume seemed a leaden box, and I was drenched with perspiration. I felt as if my legs and back had been beaten with sticks. Finally, Lao Li led me to the small back room. All I wanted to do now was close my eyes for just ten minutes, but I had to change immediately for the ceremonial dinner. The fourteen articles of clothing were removed, and I felt for one second the pleasure of being naked and unburdened. My husband remained dutifully closeted behind a screen during the undressing; it would have been unthinkable for him to see even the tops of my shoulders.

Seated twelve to a table, the guests filled the three floors of the Green Pavilion. The restaurant next door, which we had also taken, was full as well. Outside, Nanking Road was literally blocked by all our guests' cars, creating an incredible traffic jam in that part of Shanghai.

It was now late afternoon, and the next ritual, which preceded the actual serving of the wedding banquet, commenced on the ground floor of the restaurant.

We would now begin the toasting.

Only minutes before, Lao Li had explained what would become for me a terrifying ordeal. According to tradition, the married couple—followed by a waiter carrying two crystal shot glasses and a bottle of rice brandy on a tray—had to stop at each table and drink a good luck *kan-pei*, or "bottoms up," with each and every one of the dozen guests seated at each round table. Considering that the three-storeyed restaurant held twenty tables per floor, as did the one next door with an equal complement of wedding guests, Liu Yu-huang and I could conceivably be forced to down 1,500 ounces of brandy. But how could a girl, still only thirteen, and her frail husband manage such a colossal feat? I was horrified.

The truth was that no one actually expected us to do much more than lift the glasses to our lips during the toast. There were always some male guests, however, who, having had a bit too much brandy themselves, would always insist as a matter of honor that *both* the husband and wife actually empty their glasses.

Fortunately, the savoir faire of the clever Lao Li came to our rescue time and time again. At times, when Liu Yu-huang was cornered and forced to drink up, he would simply hold the brandy in his mouth, then spit it into a glass held out surreptitiously by a waiter so instructed by Lao Li. But her principal task was to come to my rescue, for there were no small number of aggressive and drunken guests who delighted in trying to force me to swallow also. Indeed, the toasting went on in an increasingly riotous atmosphere, for if the married couple was expected to observe a modest and dignified attitude at all times, there were no limits to how far the guests could go in terms of jokes and gibes and jeers. Certain particularly rowdy people even demanded that we empty our glasses two or three consecutive times! Others, convinced that I had not really swallowed anything at all, accused me of playing favorites.

"You drank with *him!*" they would shout. "But apparently *I'm* not worthy of such an honor! *Me*, you refuse! . . ."

Fortunately, at moments like these, Lao Li spared me the worst by acting the clown. She had the right to talk back to the drunkards and she always managed to shut them up; in fact, she was so skillful that we often managed to skip over several guests at a time without having to drink. Often she would even drink the toast for me, for she was not the slightest bit wary of alcohol.

Not all of the guests, however, were unkind. Many were content with the symbolical gesture, particularly those in the second restaurant who saw that we had had about as much as we could take. They took pity on us and let me raise my glass to the whole table at once so that I would not have to drink with each guest separately. My mother-in-law also helped out, for she knew from experience that this particular ceremony was apt to leave the new husband sprawled in the middle of his own vomit, and she did not intend to let things go that far. She intervened more than once in defense of her son and when she took his glass and drank it herself, no one dared to object.

At last the toasting ceremony was over and we returned to the main restaurant for dinner. Lao Li, perhaps because she was a bit drunk, turned to me and declared that she had seen a great many weddings in her life, but that in all of China she had never participated in one as big as ours. And she added that there was no doubt about the happiness which awaited my husband and me.

A long table for ten had been set up on a dais in the wedding room. The selection of guests at this table had particular significance. In addition to the newlyweds, young single people who were rich and whose parents were still alive were invited to sit there. Most of our table-mates had been chosen by the Lius from among their many cousins. Except for those at our table, the rest of the guests in the room had already begun to eat. I mounted the three steps to the head table and seated myself.

By this time, it was seven or eight o'clock in the evening. As soon as I was seated, a waiter began serving the cold hors d'oeuvres: several platters of agar and turnip slivers, glazed duck, prawns marinated in sherry. I had never been more exhausted in my life, and I was also starving. Just as I reached out with my chopsticks, Lao Li, who was still at my side, stopped me.

"No, no, no!" she whispered. "You mustn't do that! Everyone's looking at you. I am supposed to serve you!"

Those who could serve themselves were a great deal more fortunate than I. While I waited patiently, Lao Li chose a piece of glazed duck and placed it on my plate. I eagerly picked it up with my chopsticks, opening my mouth hungrily . . .

"Kan-pei! Kan-pei!"

Suddenly I was surrounded by four guests who wanted to drink with me once more. I reluctantly returned the duck to my plate, stood, and raised my glass. So did Liu.

"We hope the new man and the new woman will live to a ripe old age!"

Three courses came and went while this toasting continued. It was all right for the guests; they had already eaten their fill and could wish and hope for as much as they wanted. Liu touched the glass to his lips and thanked them. That, however, was only the beginning. One after the other, guests came forward, more aggressive than ever, calling Liu by name, scolding him for not drinking, and teasing us unmercifully. I still had not managed a single bit of food when Lao Li, seeing how exhausted we were, intervened and dragged me off to the

126

small room to change my clothes again. I was famished, I protested, but Lao Li assured me that if I changed quickly enough, I could get back to the table in time for the main courses, and that I would be able to eat in peace because toasts would no longer be permitted. I changed into a Chinese dress of pink satin with a pair of matching pumps embroidered with small phoenix birds. I returned to the dinner table just as the first, and most expensive, course, sharks' fins with crab sauce, was being removed.

Suddenly a man came up to the table. He was about thirty, slender and thin-lipped, with wrinkled skin and glasses and eyes aglitter. In one hand he held a teapot full of hot brandy, in the other a glass. He was drunk and smiled wickedly at me.

"I'm sorry," Lao Li declared, "the newlyweds have already drunk. Now they must eat, for the main courses are being served."

"Be quiet!" the man shouted angrily. "You're ruining the party! I want to drink with them!"

Whereupon he emptied his glass at one gulp. I tried not to pay any attention to this repulsive creature with the bloodshot eyes, but my husband took a little sip, thinking that would be enough to get rid of him.

"Ah, no!" the man cried. "The *new woman* must drink, too!"

"I'll drink for her," Lao Li replied, taking up a glass.

"I didn't ask *you*!" the man shouted.

This time, the man pushed Lao Li away brutally. When he filled the glass and held it out to me, I knew something thoroughly disagreeable was about to happen, but I remained calm and asked Liu in a whisper who the man was.

"Who am I?" the man roared, having overheard my question. "You don't know who I am! Why, I'm Old King! The boss is your father-in-law, right? Well, and I'm the boss's son-in-law!"

He was lying, of course, for Old King was really the brother-in-law of one of Mr. Liu's brothers. But this relationsip had gotten him a job in Liu Pin-san's central bank, and from that day on, he had boasted of being the boss's son-in-law. He was a thoroughly obnoxious, and even dangerous, character who would later delight in persecuting us.

I glanced across the table and caught the look of anger in my brother's eyes; obviously, Ching-chung wanted to spring to my defense. But etiquette categorically forbids such displays in public, and one simply had to endure whatever happened. But when Old King, his eyes glittering, continued pushing his glass into my face, one of the other young men at the table rose to his feet. He was about twenty years old, a student, like my brother.

"Our cousins have drunk a great deal," he said courteously. "Now they must be left in peace."

"As long as she refuses to drink," Old King cried, "I won't leave her alone!"

By this time, everyone in the room had stopped eating and was listening. There certainly would have been a terrible scene had my mother-in-law not appeared at that moment and taken the glass from Old King's hand.

"All right, Old King," she said softly. "I shall drink for them."

And then an incredible thing happened. At the sight of my mother-in-law, the repulsive Old King, whose teeth had been bared like those of a fox in a chicken coop, suddenly collapsed and lowered his head like a beaten dog.

"Mama," he whined. "I do not deserve such a..." he mumbled, as he stepped back, bowing and cringing, until he disappeared.

"Daughter," my mother-in-law said, bending down affectionately, "you haven't had a chance to eat a thing!"

"It's all right, Mama," I replied. "I'm not hungry anymore." This was the first time I had called Madame Liu "Mama."

"I'll stay with you now," she said. "No one will bother you any more."

And no one did. At last the dinner ended and the guests began to leave. I had to change one last time, and then take up my position next to the door to say goodbye to everyone. In a silver Chinese dress with matching shoes and purse and lots of jewelry, I bade long farewells to all the guests, most of whom I did not know. They spoke, but I heard nothing. And then, miraculously, it was over. The restaurant was empty and it was time to go home to the Lius.

My brother was one of the last to leave. Once out on the sidewalk, he stood for a long time watching the rest of the guests disappear into their cars, the slow dispersal of a world that he knew would soon be gone forever.

9

The Liu family's property stood on the great Nan-king Road, which ran down to the edge of the Whangpoo River in what had already ceased to be called the International Settlement. The house faced the race-track, soon to become the Peoples' Park. A wide strip of grass separated Nanking Road from a parallel street that served about thirty houses, among them the Lius'. The neighborhood wasn't fashionable, but the powerful Liu Pin-san insisted upon remaining there for superstitious reasons. It seemed that once, long before he became rich, a horoscope-reader had declared this particular area a lucky one for him, and he now refused to leave the house that he believed had brought him such good fortune.

It was about eleven at night when our car reached my new home. Our families, including my sisters and brothers, brought up the rear. A few close friends of my in-laws, who had gone on ahead, were already waiting for us at the door.

We crossed the courtyard and entered the drawing room on the ground floor, which was already crowded with people. At the sight of them, I couldn't help feeling nervous, even though I was sure that, given the lateness of the hour, I wouldn't be subjected to further jeering and teasing. I was, however, sorely mistaken!

"There she is! There she is!" the cry went up from the crowd.

"Just be calm," the ubiquitous Lao Li whispered, "and patient. And whatever you do, don't get angry. They're going to do everything they can to upset you—deliberately, because that's the custom. And all that is good. It's like yeast for the house. The more they heckle you, the more prosperous your household will be."

My husband had already been surrounded and carried off in the direction of the nuptial chamber by a noisy throng, a victim of an event known as Initiating the Bedroom. Pushed and shoved up the stairs, we both eventually found ourselves inside our room, which was filled with people. The guests had now reached a peak of vulgarity which, while contrary to usual Chinese behavior, was permitted, even encouraged, on these occasions.

To begin with, they asked my husband to tell the story of our courtship. Poor Liu Yu-huang! Even if he hadn't been so timid, how could he possibly have talked about love when ours was an arranged marriage? But his silence only egged them on.

"It was our families who brought us together," he finally said uncomfortably, hoping to end the jokes and questions.

Unsatisfied, the guests turned to me. They wanted my husband and me to kiss each other in front of them. This, in a country where kissing in public is never done! They pushed us together; we retreated. But there was nothing to be done and in the end, Liu kissed me on the cheek.

"No! No!" everyone screamed. "On the mouth . . . on the mouth!"

On any other occasion, of course, it would have been scandalous to do what they wanted. But all this insistence and noise and shoving was their way of wishing prosperity to our family.

"Her family is going home," Lao Li's voice rang out suddenly above the general din. "Let the newlyweds see them out."

They let us go so I could say goodbye to my parents.

How difficult it was for us to part! We stood on the doorstep, our eyes filling with tears.

"Obey your husband," Hui-i said to me. "And be careful not to catch cold when you change your clothes. It's so easy to catch cold."

"Don't worry," my mother-in-law replied. "I'll be here. I'll take care of her as if she were my very own daughter."

"My daughter is very young," Chung-ai said to her. "If by chance she should say something foolish, I beg you to excuse her. Fortunately, you will set a fine example for her, and you will show her how to behave. She will need your advice and your kindness."

Let there be no mistake: This was not just an exchange of polite formalities. My mother was a peasant, and her attitude toward Madame Liu was one of respectful humility, a posture befitting a peasant in the presence of a great lady.

I said my goodbyes to my mother and father, to Ching-chang, my youngest brother, to Ching-ling, my sister and dear accomplice, and finally, to my beloved brother Ching-chung, who seemed particularly anxious to leave. Only my youngest sister, Ching-ching, was left. She was only four and took my sleeve, trying to pull me away home with her. My mother tried to explain that this was my home now, but she began to scream and they had to bundle her quickly into the car, fearing that her tears might have a bad influence on me.

Once my family left, the guests forced me back into the bedroom. By this time, though, I found that their antics at least distracted me from my unhappiness. Suddenly the jeering stopped and a respectful murmur ran through the crowd. Liu Yu-huang's Uncle Sen had appeared. He was the director of the Chungking Bank, Liu Pin-san's largest enterprise, and my husband hurried to introduce me. I was to call him Great Uncle, not just uncle, for according to tradition the new wife must out of respect place herself one generation below that of her husband. Great Uncle Sen apparently smoked cigars, and I was ordered to bring him the box immediately. He chose one carefully, and I struck a match. It took me three or four tries, however, as each time I managed to light one, someone would blow it out and everyone roared with laughter. As the New

132

Woman I had no right to protest, or to laugh, or even speak. In the end, Uncle Sen took pity on me and was kind enough to light his own cigar.

It was almost one o'clock in the morning, and some hecklers were still trying to force my husband to drink, when my mother-in-law appeared to supervise the final ceremony—to thank those who had prepared the marriage bed. Custom dictates that this privilege be given to a couple who have had an especially happy life together. My in-laws had chosen Uncle Sen and his wife; their elderly parents were still alive, a fact which signified great good fortune, they also had both male and female children, they had never known misfortune, and they were rich. Thus they had been chosen to prepare the marriage bed the day before, and now we prostrated ourselves at their feet.

"When you were younger," Madame Sen said to me, helping me up, "I used to watch you riding by on your bicycle every day. And now I've made your marriage bed. I can only wish that your happiness will be even greater than mine."

At last the guests, including the indefatigable Lao Li, were obliged to leave. A delicious calm invaded the house and, except for my servant, Ah-san, I was alone with my new family—a family that included nine children. To be sure, not all of them were at home, but there were enough of them present to make me apprehensive. As the newest member of the family—an in-law at that—I was their inferior, and the kind of life I would lead depended a great deal on how I might be treated by these brothers and sisters, whom I could not refer to as "brother" and "sister," but rather "uncle" and "aunt," once again placing myself in the humble position of a later generation. By the same custom, I was supposed to call my in-laws "grandmother" and "grandfather," but the Lius were generous enough to permit me instead to call them "mother" and "father."

Their eldest daughter, Liu Yu-ying, was in her thirties. An ugly scar, the result of an automobile accident, creased her forehead and a childhood case of meningitis had left her partly deaf. Embittered by her bad luck, she had become increasingly unattractive with the passage of time, and she had remained unmarried. The sons of the rich had no reason to be interested in her, and she had no interest in the poor. Because of her misfortune her family had spoiled her incredibly, and her bitterness had made her jealous and catty. The antagonism between us was immediate. My second sister-in-law, Liu Yu-chen, was a fat girl who had been married at the age of fourteen to a worthless husband, without education or profession, who was perfectly content to sit back and devour his father-in-law's fortune. Aside from these two unhappy women, who were unfortunately destined to play significant roles in my life, there were two other girls, both older than I, and two much younger children, a boy and a girl. Three other children were absent; one was studying in the United States, the others were away at school. Mercifully, the introductions were brief, for I longed to go to bed.

Followed by Liu Yu-huang and my servant, Ah-san, I climbed the stairs to our bedroom. Knowing that neither of us had eaten all day, the servants had prepared a light meal. We sat opposite each other at a small table, and were waited on both by Ah-san and Ah-yu, my husband's servant; in the Liu family, each child had his own domestic. We ate in a heavy silence.

"Are you tired?" my husband asked.

I nodded. I was filled with such a sad and empty feeling that I could hardly swallow, much less speak. But Liu Yu-huang wanted to talk.

"I can't tell you how beautiful you look," he began.

I lowered my head.

"Are you still hungry?"

I lowered my head again.

"You should eat more," he said. "Why won't you talk to me? Aren't you happy, Ching-li?"

I remained silent.

"If you don't feel well," he went on anxiously, "just tell me, please. You're frightening me."

"I want my mother and father!" I heard myself say.

"Ching-li," he smiled. "You're not a baby anymore. Once you're married, you don't call for your parents."

"I want them! I want to see them!"

"But we'll go to see them."

"Now?"

"No, Ching-li, not now."

"Tomorrow?"

"Not tomorrow either," his servant Ah-yu answered. "The wife may only visit her parents three days after the wedding."

Three days! How could I wait three days when the only time I had ever left them had been on that trip to Hangchow? Even then I'd been accompanied by my brother! Both servants tried to console me, but I knew I would have to wait the required time. I suddenly remembered that my mother had instructed me to give Madame Liu the obligatory gift from daughter-in-law to mother-in-law, a luxurious goose-down quilt and the two embroidered pillowcases, on the wedding night. I carried them to Madame Liu, whose room was separated from ours by only a small sitting room.

My mother-in-law smiled happily. "You are a good girl. Now go to bed. You must get up early tomorrow."

It was already tomorrow, of course, almost two in the morning, in fact. I bade my in-laws goodnight, but scarcely had I left the room when my mother-in-law called me back. She had an important question to ask.

"When did you last menstruate?" she inquired.

I thought the question odd, but then I had discovered so many unfamiliar customs today that I replied promptly.

"It ended two days ago."

"Give me your supply of sanitary napkins," she ordered.

In China, sanitary napkins are made of narrow strips of cloth sewn together by the girl's mother. The cloth covers a certain thickness of rice paper, and the whole is held up by a belt around the waist. Ah-san brought them to my mother-in-law, who informed me that she would keep them. Only later did I realize that if I did not ask for them, she would know I was pregnant.

In our bedroom, the two servants had already pulled back the bedcovers, wishing us both goodnight and closing the door behind them.

I was now alone with Liu Yu-huang.

Staggering with exhaustion, I could see only the bed. It was so soft and inviting that, still dressed in my pink satin, I lay down and immediately fell asleep.

Someone was knocking at the door. Where was I? Slowly, the unfamiliar room came into focus and, sitting up in bed, I saw my husband rise to open the door. From the look of things, he had spent the night on a sofa in the room so as not to disturb me. Glancing down, I saw that he had even put a blanket over me, and that I had neither undressed nor washed before falling asleep.

Ah-san entered. "It's six o'clock in the morning!" she gasped. "Why are you still dressed?"

Ah-san had wakened me so early because my in-laws rose between six and seven every morning, and the daughter-in-law had to be up before them. Despite the number of servants, tradition demanded that I serve them.

My husband quietly slipped out of the room while Ah-san brought in a basin of hot water, which she placed on the marble-topped dressing table in front of the mirror. In this old house, there were no bathtubs. I washed, changed my clothes, and applied a little makeup. From the sitting room next door I could hear my in-laws coughing. I would have to hurry. Ah-san then brought a tray that held two small teapots (one drank directly from the spout) along with two bowls of an expensive and exotic type of white fungus called "silver ears," and two bowls of longans floating in ginseng juice. I followed her into the next room where I greeted my in-laws, placed the tray between them, and then waited, standing, until they had finished eating. By custom, the daughter-in-law must serve her in-laws in this way for three days after the wedding, as well as for a three-day period following each anniversary and each holiday. Altogether, this made ten solemn occasions, eight of which were to celebrate the changing of the seasons. If a daughter-in-law failed to fulfill any of these functions, she would be considered disrespectful toward her in-laws.

Once the breakfast was finished, Ah-san brought in an enormous package of silk shoes, fifty pairs, which would be distributed to the entire family. But first, four pairs had to be chosen by my mother-in-law.

"Now go eat your breakfast," Madame Liu said to me after the selection had been made. "And then we'll go together to see my sister-in-law."

We spent the entire day handing out presents, as well as certain required dishes, to my father-in-law's many sisters and brothers, and to my mother-in-law's two brothers and two sisters. As we made our way around the city, I was often tempted to telephone my parents, but knowing such a thing was forbidden, I did not dare try.

On the first evening of my married life, a dinner with thirty guests was held at the Lius, followed by a round of mahjong during which I was constantly on call, serving tea to everyone present. But that was only the beginning. In rich families, it was customary for parties and celebrations to go on for several weeks after the wedding.

When everyone had finally gone home and I had wished my in-laws goodnight, I found myself alone with my husband for the second evening. This time, however, I was not to go to sleep quite so easily.

I performed my ablutions, making sure that my husband's back was turned. Once I was in my pajamas, I noticed that Liu Yu-huang was watching me carefully, and I desperately tried to hide my bare feet. Strange as this may seem to a Westerner, it was shocking to a Chinese that a man should see them. Then I began to wonder anxiously how I would ever go to sleep with a man lying next to me in bed. Liu Yu-huang detected my apprehension. Perhaps he was afraid he might have to spend another night on the couch.

"All women sleep next to their husbands," he said, convincingly.

After all, I thought, my parents sleep together, so as quickly as I could, I slipped my bare feet under the covers. In any case, it was too cold to do otherwise, for it was the month of January, and the house had no central heating.

Liu Yu-huang got in beside me. But instead of lying down, he leaned over and began to kiss me gently on the forehead, the cheeks, then on the forehead again, then the cheeks. I let him, thinking that Mama and Papa surely kissed each other before they went to sleep and since Liu was my husband, he had the right to do the same.

He reached out, switched off the light, and continued to kiss me, squeezing me tighter and tighter in his arms.

Suddenly I felt a stiff object pushing against me. I screamed, sat up, turned on the light, and lifted the covers. In a flash, I saw that the object in question was part of Liu Yu-huang. I took a colossal leap out of the bed and found myself a good few yards away from the husband who now appeared to be some kind of terrible monster. Seeing me trembling like a leaf, Liu got out of bed. Afraid that I would catch my death of cold in the freezing room, he tried to wrap me in the blankets. But the closer he came, the more I backed away, horrified at the idea of being touched by this grotesque creature.

"But what's the matter with you, Ching-li?" he cried desperately.

"Don't you come near me!" I gasped, sobbing hysterically. "You're a monster! You're not a normal man!"

And then he understood. The blanket over his arm, he patiently began to explain.

"Ching-li," he said, "I assure you, I am not at all abnormal. All men are made like me."

"You're a liar!" I cried. "My little brother doesn't look like that!"

I had had occasion to see Ching-chang naked when his diaper was being changed, and he certainly had nothing as monstrous as what I had just seen! When I told this to Liu, he could not help smiling, despite the discomforting situation.

"But Ching-li, he's just a baby! I'm a grown man."

But I refused to listen. Huddled against the wall in the far corner of the room, I continued to shiver, as much from cold as from terror. I was ready to spend the whole night like this and die of pneumonia, rather than get back into bed next to that horror. Once more, Liu attempted to approach me, but when I cried out, he stopped dead.

"Don't shout," he whispered anxiously. "You'll wake our parents. Just take the blanket," he said, tossing the blanket at me. "I'll be back in a minute."

138

When he returned, he held a book open in his hand.

"Come here," he said. "I'm going to show you something which will prove that I'm absolutely normal."

I refused to come any closer, so he slid the book across the floor and told me to look at it. It was a medical text, opened to an anatomical drawing of a man. I studied it carefully, then began to turn the pages. It was clearly a serious book and it reassured me, but not sufficiently to relieve my fears.

"Now you can come back to bed and cover up," Liu Yu-huang said, seeing that I had calmed down somewhat. "I swear I won't touch you. In fact, I'll sleep on the couch like last night and you can have the bed to yourself. All right?"

Silently, I slid back into bed. Since there were a great many blankets, I did not have to worry about Liu Yu-huang's catching cold, but I still wanted to sleep with the light on. In vain, I told myself that since the pictures I had just seen clearly represented normal men, Liu was obviously not a monster, but I had suffered a terrible shock and even after I had fallen asleep I was haunted by those pictures and the sight of Liu Yu-huang.

Thus passed my second night as a married woman.

If I now feel compelled to describe these first nights as a bride, it is only to illustrate how, for hundreds of years, children of both sexes in China were delivered into marriage without the slightest suspicion of what was in store. Millions of young girls like myself were married for gain against their will, in total ignorance, to strangers—a situation that was not extinguished until after the Liberation.

The third day of my marriage brought with it both pleasure, in the form of a visit to my parents, and the rendering of two final bridal rituals. Before I could visit my parents I was first obliged to cook breakfast for my in-laws, followed by the traditional sewing of the "Seven Panties." In the Chinese language the phonetic pronunciation of words may be identical, although in the written word their ideographs, or characters, are as different as their meanings. Thus the sound of the word for "seven panties," or chi-ku, is almost identical to that of the phrase "seven misfortunes," or chi ku, and the making of seven panties was a symbolic gesture for warding off misfortune from my in-laws.

In the Ningpo region, Madame Liu's native city, all new daughters-in-law were required to sew seven pairs of panties for this purpose. So, on this third morning, my mother-in-law handed me needle, thread, and material. Unfortunately, I no more knew how to sew than to cook, but since daughters-in-law are expected to obey in silence, I dared not say anything. But whatever was I going to do? Once again, my good fairy, Ah-san, came to the rescue. However, as she cut the cloth, I suddenly decided that I should try to do the sewing myself. After a short while my fingers had been pricked so often that I had to put bandages on them.

"That will never do," my mother-in-law said when she saw the trouble I was in. "At this rate, the sewing will never be finished, and you'll wind up destroying your fingers! Why don't you try knitting instead?"

Knitting was no better, however, I kept dropping stitches and unexpected holes kept appearing in the most unlikely places. I kept having to undo everything and start all over again. (It was only much later, at the end of several months, that I managed through sheer obstinacy to finish those seven famous pairs of panties, so indispensable for keeping misfortune away from my family.)

Finally I could visit my parents. Liu Yu-huang accompanied me. When the door opened, there was such an explosion of joy and tears from my parents and brothers and sisters that one would have thought I had been gone three years, instead of just three days. After the initial clamor had calmed down, Chung-ai took me aside and led me into her room for a private chat. She wanted to know if I was happy, if I had everything I needed, how I was getting on, and so forth. When I described the details of the previous night's trauma—my flight from the conjugal bed, my terror, my husband's explanations, my nightmares—she raised her arms to heaven.

"What a fool your husband is!" she cried.

"Mama," I replied. "It's not *his* fault. Why didn't *you* tell me anything?"

"That's *his* job," my mother said. "He's the one who should have explained things to you from the very beginning; he's the one who should have told you what the wife's duty is . . ."

In fact, Chung-ai was sincerely horrified. Having thought of everything else, she had failed to imagine such a grotesque eventuality. She was both anxious about me and annoyed about what had happened. After all, I had definitely not fulfilled my obligations as a wife and such a failure was very serious indeed.

"You absolutely must sleep with him tonight," she told me. "You must! To do otherwise would be unthinkable!"

After serving us an excellent dinner, she hurried Liu Yu-huang and me out the door, urging us to go to bed early. Once again, I was overwhelmed with unhappiness at having to leave my family and return to my husband's home.

When we arrived at the Lius', the house was full of company, and once more I had to serve tea to the mahjong players until very late at night.

Later, lying beside my husband in bed, I at last consented to become his wife in more than name.

It is not without some hesitation and embarrassment that I recount an event which has undoubtedly left other women with much happier memories, but which, because my body was not yet completely formed, has left me with a painful memory of an ordeal that made me ill for a week afterward. During this period, however, Liu Yu-huang was full of solicitude. Then he revealed something to me that upset me even more.

"Ching-li," he said to me one evening when we were lying side by side in bed, "I have a confession to make. You must listen to me carefully. Imagine that one night, you wake up and find that my body is as cold as ice. If such a thing happens, I beg you first of all not to be frightened."

"If you're cold," I replied, "all we have to do is get more blankets."

"No, Ching-li, that's not what I mean. If I'm cold, it will mean that I'm dead."

"Please, Yu-huang," I begged. "Don't joke about such things. I'm terrified of anything that has to do with death."

"I assure you I'm not joking," my husband answered. "I once knew a man, one of my friends, who died in the middle of the night while he was holding his wife in his arms."

"Please," I said, becoming more and more frightened, "just because this happened to one of your friends, it doesn't mean that you have to imagine . . ."

Unnerved, I rolled over and closed my eyes.

"Listen, please, Ching-li," my husband persisted. "You can go to sleep afterward. My friend had a heart disease. So do I. People like me can die at any moment. All they need is some kind of shock, a strong emotion . . ."

Horrified by this revelation, I jumped out of bed and began pacing back and forth. It appeared that I had married a man who had hidden everything important from me. Only now, *after* the wedding, did he tell me he was suffering from a fatal disease! No sooner had I taken off the marriage veil, I thought, than I would have to put on mourning. I was struck dumb, and all Liu could think to do was to urge me to come back to bed and sleep. Sleep? Sleep was out of the question, for now that I'd been so brutally enlightened, I wanted to know more about the origin of his disease, its symptoms, and whether it really was serious or not. And so he told me that in fact he had suffered from a heart condition since birth, also that he had had typhoid fever, meningitis, and even smallpox (light scars were still visible on his face). Then, when he was eleven years old, he had been unable to walk for some time because of pains in his legs. But it was only after the age of seventeen, when he began to experience painful attacks of rheumatism, that his heart had given its first serious warnings. It seemed that one fall evening, while he was still a student, he had gone drinking with some of his friends. Afterward, walking in the park along the Whangpoo, he felt faint and was obliged to lie down on a bench. It was cold and damp by the river, he was dressed lightly, and once back in his room, he was struck by a violent heart attack, followed by a long period of hypertension and continual migraine headaches. His heart had increased dramatically in volume. He even showed me the X rays.

Perhaps the reader will find me cruel when I admit that at the end of his confession, anger won out over compassion. After all, I had married out of obligation, not love, and I hadn't even been given a healthy husband! Instead, they had forced me to marry an individual who was seriously ill and had abandoned me to a life hovered over by the specter of death.

"Why did you let me marry you without saying anything?" I demanded. "Why didn't you tell me the truth before?"

"But I never hid anything from you," Liu Yu-huang protested, surprised. "I talked at great length with your mother; I told her that my heart was weak. She never answered me, but how was I to know she would keep my real condition a secret? Anyway, once we were married, I wanted to be sure you understood the situation. And now you do. I beg you not to be afraid. If I take good care of myself, and if we live quietly and peacefully, everything will be fine. And since I love you deeply, I have every reason in the world to take care of myself. I do so for you."

In fact, he did take good care of himself. Not only did he take vitamin tonics every day, but he ate only the choicest delicacies such as swallows' nests and ginseng, a plant that was thought to cure everything under the sun.

The morning after this confession, I rushed to tell my parents the disastrous news. Speechless at first, they remained silent a long time. Then Chung-ai found her tongue and began cursing Mr. Chen and Mr. Yuan, the two intermediaries, calling them crooks and bandits. The words, appropriate as they may have been, were a little late in coming. I did not even bother to remind her that Liu Yu-huang had told her the truth and that apparently she hadn't thought it necessary to confide it to me. For I was familiar with my mother's ways and not really surprised at her unconscionable behavior. In any case, there was no use crying about it now. My father, on the other hand, was grief-stricken and ashamed. I almost regretted having brought to his attention a problem no one would now be able to resolve.

A week after Liu Yu-huang's revelation, I went back to school. For I was married while still a schoolgirl, and a schoolgirl I had resolved to become once again. In fact, the only promise I had exacted from the adults was that I be permitted to continue my studies. And since my school was much farther from the Liu house than my own, I now had the right to a chauffeur-driven car, which took me to school every morning.

Even though I had to get up early to serve my in-laws and even though I went to bed late at night because of my schoolwork, I nonetheless seized every occasion I could to go to my parents' house and practice the piano. There was no instrument in the Liu house, and after all their expenditures for the wedding, I didn't dare ask for one. Inevitably, I exhausted myself, for my health had never been very strong and I had not yet finished growing. I even fainted one day at school, but I kept at my work. In my joyless existence, it was all I had.

A daily routine gradually emerged in the house on Nanking Road. One morning, as I was serving her breakfast, my mother-in-law asked me to sit down beside her.

"New Woman," she said, sighing deeply, "my health is deteriorating rapidly. I have very high blood pressure..."

I knew this already. Had not her precarious health precipitated a marriage that had originally been postponed for three years—and this only to help her get well?

"We must never forget that death can take me any time now," she went on. "My time may be almost up. Which is why, New Woman..."

I knew what she was going to say before the words were out. The day before, she had remained closeted with her goddaughter, a young and vicious gossip called Chao-mei. Thin-lipped and plain, Chao-mei was violently jealous of me, but she contrived to hide it under a sugarcoated façade. Her husband had apparently grown tired of her and she spent all her time flattering my mother-in-law, who loved every minute of it. Since I had joined the family, she constantly pretended to be concerned about me, and particularly about whether or not I would ever get pregnant. This was supposed to happen as soon as possible but, she wondered, *could* I get pregnant? Would my delicate health permit such a thing? (The chauffeur had told everyone about my fainting at school.) Chao-mei ordered vitamins and tonics for me, and advised me to see a gynecologist. My mother-in-law had heard nothing else the whole day long, which I knew, and thus I was not surprised by what she was about to say.

"Yes, New Woman, that's why I hope so desperately to have a grandson before I die."

She also reminded me that the parents' ultimate happiness depended upon there being three generations alive and

144

present under the same roof, and at the moment her house sheltered but two. With the greatest respect, I commented that I had hardly been married a month and that there was no reason for concern about my not being pregnant yet. But her only response was that she had made an appointment for me with a woman who was reputed to be the best gynecologist in Shanghai, and who also happened to be a good friend of hers.

So one day after school I went to see the doctor, who turned out to be an imposing but quite gentle gray-haired woman. She checked my vital statistics and then examined me.

"Do you really think you cannot have children?" she asked.

"I'm not the one who's worried about it," I replied. "It's my mother-in-law."

"Go home," she smiled kindly, "and tell your mother-in-law that if you're still not pregnant ten years from now, then you should come back and see me. Because ten years from now will not be too late; in fact, it will still be rather soon!"

Once back at the house, I told my mother-in-law what the doctor had said. And for once, she had nothing to say.

A few days later, I was indisposed and with great apprehension I went to Madame Liu and asked for my sanitary napkins. My fears were not misplaced for her face darkened with anger. This was my first taste of the hostility that I would experience many times in the years to come. The next day, I rushed to complain to my own mother. Chung-ai thought my mother-in-law was perfectly absurd to expect me to become pregnant in just a few weeks, but I was nonetheless admonished to maintain a respectful and patient attitude. Yet despite all my patience and respectfulness, Madame Liu's irritation with me never changed, and I realized that until I became pregnant, she would consider me an unsatisfactory daughter-in-law. In desperation, I begged my mother to pray to Buddha for me; I was so unhappy about my mother-in-law's anger that I wanted to become pregnant as soon as possible. My mother promised to do as I asked. She saw how miserable I was and realized that although I had been uncooperative before the marriage, now that I was married, I wanted to be a perfect daughter-in-law.

And so Chung-ai went off to her temple and prayed for me. She also asked the chief nun to read my horoscope. The woman mixed the joss sticks, and the one she finally selected clearly indicated that not only would I be pregnant soon, but that I would have a perfect baby, endowed with great intelligence and a brilliant future. After my initial discouragement, hope returned at last.

But my period had given rise to certain worries. Instead of lasting a few days, it had gone on for two weeks, despite medical efforts that were made to stop the bleeding and the special drops I was ordered to take all day long. Gradually, I lost my appetite; even the slightest smell of food made me nauseous. And I was continually tired. Not only had the wedding itself been an exhausting ordeal, both physically and emotionally, but I had been working overtime on my schoolwork in preparation for the exams that would take place during the next to last year of high school.

And so I went to see another doctor. This doctor was as astonished and as disturbed as the first to see how young I was. But his prognosis made me jump.

"Perhaps you are pregnant," he declared, albeit with some hesitation.

Nothing was certain, of course; it was only a possibility. And he added that since my body was not yet completely formed, there were some risks involved, notably that of a miscarriage.

The doctor's prognosis astounded my mother-in-law, as she had never heard of a woman having her period and being pregnant at the same time. But since that was what he had said, it had to be taken seriously. Above all, a miscarriage had to be avoided at any price. So she ordered me to bed immediately. Further analyses were made and this time, the results were definitive. The doctor had not been mistaken; I was indeed pregnant.

Now more than ever I was obliged to take care of myself; in fact, I had to spend most of my time lying down. In any case, I was so weak that I had no choice. In spite of everything, my life still might have been pleasant; one would have thought that once my mother-in-law knew I was pregnant, she would have abandoned her hostile attitude and become more generous and affectionate. On the contrary, my pregnancy altered

146

nothing, because the one thing my mother-in-law could not tolerate, in spite of my condition, was that my husband should show any solicitude to me. Madame Liu's true nature had finally surfaced. For in my confinement, the one person I counted on to talk to and distract me was my husband. He loved me deeply, but he was *adored* by his mother. Married at fourteen, Madame Liu had had to wait four long years for her first child, a girl who subsequently died in infancy. Later a second girl was born, then a third and a fourth. Madame Liu's mother-in-law, assuming that the conjugal union was hopeless, encouraged her son to take a mistress. My mother-in-law suffered terribly. She prayed desperately to Buddha until finally, a fifth child was born, permitting her to throw the mistress out. For this fifth child was a boy. But Liu Yu-huang, my husband, was a sickly youth and had been coddled and protected like a baby chick from the moment of his birth. He was doubly precious to his mother because his father, Liu Pin-san, was a very busy and powerful businessman who led a full life, and was frequently absent. Thus, over the past twenty-six years, a passionate and jealous attachment had formed between Liu Yu-huang and his mother, an attachment that created a precarious existence for me.

It wasn't long before I noticed that whenever the son was attentive to me, the mother invariably made a scene. And now that I was forced to stay in bed, not only did I no longer have to serve my in-laws, but my husband multiplied his attentions. My mother-in-law couldn't tolerate it. If Liu Yu-huang remained with me a moment longer than usual in the morning, she raised the roof. Wasn't he ashamed, she cried, staying in bed at such an hour? Whereupon, like a pet dog, he jumped to do her bidding.

For a long period of time, I could not tolerate the sight of food. And then, quite suddenly, the vision of one particularly delicious dish flooded my memory—the noodles-and-chicken specialty I had been served months ago at the Green Pavilion when I first met Liu Yu-huang. We had had to leave just as I began to eat, and now it seemed that this was the only food in the world that might appeal to me. When my servant Ah-san appeared at the door with my lunch, Liu Yu-huang ordered her to take the plates back to the kitchen. He would go himself to the Green Pavilion and get me what I wanted. Unfortunately, my mother-in-law overheard his offer and burst into a violent temper tantrum. What was this? Who did I think I was, an empress? When she herself was pregnant, she'd eaten her noodles plain, and now here I was, ordering special food from outside the house! Liu Yu-huang apologized profusely and did everything he could to calm her. But only a promise that he would not ever go out and buy me the Green Pavilion's chicken and noodles would suffice.

More than ever now, my husband stayed away from my room. His mother couldn't bear his coming to see me during the day and whenever she caught him, she would berate him.

"You have the whole night to be together!" she would complain. "You ought to be grateful that I let you sleep with your wife without keeping the door open!"

Indeed, this particular arrangement was not unusual in China then. The Liberation had not yet taken effect. In fact, the husband's mother often slept in an adjoining room, with the door open, so that her son's passion would be tempered, or at least silenced. In many cases, these women were widows who had no one left but their sons.

Whenever my husband chanced to give me the slightest caress, my mother-in-law would give him a terrible look, reminding him of the old proverb: Husband and wife in bed, master and servant out of it.

10

The year I was married, China was on the verge of a great leap into the future, one that would transcend several centuries. During all those months when my family was deciding to unite the houses of Chow and Liu, only my brother Ching-chung had realized that the face of our world was changing. Now these dramatic events were about to become a matter of great importance to our family.

Chiang Kai-shek's Kuomintang, in power for over twenty years, had now ceased to exist. All of mainland China had been liberated since December, 1949. Through posters and improvised plays, the populace learned how the remnants of the Nationalist forces, swollen by ranks of corrupt functionaries and gangsters who had grown fat on the poverty of millions, had rushed off to Taiwan, taking as much of their loot with them as they could carry.

In the month of March, Chiang Kai-shek reassumed the presidency of the republic on Taiwan, while on the mainland the son of a peasant from Hunan, Mao Tse-tung, had become chairman of the People's Republic of China. His portrait, along with those of his commander-in-chief, Chu Teh, and of Chou En-lai, the new prime minister, began appearing all over the streets of Shanghai, plastered onto the walls of public buildings, in the shops, and on the trams. They were going to reorganize the whole country, it was said, with help of the Red Army and all the peasants and workers. And if there was any country that needed reorganization, it was certainly ours! As long as anyone could remember, there had been nothing but war and destruction. And as far as the previous rulers were concerned, they had left behind them little else but ruins. Indeed, inflation had so soared that a trip to the market required suitcases full of bank notes, and employees chose to be paid with pots and pans rather than bundles of currency. Whole neighborhoods had been turned into flea markets where everyone bought and sold and swapped and bargained, in an effort merely to survive.

Early in 1950, Shanghai had still not experienced any noteworthy transformation, nor had a single drop of blood been spilled. For just as the Red Army had entered the city in May of 1949 with nothing more serious than a few skirmishes, so had the new government assumed power in the city with neither protest, on the one hand, nor vengeance on the other. To be sure, students had plastered the city with posters, but only to inform the population of the Red Army's victories and to caricature Chiang Kai-shek and his entourage of millionaires who had been kicked out once and for all. And if they had paraded up and down the streets, it was only to celebrate the Revolution and to cheer its leaders. Moving cautiously, the Party that now ran the country was determined not to do anything precipitous; in fact, it was not to show its real authority until the summer of 1950. And so the old world and the new continued to live side by side, neither paying attention to the other. Indeed, the very fact that a wedding like mine could have taken place in a city that flew the Red flag was a striking example of this peaceful coexistence. In addition, nothing had changed in the shops, restaurants, or movie theaters. So the old remained intact, while the new moved in beside it.

The most obvious of the changes—and this was something I had noticed before being obliged to take to my bed—was in the matter of clothes. If the bourgeoisie of Shanghai still dressed up when they went out in the evening, they also sported more discreet attire in the daytime. For the Chinese style of dress was already beginning to reflect that uniformity which was one of the hallmarks of the Revolution.

What first struck the population of Shanghai, however, was the appearance of the Red Army. Soldiers rapidly became a familiar sight, although at first they were objects of great curiosity—a suspicious curiosity to be sure, for the Chinese automatically assumed that any kind of soldier was a thief. Before long, however, people began to realize that the three commandments of the Red Army—not to lay hands on so much as a pin belonging to the population, to consider the people as its family, and always to return what had been borrowed—were not simply empty words. On the other hand, if the soldiers astonished us, we the people of Shanghai astonished them even more. Many of the troops were from the north and were thus unable to speak our language; only those who knew how to write could manage to make themselves understood by shopkeepers, for written Chinese is the same throughout the country, regardless of dialect. Most of them, however, were peasants who had never in all their lives seen any of the goods displayed in the windows of Shanghai's shops, things such as refrigerators, or European-style bridal gowns . . .

The period of transition was drawing to a close during this spring of 1950. Of this we were all aware because none of the new measures taken by the government remained secret for very long. On the contrary, each policy decision immediately became the subject of endless analysis and commentary, not only in the newspapers and on the radio, but on all the walls and sidewalks of the city. Even those acts that would seem particularly brutal to foreigners—such as the public trials and confessions—bore witness to the leaders' resolution to conduct their business out in the open, to persuade the people to their cause by educating them and by keeping them informed, and always to choose reason over force. Even the worst gangsters were thrown into prison not so much to be punished as to be reeducated.

The reorganization of such a huge country was a herculean task, necessitating whole armies of volunteers. The peasants were the first to be organized; in fact, "peasant power" had existed for a very long time in those vast areas of China where the Red Army had found its greatest support. Now the new state took over completely the government bureaucracy, the post office system, the railroads, and in Shanghai, even the big universities like St. John's, where my father had studied. All foreign teachers and administrators had to leave the country and were obliged to announce their departure both in the English and Chinese newspapers so that any creditors might be forewarned. Before issuing visas, the government wanted to make certain no debts were left behind.

One of the major problems facing the new People's Republic, however, was that China was an illiterate country. Thus, even though my brother Ching-chung was only twenty years old, he had been singled out by the party for an essential service, that of instructor.

My brother might now be a Party official, but my husband was still the scion of one of the richest capitalists in China, a fact, however, that worried neither him nor the rest of the Liu family. In general, those who had the most reason to fear the Liberation Army—the warlords, bankers, and bandit leaders, those who had been the most corrupt or the most seriously compromised—had already fled to Taiwan. Later, apprehension about the future would drive other members of the privileged class to seek refuge in nearby Hong Kong, but for now those who remained behind were surprised to discover that they were not being interfered with and could carry on business as usual, and that the Communists were permitting non-Communists to participate in their government—including the left-wing faction of the Kuomintang, the Kuomintang Revolutionary Committee. This group, made up of those who chose not to follow Chiang to Taiwan, was headed by Madame Sun Yat-sen, widow of the first president of Nationalist China and Chiang Kai-shek's own sister-in-law.

Afterward, even when the capitalist system had been destroyed and the feudal system of property ownership had given way to proletarian control, the government still allowed landlords to keep their portions of redistributed land, and did not confiscate any land actually cultivated by the owner himself. Far from destroying the capitalists, the government wanted to enlist their aid in the reconstruction of the country, and all social classes were invited to join in what the government referred to as the United Front.

In any case, my father-in-law, Liu Pin-san, considered himself a patriot and he believed that Mao Tse-tung was clearly working for the good of China.

The fact that the new government badly wanted to persuade capitalists to join the common effort seemed evidenced by a large issue of government bonds in the spring of 1950, which the government promised to reimburse in the form of annuities, plus interest. Unfortunately, bond sales fell off during the month of May, and one day early in the month, my father-in-law, Liu Pin-san, was called to the Park Hotel, a luxurious twenty-four-story edifice in downtown Shanghai, where the government had installed its Loan Offices. Liu Pin-san had been ordered to appear at nine in the morning, but by lunchtime he still had not yet returned. I was in my bedroom on the second floor, where I had been confined for the past three months, still pregnant, but terribly weakened by a continuous loss of blood no medication seemed able to stop. If I wanted to have the child, I was told, I would have to remain bedridden until the birth.

My servant Ah-san told me of my father-in-law's detention, an event that had obviously made the whole family tense with anxiety. In addition, my bedroom was right next to the small sitting room where my mother-in-law spent most of her time. She was becoming increasingly anxious and I could hear her ask, "What could be going on? Why hasn't he come back yet?" Lunchtime came and went, as did the afternoon. The dinner hour arrived, but Liu Pin-san still had not appeared. Madame Liu could not stand the suspense any longer, and since the Park Hotel was but a short distance away on Nanking Road, she set out for it on foot.

Received by a functionary in a Mao suit, she asked him if her husband was still being detained; when the official replied in the affirmative, she asked if he might not be able to come home for dinner. The official informed her politely that Liu Pin-san would surely not have enough time for dinner. Madame Liu had no idea what he meant and she demanded to see her husband. Again her demand was refused. She returned home, but an hour later she went back to the hotel with a package of food. The same official met her with the same refusal.

"But this isn't a prison!" Madame Liu exclaimed. "And even if it were, I assume even prisoners eat sometime?"

The official finally agreed to take the package.

"It will be given to your husband," he said. "But don't rely on his returning home tonight."

In those days, my brother Ching-chung was in the habit of visiting me every evening after work. Only family visits like his were keeping me from dying of boredom while confined to my bed. That night, he arrived somewhat later than usual. I heard him enter my mother-in-law's sitting room. I could hear them speaking.

"Before his victory," Madame Liu cried, "everyone said how bad Mao was. My husband's friends have been telling him for months now to get out, but Liu Pin-san has always refused. And why? Because he's a patriot, that's why! He loves his country. He thinks Mao will be good for China. And now, here he is, arrested like a common criminal! Maybe his friends were right! Maybe the Communists are bandits!"

Ching-chung was embarrassed and disturbed by what my mother-in-law said, but he had complete faith in the new regime. After all, didn't he spend most of his time proselytizing others?

"You mustn't worry," he comforted her. "Haven't you heard that the Party will not take so much as a pin from you? I assure you, they would never harm a good man. Perhaps there's been an error; perhaps it's as simple as that. Do you realize how much work lies before us throughout the entire country? How can we help making mistakes when the job before us is so enormous? I'm sure everything will be set right by tomorrow. You mustn't worry."

But my mother-in-law did not see things the same way as Ching-chung. For the past month there had been bad signs. Her husband's shining forehead, for example, had begun to lose its luster; it had even changed color, to a dull brown. To Madame Liu, this phenomenon could only mean misfortune.

154

Since Ching-chung was an official of the Party, she now insisted upon itemizing Liu Pin-san's virtues.

"Have they forgotten what my husband once did for someone who is today a very important Party official? Have they forgotten that during the Long March, this man's family was dying of hunger and who, I ask you, who took care of them all those long years? Liu Pin-san, that's who! And he risked his life doing it! Everybody knows what would have happened to him if the Nationalists had found out that he was protecting the family of a Communist! And what about all those peasants Pin-san helped? And this is his reward—being shut up in the Park Hotel! Why, he isn't even allowed to see his wife!"

Ching-chung knew she was telling the truth about the family and the peasants Liu Pin-san had taken care of. All he could do, however, was to assure her that everything would be all right.

Unfortunately, this turned out not to be the case, for on the following morning, the whole situation took a disastrous turn. Everyone in the house was already up when a terrific clamor broke out in the street. My brothers- and sisters-in-law rushed to the windows to see a huge crowd gathered together in front of the house.

"Come out, Liu Pin-san!" they were shouting. "Come out!"

Eventually, a small group of three or four men separated from the mob, crossed the courtyard, and knocked at the front door. The frightened servants opened it and told them that Liu Pin-san was not at home. Then they asked who these men might be.

"We are workers from the Tsong Chin cotton factory," they replied.

My father-in-law owned stock in this company and was also a member of the board of directors. The Party, however, had just turned over the factory to the workers and they, along with the workers in other enterprises, had spontaneously set out to find their directors with the idea of putting them to work on the assembly lines. The only trouble was that most of the directors—particularly the most notorious ones—had already fled to Hong Kong.

It was, in fact, incredible that the workers were not more violent, for Shanghai had been a big industrial city and in the past, its leaders had suppressed strikes immediately with particular savageness. But vengefulness was being channeled into nonviolent acts of "reeducation," a word that recurred often during this particular period. More banker and landowner than industrialist, my father-in-law had not played a major role in the running of the Tsong Chin factory. But as the workers could find none of the company's officers, they had decided that Liu Pin-san would suffice. When they were informed that he too was absent, the workers would not believe it; the little group of spokesmen insisted upon entering the house and searching all the rooms, for they were convinced that the master could not possibly have left home so early in the morning. They even interrogated my mother-in-law, who calmly replied that he simply was not there, and then refused to discuss the matter any further. To my own fright, they also invaded my bedroom, but they were very polite, taking great care not to break anything. At the same time, they were clearly proud of themselves and anxious to show how dramatically things had changed.

"We'll be back," they declared when, having found nothing, they went out the door.

My mother-in-law now could not decide whether she ought to complain about her husband's arrest or be thankful for it. Given the workers' invasion, it was a stroke of luck that he'd been detained at the Park Hotel—as long as he would be freed eventually, that is. Better, she decided in the end, not to even imagine Liu Pin-san being led triumphantly to the Tsong Chin factory by the workers. His self-esteem would never have withstood the shock and he would surely have died of shame.

When we found ourselves alone at last, an argument broke out between my mother-in-law and two of her daughters. One, Yu-chi, was seventeen and the other, Yu-ming, about my own age. Both were sympathetic to the new regime. They tried to reassure her that Chairman Mao would never have told workers to behave as they had and that such behavior represented the customary excesses one might expect in the early stages of any major upheaval. But, all the girls managed to do was provoke Madame Liu again.

156

Lunch came and went. Liu Pin-san had still not come home; once again his wife set out for the Park Hotel to take him something to eat. When the officials refused to accept the package, she returned home, but went back again with dinner in the evening. When she inquired once more why her husband was still being held, they replied that it was his own fault.

"His freedom depends only on him," they said. "It depends upon his behavior and not upon us."

It was impossible to find out what was happening. On the second evening after Liu Pin-san's arrest, Ching-chung came for another visit. When she saw him, Madame let loose all her venom against the Communists.

"You must understand that for generations, the workers have had a very hard life," Ching-chung replied patiently. "Their capitalist bosses have always dealt harshly with them. Didn't Chiang Kai-shek have ten thousand of them killed during the Shanghai strikes of 1927? So today the workers are in a celebrating mood. To be sure, they've lost their heads, they've acted excessively. They don't really understand that a man like your husband is an exception, but how do you expect them to distinguish between him and all the other bosses? In any case, I'm sure no harm will come to him."

At last, on the morning of the third day, the phone rang. It was Liu Pin-san.

"They're letting me go," he told his wife. "I'm very tired. Can you come get me, and bring my son."

The whole household was overjoyed by the news, but my mother-in-law kept her head. She remembered that the workers had promised to come back and get him, and she decided that it was impossible for her husband to return home. My sister-in-law Yu-chi was immediately sent to reserve a room for him in a hotel not far from the house, and Liu Pin-san was driven there directly after leaving the Park Hotel. Only when he was safely ensconced in his own room did he tell his wife and son what had happened.

It appeared that his detention had to do with the government bond issue. Given the small number of subscribers, the government had decided to appeal directly to those who controlled most of the country's capital, beginning with the

157

wealthiest. Since Liu Pin-san was among the top ten, he was one of the first to be summoned. The well-known Shanghai millionaire Tsu had been "lodged" in a room right next to his. At first, the officials had politely requested that my father-in-law buy $100,000 worth of bonds, in cash. He replied equally politely that it was absolutely impossible for him to raise such a sum. Then they asked him to sign a promissory note and take a few days to get the money together. When Liu Pin-san continued to refuse, the officials began spelling each other in an effort to persuade him, reminding him that it was an entirely risk-free loan, that the state would pay yearly interest, and that the whole investment would be reimbursed in ten years. But Liu Pin-san firmly maintained that he simply did not have $100,000. After forty-eight hours, however, he finally relented, signed the note, and was promptly released.

That afternoon, my brother came to the house again, for he was genuinely worried about my father-in-law.

"Your beloved Communists are nothing but a bunch of extortionists!" Madame Liu cried.

"On the contrary," Ching-chung replied with the utmost gentleness, "they love their country and are trying to rebuild it. But when they see that the capitalists don't want to contribute to the effort, they have no choice but to force them. Mao didn't want it to come to that; he tried as best he could to convince them to cooperate. And in any case, the Communists aren't pocketing that money; it's for the country, which is a far cry from what went on under the previous government. You must try to understand and be patient, Madame Liu."

But my mother-in-law didn't deign to reply; in her opinion, there was no point talking to a madman. And, as it turned out, she had been right to hide her husband in a hotel. The very next morning the same group of workers knocked at the door. Once again, they turned the house upside down, but had to leave empty-handed.

It was clear, though, that Liu Pin-san's days were definitely numbered. That afternoon, after lighting the candles and incense and placing the twelve dishes in their proper positions, my mother-in-law knelt down before the ancestral altar in her sitting room and bade her farewells. The decision to leave had been made, but she was deeply disturbed about what would become of me and the grandchild she so ardently desired. Asking my mother to come and see her, she told mother that she and her husband were leaving that evening for Hong Kong. She explained that since it was only Liu Pin-san's safety that was at stake, all the children would stay behind for the present. It had been decided that they would leave later, accompanied by my husband. As for me, it was out of the question that I undertake a thirty-six-hour trip, and Madame Liu asked mother if she would consent to keep me with her until they could decide what to do next. It was impossible to say at the present time whether they would be staying in Hong Kong or would be able to return to Shanghai. At that time there was free access between Hong Kong and the mainland, and many rich businessmen had fled to Hong Kong so that they would be nearby and able to return easily if events permitted.

"Once you leave, you might stay away forever, or at least for a very long time," Chung-ai replied, stunned by my mother-in-law's announcement. "And in those circumstances, it wouldn't be fair for me to take my daughter from you. Her place is with her husband, even when conditions are difficult. All I ask is that you not abandon her. If your own children are staying here, then Ching-li must remain with her husband. But I'll come to see her every day and of course, I'll see to it that good care is taken of her."

"I don't want to leave my children or my daughter-in-law either," Madame Liu replied. "But I must get my husband settled first, and that ought to take at least a month. We're not young anymore and we don't know Hong Kong. But if all goes well, we ought to be able to send for the children a month from now."

Chung-ai took her leave and returned home with a heavy heart.

After having got together the $100,000 he had been forced to promise the government, Liu Pin-san gave the money to my husband, who took it to the officials at the Park Hotel. Then my father-in-law reserved seats for himself and his wife on the train to Hong Kong, taking care not to book places in the sleeping car, a luxury that was available only to the very wealthy and would surely have drawn attention to them. He was also very careful in his choice of clothing; thus, dressed in everyday Chinese clothes and carrying a minimum of luggage, my in-laws set off for Hong Kong, melting in with the common travelers.

I was now alone in the house with my husband and the rest of the Liu family. Mother came to see me every day and, with my husband's agreement, called in doctor after doctor to examine me. But neither Chinese nor European doctors could stop the bleeding. Whenever I tried to get up from my bed, the trickle became a flood. In addition, the accumulation of both injections and Chinese medication had weakened me even further, and I was forced to remain stretched out on my back with my head lower than my body, forbidden to turn either left or right. At the same time, my belly had grown larger, as if my child were clinging desperately to keep his life from draining out of me.

One evening after her daily visit, my mother was returning home even more depressed than usual, tormented by worry over what was going to happen to me and my child. In the street, she ran into a distant relative of hers, an older woman whom she had not seen for years. The woman was delighted with the reunion, but she was also struck by Chung-ai's troubled expression and asked her what was wrong. Mother poured out the whole story. Far from being alarmed, her elderly relative merely smiled.

"That's nothing," she replied. "We'll have her up and about in twenty-four hours!"

She gave my mother a recipe with ingredients I shall never forget: seven ginseng roots, seven dried longans, and a pill that combined the extract of various plants which were sold by one particular Chinese herbalist. The round ends of the ginseng root had to be boiled with the longans, and I had to drink the concoction with one of the pills. The relative maintained that only one dose was needed for the blood to stop flowing, but she recommended that I repeat the treatment three times, then once a month until the baby was born. In addition, I was to eat pigeon eggs every day.

My mother was dubious. Hadn't she already given me just about every drug known to man? But she thanked her relative and, perhaps because of her lingering superstitious beliefs, she went off to purchase the required ingredients. There was no problem with ginseng, as my husband had his own supply of this expensive plant in a special box. When everything else had been acquired, mother prepared the recipe and I swallowed my first dose that evening. By the following morning, the hemorrhage had miraculously stopped, but I dared not get up right away and so, following the relative's advice, I continued the treatment for three subsequent days. On the third day, I got out of bed for the first time in three months without the faintest drop of blood. I was overjoyed, not only because I was on my feet at last, but because I knew now that my baby would live.

My mother continued bringing me pigeon eggs and offering up thanks to all the gods in heaven, as well as to her relative, and we finally began to receive news of my in-laws. Apparently the population of Hong Kong had swollen considerably since the Liberation, which had created an influx of fleeing Chinese, including a great many people from Shanghai. Finding a place to live was thus extremely difficult. In addition, both because he felt he should watch expenses, and because he was afraid of attracting undue attention, my father-in-law was reluctant to rent a too-comfortable apartment, even though he had the means to do so. And so they settled into a second-rate hotel in Victoria, in the center of Hong Kong. All my father-in-law wanted to do now was send for his family— particularly since he had heard from his son that I was well again and would be able to travel.

So Liu Yu-huang decided that we should all leave for Hong Kong as soon as possible. When we told Ching-chung of our plans, I could sense his disapproval, but he said nothing. How was he to know that he would later suffer the consequences of our decision, one he had not made and of which he had in fact thoroughly disapproved?

As for me, I had barely recovered from the shock of leaving my parents' home, and now I would have to leave for an unknown city, abandoning Shanghai, where everyone I cherished lived. My parents shared my anguish, but there was nothing to be done. With my in-laws gone, Liu Yu-huang was the head of the family. He was responsible for planning the trip, for winding up his father's affairs, and for persuading one of his married, but childless, uncles to come live in the house once we were gone.

The arrangements did not go as smoothly as my husband had planned, however, for the moment he announced his decision, a terrific argument broke out among his sisters and brothers. The two youngest girls were Communists at heart, and there was no question of their leaving the country, even if their parents demanded it. But the most painful problem was posed by my husband's oldest sister, Liu Yu-ying, the scarred old maid, who adamantly refused to budge because she was in love!

It seemed that a short time earlier, she had met a man called Chang, and had fallen hopelessly in love with him. Known to everyone as Jim—he had added the American name himself, no doubt considering it fashionable—he worked as a secretary in a hospital. Given his modest salary, it was difficult to see how he could have become the playboy he was. And yet that was how he was known throughout the city. He never went anywhere without an entourage of pretty girls, usually nightclub dancers, and all he cared about was high living and lots of luxuries. Chance brought him together one day with Liu Yu-ying, and although she hardly resembled his usual type of woman, she *was* the daughter of a millionaire. He began to court her assiduously and, without a moment's hesitation, she fell into his trap. My husband and his friends tried in vain to warn her about this Don Juan who was obviously only after her dowry and all the money she represented, but she refused to listen. Indeed, she had come up with an ingenious explanation for Chang's interest in her, as much to convince herself as to silence his detractors. She claimed that Jim was fed up with going from one girl to the next, that he wanted to change his way of life, and that he dreamed of finding a nice, simple

162

woman from an honorable family with whom he could settle down in domestic bliss. This was clearly what he had told her, and she wanted desperately to believe him, for time was not on her side. Some years before, a marriage broker had actually found her a fiancé, but when the boy in question saw her scarred face and discovered that she was also partly deaf, he had the engagement annulled, a terrible humiliation that hurt her deeply. Now she was thirty-one, an old maid, and suddenly a man actually wanted to marry her! There was no question of her leaving Shanghai.

When my in-laws were informed of this scandalous relationship, and of their daughter's refusal to leave, they responded by ordering her not only to come to Hong Kong, but to do so *immediately*, even before the other children. My husband was instructed to drive her to the train and personally escort her to her seat, for everyone knew she was perfectly capable of some wild maneuver that might compromise everyone else's departure. My husband bought a ticket for her right away and one for one of his younger brothers, then saw both of them safely to their seats, a difficult job since my sister-in-law cried and screamed all the way to the railroad station. There was no recourse, however, for a parental command represented the final law.

As for my second sister-in-law, Yu-chen, the one who had married that worthless individual who was living off his father-in-law's money, she would be staying in Shanghai. The two younger sisters, Yu-sao and Yu-chi, who had Communist sympathies, were going off to the university in Peking, which left only my husband's youngest sister, Liu Yu-ming, who was fourteen years old, and my nine-year-old brother-in-law, Liu Yu-shen. It was understood that we would bring both of them with us to Hong Kong.

And so at the end of May, 1950, the day of our departure finally arrived. Dressed in workingmen's jackets and carrying only a few suitcases, my husband, his little brother and sister, and I set off for the station, accompanied by my own family, all of whom were shedding copious tears. Like my in-laws, we had not dared reserve places in the sleeping car, and so the trip was to be made on the hard wooden benches of a packed third-class car. My mother wept at the sight of my belly, which was just beginning to round out, and at the thought of the thirty-six hours I would have to spend under these trying conditions. Indeed, the Shanghai railroad station was already the source of one sad memory for me, that of my father's perilous trip to Chungking so many years before. But our own departure was even more painful, for I had no idea whether I would ever see my family again. A thousand knives cut into my heart as the train jerked into motion, while out on the platform, my brother Ching-chung continued running alongside the train, his face bathed in tears, until he was completely out of breath.

I was still crying when we reached Hangchow. An elderly woman who was sharing our compartment leaned forward and tried to console me.

"You must stop crying," she said. "It's very bad for your baby."

Although I was still too young to know what being a mother really meant, I was sincerely moved by what she said, and out of intuitive love for my unborn child, I forced myself to stop.

I will not go into the details of our calvary, of the hot and humid night during which my husband, with his weak heart, and I sat squeezed together on a hard bench so that the younger children would have room to sleep. Not once in the entire thirty-six hours were we able to close our eyes. We found the energy to stay awake only because of our responsibility for Liu Yu-ming and Liu Yu-shen. When we reached Canton, which was the next-to-the-last stop before our destination and only an hour from the border, we had to change trains. The station was packed with soldiers, but none of them so much as glanced in our direction. Finally we reached Sham Chun, the frontier outpost for the so-called New Territories, and saw our first English soldiers from Hong Kong. It was like a sudden leap into the past, for with their flat hats and elegant uniforms, they reminded us of the long-ago days in Shanghai before the war. The rest of the trip, in the southern heat and humidity, exhausted us completely, but two hours after crossing the border we arrived at last in Hong Kong.

After barren countryside and squalid suburbs, Hong Kong,

164

with its big buildings, its movie theaters, its hotels, and its traffic, seemed an exact copy of Shanghai. The only difference was that the people, who were predominantly Cantonese, were shorter than the inhabitants of Shanghai and spoke what seemed to us an utterly incomprehensible language. As Shanghainese, we were virtually in a foreign country.

My in-laws, along with their eldest daughter Liu Yu-ying, were waiting for us at the Kowloon railroad station. Ordinarily discreet and not given to displays of emotion, they were obviously overjoyed and immensely relieved to see us. Together we took the ferry for Hong Kong, and then a taxi from the quay to the hotel.

My in-laws' hotel was not only rundown but dirty. I knew my father-in-law disliked spending money, but this time he had really been shamefully stingy. He may have been in exile, but I knew he certainly did not want for funds. And yet all he had done was take two big bedrooms—one for the women, the other for the men. The first was occupied by not only my mother-in-law, but by my two sisters-in-law and me as well. The second housed my father-in-law, my husband, and his two younger brothers. We had to use a communal bathroom on our floor.

I could have borne this discomfort and deprivation in a foreign city with joy if we had been a warm and close-knit family, confronting such adversity with love and understanding, or if I had felt even the slightest kindness or affection among them. Unfortunately, our first day had not even ended when it became obvious that the atmosphere within the family was even more upsetting than that of the hotel. Finding herself suddenly deprived of her numerous servants, my mother-in-law had lost her dignity. She had become a bitter old woman who spent all her time whining and complaining to her husband, who did his best to console her, but still refused to move to more commodious quarters. As for my older sister-in-law, Liu Yu-ying, all she thought about was her abandoned Don Juan, her beloved Jim, whom they had forced her to leave behind. And when she wasn't crying, she would sit and stare at us as if we were her worst enemies. The temperature and the humidity of Hong Kong were very unhealthy for my husband's heart and for his rheumatism, and he was frequently sick. As for the younger children, they were miserable living in a hotel, and could not understand why the faces around them looked so somber all the time. Aside from my father-in-law, who remained perfectly calm and serene, I was the only other reasonable human in the family. I realized that our situation was unfortunate, but I could do nothing to change it, and so I spent my time listening patiently to the lamentations of the others, in the hope that once the initial shock had passed they might eventually adjust.

Besides, I had other things to worry about.

Chinese women of the old school cared for their hair in a very special way. Although they washed their hair only two or three times a year, they combed it every day for hours at a time with a fine double-toothed comb fitted with small pieces of cotton which picked up the dirt, and which of course had to be changed frequently. Back in Shanghai, my mother-in-law had had a servant who spent at least an hour daily combing her mistress's hair. This daily pleasure, rather like a massage, was something my mother-in-law could not bear to do without. She had in fact done without it since arriving in Hong Kong, but of all of her deprivations this was to her the worst. She had thought of asking her eldest daughter to do it, but confronted with Liu Yu-ying's sour and haughty temperament, she didn't dare. Thus, the task fell to me. And so every morning, I had to stand and comb her hair, even on those days when I felt as if I would faint from exhaustion. Since there were neither housekeeping nor cooking duties to worry about, as we ordered our meals from a nearby restaurant, I spent my mornings divided between combing my mother-in-law's hair and visiting a cousin of my mother's to whom my parents addressed all my mail, because we were unsure as to how long we would be staying at the hotel. Thus, fresh tears were shed every day as I read the precious news of my family.

After several days had passed, my father-in-law finally admitted that we would have to move. When he went out looking for an apartment he took me with him—not only because he was tired of his family's complaints and found my behavior refreshing, but also because I spoke English. Aside from Cantonese, a dialect that none of us knew, English was the only other useful language in Hong Kong. Finally, after a difficult week of searching, we found a suitable apartment.

The cheapest and most elementary furnishings were rapidly assembled, and within forty-eight hours we were all installed. In comparison with the two hotel rooms, the new apartment seemed palatial, but there was one serious drawback—we had to do our own cooking and cleaning. And as Madame Liu's only responsibility in Shanghai had been to play mahjong, she made us pay dearly for giving any help in the housework by whining and complaining. As for my wet-eyed older sister-in-law, Yu-ying, one dared not ask her to lift a finger—we were thankful enough simply for those brief moments when she stopped moaning about her Jim. Thus, as the new woman, all the household duties fell inevitably on me. Typically, my day was spent combing my mother-in-law's hair, making the beds, cleaning the apartment, doing the marketing, and preparing all the meals.

We did not live near any markets, so I had to undertake a long expedition every morning, returning laden with bags and packages under a stifling June heat. Moreover, since my mother-in-law was too parsimonious to buy a refrigerator, I usually had to market twice a day, for in that heat perishables bought in the morning would be spoiled by dinner. As far as preparing meals was concerned, since my mother had not taught me to cook, Madame Liu and Liu Yu-ying never failed to make a scene if the food was either overcooked or under-done, too salty or too sweet. I therefore bought a cookbook and applied myself with great energy to the task of mastering it in the hope of pleasing the Lius.

If it wasn't my cooking that provoked angry outbursts, it would be something else. My sister-in-law Liu Yu-ying fought with her younger brother all the time, and since he always managed to stand up to her, she inevitably wound up turning her anger in my direction. What made it worse was that although a sister-in-law had the right to say whatever she wished to the new woman, the latter was prohibited from replying. I tried my best to find excuses for this frustrated and pathetic old maid, but it became increasingly difficult to put up with her. To be sure, my husband suffered greatly at seeing me working so hard and being treated so shabbily, but knowing that any intervention on his part would provoke his mother's anger, thus making my life even more difficult, he kept silent. In any case, his ill health was already a heavy enough burden for him to bear.

A few days after we moved into the new apartment, my sister-in-law, probably because she couldn't find anything else to complain about, accused me of making fun of her.

"I can't stand Ching-li's attitude toward me any longer," she complained. "I'm going back to Shanghai! I refuse to live another day in the same house with her!"

My mother-in-law didn't want Yu-ying to leave, but she was easily persuaded that I had in fact been behaving badly, so she asked my father-in-law to take me to task. There I was, little more than a child, pregnant, weak, and doing my best to satisfy everyone, and this was how I was rewarded! On the verge of a nervous breakdown, I wrote to my parents, describing the kind of life I was leading. A few days later, my brother arrived in Hong Kong.

Before leaving Shanghai, Ching-chung had quit his job as an instructor, unfortunately unaware of the serious consequences that would later result from his actions. Once in Hong Kong, he was met at the train by our long-lost "Uncle" Yao, my father's childhood friend who had shared our house in Shanghai. He had been living in Hong Kong for quite some time, and since he had escaped from Shanghai with his fortune intact, he had been able to buy an amusement park called the Lichee Corner, which included two theaters, one for plays and one for movies, as well as an amusement park. In addition he had acquired a small textile factory and, with his two wives and their respective children, he was living quite comfortably in a nice house. Unlike my in-laws, he spent his money freely.

Ching-chung could not stay with us, both because there was no space and because custom imposed a proper distance between the families of the husband and wife. I, of course, was the only one who knew the reason my brother had left China and come to Hong Kong. As far as my in-laws knew, he was only visiting me. But when my brother saw how weak I was and under what duress I was living, he didn't have the heart to return to Shanghai, and since he couldn't stay in Hong Kong without finding work, he turned to Uncle Yao. By chance, Yao needed someone he could trust to run his textile factory, and although Ching-chung was too young to be called a director, he was given the title of assistant director, one which was not only honorable but which also afforded him a reasonable living.

Ching-chung came to see me every day. He also wrote to our father, telling him why he was staying in Hong Kong and how discouraged he was by my condition. It was a frustrating experience for both of us, as all he could do was passively observe my plight. But his letter moved Hui-i, who soon arrived in Hong Kong himself.

By this time I was five months pregnant and still working as hard as before. I had no appetite and had lost weight. The only food that interested me was milk. Unlike most Chinese, I had always loved milk, but my in-laws thought milk an abomination and refused to purchase any. I didn't dare buy any on the sly when I saw how carefully the change from my marketing was counted. As for my husband, he didn't work and so had no money of his own. My poor father, who had complied with the ban against taking money out of China, didn't have a cent, but in order to buy milk for me he sold the ring he wore on his finger. Nevertheless, I still cried when I was alone at night, and sometimes in my father's arms when he visited, for his unhappiness made me even more miserable than my own.

Several days later, he asked to see the Lius, begging them to let my husband and me return with him to China. He tried to make them understand that he was certain my husband and I would be able to live perfectly happy in Communist China.

My in-laws, however, were intractable. Not only could my mother-in-law not tolerate the idea of being separated from her son, but my father-in-law, after that encounter with the Communists at the Park Hotel, had lost all confidence in the future for people like him or his son.

"I believe in Mao Tse-tung," Liu told my father, "but not in the people. How do I know what they might do to my son? Didn't my workers turn my house upside down twice looking for me? And what do you think would have happened if they'd found me? No, my children will never return to China!"

Hui-i left the house in a state of profound depression. What could he do? He could neither stay here, away from the rest of his family, nor could he imagine bringing them to Hong Kong. Since he was prohibited from taking money out of China, what could they possibly live on? And so, deeply discouraged at his inability to make my life easier, he finally had no choice but to return to Shanghai.

My life went on in the same way as before until about three weeks later, when my father suddenly returned to Hong Kong with some marvelous news. Apparently, there were no longer any obstacles to our returning to China, for Mao Tse-tung had announced in all the newspapers that all nationalist bourgeois who desired to return to the mainland would be well treated. Liu Pin-san himself had had a role in this new policy, albeit a small one. During his internment at the Park Hotel, my father-in-law, astonished at the treatment he was receiving, had informed the officials of the services he had rendered to a former employee of his who had left his bank to join the Long March. He also reminded them of the risks he had run in taking care of the man's family during all those years of struggle. And now Liu's story had finally been dramatically confirmed.

For this employee, whom I shall call Soong, had become one of Mao's most intimate advisers in Peking. It took several weeks for the story of his former employer's arrest to reach him, but when it finally did, he was most disconsolate and told Chairman Mao that not only had Liu Pin-san shown his patriotism and his sympathy for the Communists' struggle by risking his life to help the family of a soldier in the Liberation Army, but that he was one of the very few among the wealthy who had not tried to leave the country when the Communists took power. With Mao's permission, Soong had sent Liu Pin-san a letter of apology from Peking, unaware at the time that he had already left for Hong Kong. The letter arrived at the house on Nanking Road and was opened by Liu Pin-san's brother-in-law, who rushed to show it to Hui-i. My father brought the letter with him. It said that Liu Pin-san's arrest "must be considered an error both of the government officials and of the people who did not yet know how to continue their struggle correctly" and it assured Liu Pin-san that "in the future, such unjust actions would be strictly forbidden."

"And so," my father concluded, "if even *you* are now permitted to return to China in perfect safety, then surely your children can do the same. And so I must again ask you to let your son and his wife return with me to Shanghai."

My father-in-law replied that he would have to think about it. It was just possible that things might be worked out.

Liu Pin-san didn't think about it for very long. From what he had just learned of the government's policies, his properties were being redistributed among the people, but he himself was considered part of the people and would be able to maintain a fair share, thus recovering at least a part of the assets he had left behind. And since his son was familiar with his business holdings, he imagined Liu Yu-huang to be just the right person to take care of his affairs. Liu Pin-san's decision to let us return to Shanghai was obviously carefully calculated. He saw that his son and new wife would be able to live quite handsomely on the revenues from his businesses. Indeed, more than one Chinese capitalist remained quite prosperous until 1965, the year the Cultural Revolution began to swell.

And so after an agonizing two months in Hong Kong, I was at last able to return to Shanghai with my father and husband, delivered once and for all from the persecutions of both Madame Liu and my detested sister-in-law Liu Yu-ying. Unfortunately, Liu Yu-ying followed shortly thereafter. Her complaints about her abandoned Jim, and the impossibility of living among people who spoke only Cantonese, had finally worn her parents out, and they consented to her departure as well. When all of us had returned to Shanghai, Ching-chung had no further reason for staying in Hong Kong, and he resigned his job as well, coming back to Shanghai as quickly as he could.

11

Nothing much seemed to have changed when I returned to Shanghai.

My husband and I were now sole masters of the Liu house on Nanking Road. Since Liu Yu-ying, my redoubtable sister-in-law, had not yet arrived from Hong Kong, the only people living with us were my husband's uncle and his wife, who had been taking care of the house since our departure. Discreet and helpful, these good people did not bother us in the least; in fact, we were delighted to have them stay on.

But the house was much too big for a woman to handle alone, particularly a pregnant one. And so I asked my husband to engage two servants, one to do the housework and the other to cook. For the first time I experienced the wonderful sensation of freedom. I could walk in and out of every room, open all the forbidden cupboards, look through all the drawers, and not only was I indisputable mistress of the house, but for the first time since my marriage, I had the right to go to a restaurant or to the movies with my husband. Formerly he had been permitted to accompany me only to my parents' house!

One day, as I was putting some things away, I chanced across a small illustrated book with the portrait of a strikingly

172

beautiful woman inside. The picture made a great impression on me, and I asked my husband to tell me who she was and what the book was about. Liu Yu-huang explained that the woman's name was Chen Mei-li and that she had been a hostess in a famous Shanghai nightclub called the Parliament. A hostess in appearance only, she was a Chinese agent whose mission, from 1937 to 1939, had been to extract information from the Japanese officers and Chinese collaborators who frequented the club. It was no accident that Chen Mei-li's portrait appeared in the Liu household. One of my father-in-law's younger brothers, Liu Pin-chen, young, handsome, and extremely wealthy, had met the woman in question at the Parliament. He found her not only beautiful, but intelligent and sensitive as well. It was, in fact, love at first sight for both of them. Unfortunately, however, they aroused the suspicions of a Japanese officer who was also desperately in love with Chen Mei-li. One night, when the officer was present, Liu Pin-chen arrived at the club and sat down at Chen Mei-li's table. The orchestra was playing a slow waltz, and although Liu was careful not to say or do anything which would betray his feelings, he and Chen Mei-li could not help exchanging glances. That was more than enough for the Japanese officer; in a flash, he had whipped out his revolver. Chen Mei-li, seeing the danger, threw herself on her lover, protecting him with her own body. Both were severely wounded in the ensuing fusillade, and in the midst of indescribable confusion, the two lovers were taken to the hospital. But whereas Pin-chen survived, Chen Mei-li died on arrival. Every newspaper in the city had carried the story, but it was only after the war that her true identity as a spy was revealed. The story fascinated me, and I now viewed Liu Pin-chen, whom I hardly knew and heretofore had thought of as rather dull, in quite a different light.

My brother, Ching-chung, had finally returned to Shanghai. However, it was not long before he was made to realize that his concern for me had cost him the Party's faith. Because of his lengthy stay in Hong Kong, his devotion and loyalty were questioned, he was pronounced no longer worthy of the tasks entrusted to him, and he was summarily suspended from any further activity while the party deliberated his fate. I felt great guilt and frustration, as I could do nothing for him.

At the same time my husband, Liu Yu-huang, while supervising all of my father-in-law's business enterprises, had also gone to work in one of Liu Pin-san's banks as a director, thus allowing us to live very comfortably. Since I was still pregnant and couldn't continue attending school (although married and pregnant, I was still only turning fourteen), tutors were hired to come to the house, primarily to give me English and piano lessons.

While for us life seemed as untouched as before the Sino-Japanese war, let alone the Liberation, in actual fact China was going through a series of dramatic changes. To begin with, the emphasis was on the creation of a new Socialist man, who would discard the old garments of Confucian belief and live instead by the Five Loves—love of fatherland, of people, of labor, of science, and of public property. These tenets were publicly proclaimed, printed, and plastered all over China on wall posters, to be analyzed and discussed at great length by the entire population, albeit in small, separate study groups such as those formerly headed by my brother.

However, one of the most dramatic changes that took place—and one that I wept over with great bitterness, coming as it did only five months after my wedding day—was Mao's edict against any arranged, and therefore forced, marriages. The bitterness, rage, and unhappiness I felt is indescribable.

Accompanying this decree, Mao also outlawed other similar, and possibly worse, barbaric practices such as the drowning of newborn female babies, polygamy in the form of concubinage, and slavery through the sale of women into servitude or prostitution. Mass meetings and campaigns were held throughout the country, and long articles about prostitution began appearing in newspapers, accompanied by the personal stories of young girls who had been sold as children into the possession of older women, themselves former prostitutes. Unlike the situation in the Western world, procurers in China were typically female.

Out of curiosity, I myself attended several of these mass

174

meetings which marked the end of prostitution in China. Indeed, Shanghai had been an international capital of vice, and the prostitutes, highly concentrated in the brothels of Second, Third, and Fourth streets, numbered in the thousands. The meetings were sometimes held in public auditoriums or restaurants, but more often in open areas. The standard procedure was simple enough. A political commissar stood on a podium and pointed to a group of procurers who had just been arrested. At the same time, he invited a newly liberated prostitute to take over the meeting and to tell her story in her own words. Invariably the girl was a peasant, purchased in her village by traveling female procurers. Her family was usually fatherless, the children numerous, poverty and starvation rife. The mother was always told that her daughter would be given work in Shanghai, that she would earn a decent salary, and that she would even be able to send money home. Typically, the poor woman understood little of what she was told, but since the people from Shanghai seemed to be promising a change for the better in what was otherwise a hopeless situation, she ended up by accepting the offer. The mother was then asked to authorize her daughter's departure by signing a paper—usually with a thumbprint—whereupon she was given a small sum of money and the girl was spirited away.

The girl's story was invariably interrupted by both her own tears and the groans from her audience. She would describe her arrival in Shanghai, her failure to understand why the "nice lady" was giving her clothes and teaching her the art of makeup, but she would learn soon enough what was in store for her: She was usually raped by one of the madam's accomplices, whereupon the madam herself would burst into the room, as if by accident, playing the role of the outraged wife, and accuse the poor girl of having seduced her husband or boyfriend. The "traitorous" girl was then forced to do as she was ordered; if she refused, she was threatened with terrible punishments, not the least of which was prison. Those who continued to refuse were tortured.

One balmy spring day, I witnessed an outdoor meeting of this sort. The speaker was a dark-skinned Chinese girl from the north. She walked to the podium, but before beginning her story, she turned around suddenly and exposed her back to the crowd. It was heavily scarred by the marks of a branding iron. It seemed she had refused to comply with the madam's commands, resulting in a torture session that had gone on for quite some time; when she fainted, she was revived and tortured again until she finally consented to obey. The girl explained that many like her had naïvely fled to the police, without realizing that the officers of the law were themselves hopelessly corrupt. Invariably, the girl was taken back to the brothel and given appropriate punishment. Indeed, more than one of these poor fugitives had died under torture.

Most of the time the guilty parties, the owners of the brothel, as well as their procurers, were present at these meetings. When the commissar pointed to them and asked the crowd what it thought such individuals deserved, the mob often screamed for their heads. They were not killed on the spot, but led off under heavy guard with the promise that they would be appropriately chastised, possibly with execution. As for the former prostitutes, the government set up a network of halfway houses outside Shanghai, where female party officials took over their "reeducation."

Mass meetings and trials of this kind were being held by the thousands not only in the cities but also in the countryside, where certain property owners and local despots were obliged to listen to the peasants pour out their long-suppressed complaints in public. The peasants' tales were always the same: a lifetime of poverty on top of centuries of suffering, and now for the first time a faint glimmer of hope and the possibility of real change. Indeed, many of these stories strongly resembled a popular revolutionary play called *The Girl with White Hair*, in which the beautiful Hsi-erh, daughter of the poor peasant Yang, is kidnapped by Huang, a despotic landowner and collaborator with the Japanese. When her father is finally killed, Hsi-erh manages to flee to the mountains, where she lives a solitary existence, kept alive only by the hope of revenge. Eventually, her hair turns white and in the end, the Red Army arrives and captures the evil despot. After a public trial, Huang is executed and Hsi-erh is revenged.

This famous play, which has been revised and staged as a

ballet, is based on facts that were well known to all Chinese. For Huang represented thousands of small landowners in the countryside, who had exploited countless peasants and their families. The trials of these landowners nonetheless served to moderate the peasants' outrage, and Party officials consistently countered the possibility of violence by explaining that there was now no further reason to be afraid of such tyrants, and that the important thing was not vengeance, but the realization that they had at last been freed—which is precisely what Hsi-erh's fiancé; Ta-chun, tells her at the end of the play.

While these mass meetings were taking place all over the countryside, the purging of religious orders was underway in the cities. For everyone knew that among the many irreproachable Buddhist temples existed some that were dens of vice and corruption. The priests in these establishments scarcely deserved the title; they were a far cry from the authentic Buddhist monks who had taken the vows of chastity and vegetarianism, in accordance with Buddhist tradition. The Communists were not attacking religion in itself, but rather its exploitation and the victimization of vast numbers of superstitious and uneducated believers.

This dramatic housecleaning was always accompanied by detailed and public trials, for the Liberation Army abhorred any sort of secrecy and was always careful to publish regular reports of its activities. One day, I went to an exhibition in Shanghai devoted to the extortionary crimes of secret societies. In a large room were displayed elegant clothing and jewelry that had been donated by credulous members of the I Kuan Society (the Society of the Unique), accompanied by written documentation and explanation. Not only had this society demanded large and regular financial contributions from its members, but its master, among various other misdeeds, had even violated his own daughter. And although this man had hundreds of disciples, they were unable to prevent his being thrown into jail. I was particularly interested in this exhibition because my mother-in-law had been a devout member of this sect, often shutting herself up in her room for hours to practice certain rites the society claimed would restore her health. Indeed, her name figured on the membership list unearthed by the police, and had she not left Shanghai when she did, she would certainly have been arrested. Curiously, she had been encouraged to join by Old King, the drunkard who pretended to be her son-in-law and who had made such an unpleasant scene with me at our wedding. But now at last, the Communists had put an end to one more racket that had made a fortune by victimizing thousands of unsuspecting faithful.

And then suddenly, one day, the public trials ended and the newspapers published the lists of those who were to be executed. Hundreds of gangsters and vice lords were shot that same day at three o'clock in the afternoon on the golf course of Hungjao to the west of Shanghai, where so many wealthy gentlemen had once played their eighteen holes. The sky was dark, hail began to fall, and many interpreted this as a sign that the gods themselves were angry at those who were about to die.

This was one of the first mass executions. The elimination of counterrevolutionary elements went ahead with particular severity during the summer of 1950, especially after the implementation of the agrarian reform. Not all big landowners were punished, however, as the case of my father-in-law illustrated clearly enough. Liu Pin-san owned a great deal of property in Ningpo and in Hangchow, but since it was widely known that he regularly gave a large part of his income to old people, orphans, and hospitals, he was never denounced to the authorities. In fact, he was given the title of "Good Proprietor," even though he had already left for Hong Kong. Had it been otherwise, had Liu Pin-san not been a generous capitalist, life might have been extremely difficult for my husband and me.

12

The close of the year 1950 was marked by two events, one international, the other personal: the Korean War and the birth of my son, Sun-po.

In spite of the presence of Liu Yu-ying, who had finally returned from Hong Kong, my life proceeded peacefully. I was happy, for even though Yu-ying's disagreeable nature had not changed, she had at least found her beloved Jim and therefore left us alone. Indeed, my tranquillity was disturbed only by my dreams. Ever since becoming pregnant I had dreamed not only of the gates of heaven opening but also, and more frequently, of snakes. As I had lost so much blood in the early stages, I was convinced that these dreams were sinister portents, announcing some terrible deformity in my unborn child. Frightened, I went looking for Chinese books on dream symbolism. I bought one and read it in secret, immensely reassured when I discovered that according to this particular text, the woman who dreams of snakes will produce an exceptional child. My fears assuaged, I began devouring calcium and vitamins in an effort to aid the prediction, to strengthen this unborn baby for whom I was now beginning to feel the blossoming of maternal love.

For this unborn child helped me forget my forced marriage

and my disappointment in the death of my childhood ambitions and romantic dreams. The baby would be my hope and consolation. And if I tended to think of the baby as a male, it was because there was no doubt in my mind that the child would be a boy. Chao-mei, my mother-in-law's goddaughter, had given me an amulet as soon as I had become pregnant—a small cloth sachet, containing the gallbladder of a bull from the north of China, which was reputed to ensure the birth of a male child. When she gave it to me, she told me the story of a woman she knew who had nine daughters in a row and who, in desperation, began wearing the amulet and had finally given birth to a son. I wore the amulet tied around my waist for five months, not removing it even when I bathed.

In September, as I neared the end of my pregnancy, my mother began to worry about possible complications and asked my husband and me to come live with her. Being old-fashioned, she insisted upon observing the fine points of traditional Chinese custom. Although a son could sleep with his wife in the house of his own parents, a woman was not supposed to sleep with a man in the house of her parents. To do so was bad luck, and in order to protect ourselves, a special ceremony was required. My mother set out the traditional square table with red candles and special dishes, before which my husband and I knelt and prayed to our ancestors to accept us into the house. In addition, we paid my mother a symbolic token rent.

Chung-ai, however, felt that rent should be more than token. Throughout our stay, she carefully noted down each mouthful of food swallowed so as to be reimbursed later. Such an absurdly detailed accounting, however, was not purely avaricious. She was also conforming to a deeply rooted Chinese belief that once a daughter is married, she ceases to be part of her parents' household. Hui-i and Ching-chung, on the other hand, could not have cared less about the proverb, and were as generous and affectionate as they had always been.

By this time, Hui-i had given up his import-export business, in part because of internal political circumstances, but mostly because all contacts with foreign countries had been cut off. With his degrees and his pedagogic experience, however, he had found a job as the principal of a high school, and although he now earned less money, he was happy to be back at his old profession. As my sister Ching-ling now boarded at the conservatory, my childhood bedroom was empty and I installed myself there with my husband to await the baby's birth.

Meanwhile, other signs favorable to the birth of a male child began to appear. For one thing, my grandparents often came to visit us. In age, the miserly Tso-hung had changed a great deal; he was now a devout Buddhist and prayed fervently for a grandson who would be born at a favorable time on a favorable day.

And then, three days before my baby arrived, I awoke one morning and found that the palms of my hands were red, just like my father-in-law's. I asked my mother what it meant, but she had no idea, and neither did my grandfather nor the servants. I began poring through my books again, convinced that it must have some significance. And indeed it did. "The woman whose palms turn red just before the birth of her child," I read, "will have a son blessed with excellent qualities."

Three days later, I woke abruptly at five in the morning with pains in my stomach. They lasted until the following evening, when they became so severe that I couldn't stand it. My suitcase was packed and off we went to Dr. Liang's clinic, where my husband had reserved a room for me.

The delivery was extremely difficult because my body was still that of a child's, and because the baby's head was very large. The door was wide open, as the Chinese saying goes, but still the baby's head could not get through. Since I screamed and groaned like a wounded animal, Dr. Liang requested permission to proceed with a forceps delivery. My father consented; he had never witnessed the birth of any of his own children, and he looked about to faint. My mother, on the other hand, objected. Given her vast experience, she preferred a natural birth which would not deform the child in any way, even if I would have to suffer atrociously. The family argument went on until finally, the exasperated Dr. Liang had me moved to a room on the third floor from which outsiders were prohibited. Once separated from my parents, I immediately stopped screaming in spite of the pain. Aided and encouraged by the doctor, I pushed as hard as I could and at 4:45 A.M., sweating and trembling, I gave birth to my child.

"Doctor," I asked anxiously, not having heard a single cry, "is it a boy or a girl? Why isn't it crying?"

"Congratulations," Dr. Liang replied. "You have a fine son. If you don't hear him crying, it's because he's extremely busy at the moment with his first bowel movement!"

That indeed was my son's first offering, and I received the news with joy, for I had heard my mother-in-law say that this was a sign of great good fortune; whereas the baby who urinated immediately after being born was sure to bring bad luck. Added to my dreams of serpents and heavenly gates, this first small gift removed all doubt about the exceptional quality of the being I had just brought into the world.

And so Sun-po was born on September 11, 1950, the Year of the Tiger. He was a good-sized baby, and his name, Po, was that of a great scholar in ancient China. Giving him that name signified the hope that he would one day follow his illustrious namesake.

My mother was particularly satisfied, because he was born close to five o'clock in the morning. According to tradition, since the tiger leaves his lair at night to go hunting, a baby born in the middle of the night would be destined to kill himself working, whereas a baby born in broad daylight would grow up to be worthless and lazy, like the tiger sleeping in the shade at noon. But one born at five in the morning promises to be exceptional, for it is the moment that the tiger, glutted by the hunt, returns victorious to his lair to rest.

Exhausted and content, I kept my child's cradle right next to the bed. I couldn't take my eyes off him. My husband slept in another bed in the same room with us, an exceptional arrangement, to be sure, but we were in a private clinic. I spent ten days recuperating before I was able to get up. My hair was finally beginning to grow out again. Nurses came and went regularly to take the baby away to be bathed and fed. One day, however, a new nurse was on duty. When she brought Sun-po back into the room, she asked where the mother was. I told her I was the mother. She looked at my child's face and two short braids, and asked me to please stop joking. I insisted I was the mother, but she refused to believe me. Our voices rose and the other nurses came to see what all the commotion was about. When they verified the fact that I was the mother, the new nurse nearly went into shock. As far as I was concerned, I lost my temper only because I had once heard a terrible story about another maternity clinic in Shanghai where there had been a terrible mix-up among the babies. In addition to its Chinese patients, the clinic also had many Indian women, the wives of those tall Sikh policemen with the red turbans in the International Settlement who were called the "redheads." Apparently, after having left the clinic with her baby, one of the Chinese women noticed that the color of her child's skin was extremely dark; she had been given an Indian child by mistake. This story haunted me the whole time I was in the clinic and I was constantly worried about the possibility of a substitution.

My in-laws in Hong Kong had been notified of their grandson's birth, and my mother-in-law wrote immediately, exhorting me to breast-feed my child for at least a month after its birth, as mother's milk was considered a baby's best protection against sickness. I did my best, but as I had very little milk, the child was literally starving. He cried and I cried, and it soon became clear that we would have to find a wet nurse. When I left the clinic after two weeks and returned to my mother's house, a placement service in Shanghai sent us Ah-ching. She had large breasts and positively radiated good health.

The story of her life, however, was not quite so radiant. The daughter of poor peasants, Ah-ching was orphaned at an early age. She was taken in by her grandmother, but obliged to earn her bed and board. Now it happened that in her grandmother's village there lived a young man, a tailor, and near this tailor lived a thirteen-year-old girl called Ah-ying, who had been engaged by her family to a baby boy barely a year old. This was a perfectly normal practice in those days; in fact, it was most advantageous for the baby's family, as the older fiancée could take care of the baby, her future husband, and serve her future in-laws as well.

Time passed and Ah-ying grew up. One day she met the

tailor, her neighbor, who was a few years older than she. They fell desperately in love but were forced to meet in secret, for she was affianced and, in those days, both risked death if their liaison were to be discovered. The tailor's mother, who knew about the affair, lived in terror for her son's life, and decided that her only hope lay in finding her son a wife. Our future nurse, Ah-ching, was twenty years old at the time, and the tailor's mother, finding her suitable, forced the tailor to marry her. This didn't stop him from spending his wedding night, and many nights thereafter, with his beloved Ah-ying. In the course of events, Ah-ching became pregnant and gave birth to a daughter. But since her husband gave her neither love nor money, and since the baby had had the bad luck to be born a girl, Ah-ching threw the hapless infant into a garbage can—a not uncommon practice at the time. The following year she had another child, also a girl, but since the new law promulgated by the Communists prohibited the murder of newborn babies, Ah-ching dared not repeat her crime. Instead, she turned the child over to her mother-in-law and came to Shanghai with the hope of selling the only thing she possessed: her milk.

I learned this story through the agency and was so moved by it that I insisted my husband hire her to be Sun-po's nurse and to make sure she was paid a good salary. Ah-ching's milk, which her own poor baby had never tasted, had an excellent effect on my son's health; he soon stopped crying and became a flourishing and contented baby.

Liu Pin-san's fears about returning to Shanghai had been allayed by the letter of apology from Peking, and he decided to come for a two-week visit. His first stop was to see this grandson whose birth had been so enormously important to him. Indeed, it was my father-in-law who had named my son Sun-po. He also brought gifts for my mother, in gratitude for her having raised such an excellent daughter. Then, as custom dictated, a celebration took place when a baby reached the age of one month. A big party was held in my father's house, and the guests filled all three floors. My son was dressed in red silk, and on his head sat a bonnet in the shape of a tiger, while his feet were shod with matching shoes embroidered with tiger

184

heads—the traditional way of protecting children who are still too young to walk away from evil spirits. Soon after the celebration, my father-in-law returned to Hong Kong.

I was perfectly happy at my parents' home, and for the time being had no intention of returning to Nanking Road. But disaster struck. It seemed that my sister-in-law's playboy lover, Jim, had gone to see her one day. He had apparently hung his jacket on a coat peg without realizing that a paper was sticking out of the pocket. With the typical curiosity of his age, my young brother-in-law, Liu Yu-hsi, who had returned from Hong Kong and was now at Nanking Road, pulled the note out and read it. Unfortunately for Jim, it was a pawnshop receipt for some clothing. Liu Yu-hsi showed the paper to the uncle now in charge. Finding it scandalous that someone should pawn his clothes, the angry uncle took Jim to account. Jim, in turn, gave the boy a good dressing down for rummaging in pockets that didn't belong to him, but my sister-in-law finally had to admit that there was indeed something suspect about her fiancé pawning his clothes. Frustrated and angry, she turned all her venom on her brother, at which point her outraged uncle telephoned us at my parents' house to demand that we move back to Nanking Road and try to put things back in order.

Before doing so, however, we wrote my mother-in-law in Hong Kong. She caught the next train to Shanghai, resolved to settle the problem of her daughter and Jim Chang once and for all. But in spite of her pleading and demands that Liu Yu-ying return at once to Hong Kong, my sister-in-law remained faithful to her original intention: Jim was the great love of her life and she meant to marry him no matter what.

"If that's how you feel about it," my mother-in-law sighed, "then marry him. I won't stop you. But you can tell your lover that you'll have neither a dowry nor a trousseau. You can tell him, too, that I'll pay for a three-day wedding and honeymoon at the Park Hotel, and after that you can both take care of yourselves!"

"That's fine with me," Liu Yu-ying replied.

And so the wedding took place at the Park Hotel in the presence of Jim Chang's parents, a witness, and my mother-in-law. Neither my husband nor I was there. In fact, there were only enough guests to fill the twelve seats at one of the round tables.

On the third day after the wedding, Yu-ying, now known as Chang Yu-ying, arrived at our home on Nanking Road with a swollen face, a black eye, and a gap in her front teeth. My mother-in-law gasped and demanded to know what had happened. By this time, the whole family had come running to see what all the commotion was about, and Yu-ying replied uncomfortably that during a moment of inattention, she had been struck in the face by the hotel's revolving door. Later, however, alone with her mother, she blurted out the truth. From my bedroom, I could hear the two of them weeping.

Apparently, on the wedding night, Jim had asked his bride what she had brought by way of a dowry. When she revealed she had nothing, she was rewarded with a royal beating. In an instant, all her illusions about their exceptional love were smashed by the fists of her handsome Jim. It was too late, however, for once she was married, no one could help her. My mother-in-law gave her some money, enough to rent an apartment and buy some furniture, but only so that the outraged husband would not throw her daughter into the street. Whereupon a saddened Madame Liu returned to Hong Kong, while Yu-ying began a new and scarcely promising life.

Our own life on Nanking Road returned to normal as the prince of our hearts, Sun-po, or Paul, as we were to call him later, grew into a beautiful little boy. After Chang Yu-ying's departure, aside from the servants, there were only four people living with us, my overly inquisitive younger brother-in-law Liu Yu-hsi, my little sister-in-law Liu Yu-ming, and my husband's uncle, Liu Pin-chen, and his wife. My husband and I led an active social life. We received guests and went out every evening to formal dinners as if nothing had changed since before the war. For although we wore simple Mao suits by day, we still dressed up in the evening.

There were changes, however. Not only had I grown taller than my husband, but now that my in-laws no longer lived with us, I had my own piano. In addition, private tutoring had ceased. The state had nationalized the entire educational system, and the MacIntyre School had now become Shanghai School No. 3. In 1951, I was authorized to return there to take my final high school examinations for the Chinese baccalaureate.

Meanwhile, my sister Ching-ling had for some time been a boarder at the conservatory in the suburbs of Shanghai. One day, she introduced my brother Ching-chung to a classmate of hers; the two fell in love and were married shortly thereafter. Ching-chung's new wife finished her studies and found a job in Peking, where both of them went to live. Ching-chung taught English in one high school while his wife taught music in another. Although still suspended from the Party, he continued to be a dedicated Communist.

In the same year, Ching-ling met an engineering student at the university at Hangchow. He was charming and intelligent, and his name, curiously enough, was also Liu. Their marriage plans ran up against severe resistance from my parents, however, primarily because of my mother's deeply rooted and old-fashioned prejudices. The father was a banker, like Liu Pin-san, which was in the boy's favor, but unfortunately the father had also five wives, three of whom were still living with him. One was his official wife, the others were concubines number one and two, and, to make matters worse, my sister's fiancé was one of the concubine's sons. I defended my sister and her fiancé against my parents, arguing that they loved each other, that Mao Tse-tung had freed the institution of marriage from its barbaric constraints, that the new society paid no attention to people's origins but only to their qualities, and that it was obvious this boy was worthy of marrying Ching-ling. Thus caught between my arguments and my sister's obstinacy, my parents gave their consent, and the two were married the following year.

As for me, when not studying, I was enjoying the comforts of my situation, remaining largely unaffected by the events that were revolutionizing China. Soon enough, though, another family crisis came along to shatter my idyllic existence. My second sister-in-law, Liu Yu-chen, was visiting me one

October afternoon, and suggested we go out to eat at a restaurant famous for its crabs. I agreed, and then decided to phone my husband at the bank and invite him to join us. When I was told that he wasn't there, I thought nothing of it, and invited my youngest sister-in-law, Yu-ming, to come along with us instead. At five o'clock in the afternoon, the three of us were comfortably ensconced at a table on the second floor when I suddenly saw my husband coming upstairs carrying two crabs, this being a restaurant where the diners were able to select live crabs from water ranks.

"What are you doing here?" I exclaimed, surprised and delighted to see him. "I just called you at the bank to tell you to meet us here! How did you know?"

"I didn't," Liu Yu-huang replied. "I'm in another room with some colleagues from work."

Whereupon he turned and entered a small room, pulling the curtains shut behind him. It was the closed curtains which piqued my curiosity, and so, followed by Yu-ming, I walked over and parted the curtains, peeking through to see who these colleagues might be.

There was only one other person in the room, an attractive woman. After the initial shock, Yu-ming, who was no older than I, yanked the curtain aside and pushed me in, then began shouting at the woman sitting beside my husband.

"Aren't you ashamed?" she cried. "Aren't you ashamed to be here with a married man?"

My head began to spin; I wanted to get out of there as quickly as possible. I started to pull Yu-ming out of the room, but she was already across the room telling her older sister. We ran downstairs, followed by my husband. He continued to pursue us in the street, gasping out his explanation as best he could. It seemed that the woman was an old friend of his, a nurse he had known before he met me, and who had been in love with him although he had never reciprocated. Apparently, she'd been telephoning him at the bank, and even though he'd told her that he was now married and had no wish to see her, she kept begging to see him. At last, worn out by her insistence, he had agreed.

"You must believe me," Liu Yu-huang went on. "There's

nothing between us. I agreed to meet her out of sheer courtesy."

"Courtesy!" I exclaimed. "If you're worried about courtesy, *I'm* the one you should be making appointments to see! I'm the one you should be meeting in restaurants! Courtesy! So it's for the sake of courtesy that you take her to a private room to eat *crabs?*"

In China, when eating crabs, one takes them apart with the fingers, an act which is considered intimate and is usually performed only in private and in the presence of close friends— certainly not with people one knows only slightly.

I was shocked and bewildered by what I had just seen and could not help thinking of the nightmare of my wedding and of everything I had suffered for my husband. And now that I had resigned myself to my fate and had accepted Liu Yu-huang as my husband forever, I discovered him eating crabs in a private salon with some strange woman! Why go on living with him, I asked myself? The man had never had any particular attraction for me—neither physically nor intellectually. It was his kindness alone that had finally won me over, and if his attentions were now directed elsewhere, what was the good of staying together?

The minute I got home, I ordered Ah-ching to pack both my bags and my son Paul's. By this time, Liu Yu-huang had returned home in tears, begging us to forgive him, swearing that I was the only woman he loved, threatening that if I left him, he would surely suffer a heart attack. Well aware of his fragile condition, I tried to calm him down, but I had made up my mind to leave and I did not intend to be dissuaded. After all, it was not impossible to remake my life. Mao Tse-tung had liberated Chinese women and now they worked like men at everything from teaching to engineering. I could take up my studies again; I could even remarry. All of a sudden, I was filled with an overwhelming sense of freedom. To be sure, I was taking my little Paul with me, which meant that no matter what happened, I would still have what was most precious to me in all the world.

When Liu Yu-huang saw that my suitcases were ready and that I really did intend to go to my parents, he asked me at least to have one last dinner with him. As it was almost seven o'clock, I asked the cook to prepare a meal. My sister-in-law, who had witnessed everything from the restaurant on, took her leave. We sat down to supper, but not a word passed between us, and neither of us ate much. Afterward, I set about getting the luggage together, but just before leaving, I passed the door to our bedroom and saw Liu Yu-huang stretched out on the bed, apparently asleep. Five minutes ago he was in tears, I thought to myself, and now he's fallen off to sleep! What a hypocrite! I was so angry that I called out to him. There was no response. I walked over to the bed and shook his arm. Still no response. Terrified, I placed my hand over his heart; it was still beating. So he wasn't dead after all! And then I saw the empty bottle of sleeping pills. Rushing to the phone, I called the hospital; an ambulance arrived moments later. As Liu Yu-huang was being lifted onto the stretcher, a piece of paper fell from his hand. I picked it up and read: *Ching-li, my darling, I swear you are the only one I love and that I have never deceived you in any way. But now that you are leaving, life has no more meaning for me. And so, instead of you, I prefer to be the one to go, the first and forever. My only wish is that you take good care of our son. Adieu.*

At the hospital, the doctors were able to pump out his stomach in time, and once Liu Yu-huang had returned home, I no longer had the heart to leave him. Our life together continued as before, except that Liu Yu-huang was so filled with guilt over what he had done that he became more attentive and affectionate than ever. His strength was beginning to give out at last, and it sometimes seemed as if he realized he would soon be leaving us for good.

Early in 1953, I was pregnant again and since I had always been obsessively concerned with horoscopes—as was almost everyone in China at the time—I set out to calculate the date of my child's birth, only to discover with horror that the baby would be born under the Sign of the Dragon. Paul had been born during the Year of the Tiger, and not only do the tiger and the dragon not get along with each other, but they are destined to fight until one devours the other. There was no doubt in my mind that this second child would cause Paul no end of suffering, and I loved my son too much to expose him to such unhappiness. Strange as it may seem to a Westerner, I resolved to prevent this child's birth, no matter what the cost. It was not difficult to find the right drugs for inducing miscarriages, and although I had to do so alone and in secret, I managed to accomplish what I wanted.

In accordance with its policies, the government was to wait for quite some years before purging the country of those citizens it referred to as *national capitalists*, but whose money and expertise were so badly needed. In fact, when a foreign enterprise such as the Compagnie Française d'Électricité began to be harassed by worker agitation, the government ordered the workers to stop and obey the company's orders. After all, that particular company supplied all the electricity for Shanghai's trams.

Since returning from Hong Kong, I myself had become on paper one of the richest women in Shanghai. There was nothing illegal about our income, for my husband was his father's duly appointed administrator and had power of attorney. Revenues from my father-in-law's banks, land, and stocks continued to pile up in our accounts, including the first payment on the loan my father-in-law had been forced by the government to subscribe. The state had indeed kept its word, and the interest on the $100,000 came to a very tidy sum.

But in spite of all this, I continued to give piano lessons to children, partly to avoid asking my husband for an allowance, and partly to help my parents out from time to time. Hui-i was going through a difficult period, having tried various jobs in order to earn more money, including quitting his low-paying position as a high school principal and going to work in a small, private dye factory. But this hadn't worked out, and in the end, he had returned to teaching.

In 1953, a new stage in the Liberation brought all private enterprise under the control of the state. Although the private ownership of industry had been permitted to continue in accordance with the program of 1949, it was now to be phased out. However, the former owner still received certain compensations from the government, such as being entitled to half the value of his shares at the end of the year, and if he continued to work for his own company, he would receive both a salary and the dividends on his stock.

Thus, although Liu Yu-huang had ceased being the director of his father's businesses, he still maintained a managerial position under the supervision of a union representative. Changes of this sort were also accompanied by a process of reeducation, or *hsi-nao*, which took the form of compulsory meetings two or three times a week, in which self-criticism as well as the story and criticism of each other's background and history took place. In addition, the works of Marx, Lenin, and Stalin were studied, while the writings of Mao became scripture and individual insignificance was stressed as against party omnipotence and a new life of liberation, progress, and meaningful existence.

At the same time, a wave of attacks against counterrevolutionary elements broke over the city of Shanghai. During the month of April alone, there were countless police raids as well as huge public trials at the racetrack where Chinese and foreigners alike had once congregated to bet on the greyhounds.

For the bourgeoisie, however, the situation had not really deteriorated in any significant way and thus, speculation and trafficking began once again. The most frequent dabblers in these illegal activities tended to be functionaries and it was primarily against these profiteers that the government launched its Campaign of the Five Antis, which attacked the crimes of bribery, tax evasion, fraud, embezzlement of state property, and espionage aimed at obtaining certain economic state secrets. But even so, despite the public trials and widely publicized condemnation, those found guilty were usually sentenced to camps for reeducation rather than to corporal punishment or execution.

Only once during this time was I personally affected by these activities, and that was the long and agonizing week during which my husband was detained at the main offices of the Chungking Bank. I first learned the news when the phone rang one evening and I was instructed to bring him blankets. I knew Liu Yu-huang's conduct was irreproachable, but I had heard of so many employers being insulted, and even beaten, that I was extremely worried. And given my husband's delicate health, it was not much consolation to imagine his detention being the result of someone's mistake. He finally returned home at the end of the week, claiming that he had been treated well enough, and although he was obviously exhausted from his ordeal, he seemed relatively unconcerned, explaining that the union representatives and the bank employees had spent the week interrogating him about his father. Basically, they accused Liu Pin-san of having fled to Hong Kong with an airplane full of dollars and gold bars. How much had he taken out, they wanted to know? Who had helped him? And how had he managed to get hold of a private plane? The union was vociferous in its demands for the return of the money, but Liu Yu-huang was unable to give them information he didn't have. If his father had in fact smuggled some money out of Shanghai by plane, he certainly hadn't told his son about it. When the workers saw how ill my husband was, he was finally freed, unharmed. Whatever they may have thought of the father, the son was widely respected.

Outwardly, Liu Yu-huang appeared none the worse for wear, but inwardly the physical and moral shock of his week-long detention had taken its toll. Indeed, judging from the number of those who committed suicide during this period, fear alone caused untold damage in the ranks of the affluent, unable as they were to withstand the humiliation of public accusations and trials. My husband never went so far as to contemplate suicide, but the interrogation had drained his energies and weakened his will to go on working.

A few days later, while Liu Yu-huang was still at home recuperating, we received another serious shock. It all began again with a telephone call. It was Old King, the self-styled "son-in-law" employed in my father-in-law's main bank—that same odious individual whose conduct had been so scandalous on our wedding day. But whereas before he was content to flatter my in-laws shamelessly, passing himself off as Liu Pin-san's relative, he now had become a toady to the new Communist bank managers, and he had once again come up with an idea profitable for him but tormenting to us.

"Your husband must come down to the bank right away," he stated dramatically.

"Is that *your* order or the union's?" I inquired archly.

"The union's."

"Then tell your union representative to make his own phone calls!"

"That won't be necessary," Old King retorted. "I can speak for him."

"Well, then, I'm sorry, but Liu Yu-huang can't leave the house. He's very ill."

"That's all right. You come instead."

"I'll be right there," I replied, hanging up.

When I arrived at the bank, a mob of employees was gathered in the hallway. Two huge piles of books sat on the floor in their midst.

"There she is! There she is!" Old King cried, thrusting his finger in my direction.

Then, still pointing, he made his way over to me.

"Look at what your husband's been doing!" he shouted. "Look at what he's been reading when he should have been working! Pornography! All those books are pornography! And they all belong to him!"

His accusation was so unexpected that it took me a few seconds to react.

"I don't believe you," I finally replied. "My husband would never..."

"You deny it then?" Old King cried. "You deny it even though he probably practiced everything in those books when you were in bed together!..."

Faced with this ignoble insult, I lost my temper.

"Don't forget who *I* am, Old King!" I snapped. "And be careful before you sully my name with such disgusting and salacious lies!"

Then, turning to the rest of the employees, I went on with my tirade.

"And you!" I cried. "You're nothing but cowards! You got

194

hold of these books somehow, you read them, and now, in order to wash away your own sins, you pretend that they belong to my husband! Isn't that right? Isn't that the real truth?"

By this time, most of the employees had fallen into an uncomfortable silence. But a few of them, the younger ones, grew more aggressive.

"There's nothing further to talk about!" they cried, advancing toward me. "We know these are your husband's books, so take them home with you! We don't want them around here anymore, we don't want to dirty ourselves with your..."

Calmly, I asked one of the bank's errand boys to bring a large bag and when he did so, I dumped the books into it, firmly repeating that they were not my husband's, that all of the employees were a bunch of sheep, and that no one was man enough to admit it. Once all the books were in the bag, I announced that I was taking them into the kitchen of the bank's dining room and would burn them in front of everyone. At this point, Old King and a few of his cohorts began shoving and pushing, pulling me this way and that, by the hair, as so many employees had done to their former bosses. I kicked and screamed and swore at them, putting up a good fight. I have no idea what would have happened to me if one of the managers hadn't suddenly intervened.

"Stop it!" he shouted over the tumult in a stentorian voice. "Leave her alone! She hasn't done anything wrong."

And once again, as on my wedding day, when my mother-in-law had intervened to keep me from having to drink his toast, Old King began bowing and cringing, his face taking on the same expression of a frightened weasel.

Unwilling to abandon my original plan, however, I asked the errand boy to pick up the sack and follow me to the kitchen. There I set fire to one of the books and threw it into the gaping coal stove. Book followed book until the last volume had been reduced to ashes. Then I returned to the hallway where the employees were still standing in a group.

"Given what's happened here today," I cried, in the best oratorical manner I could summon, "the Revolution is nothing but a pretext for certain jealous and nasty individuals to take out petty grievances and vilify everyone else! Really loyal Party members don't act like this, and people like you should be prevented from doing harm!"

I had spoken fearlessly, and only when I was safely back in my house did I wonder how I'd had the nerve to stand up to all of them. I began to shake with delayed reaction.

In the meantime, my brother Ching-chung was himself running into grave difficulties with his party superiors in Peking. The old story of his trip to Hong Kong had resurfaced. Ching-chung was again called upon to justify his actions, but all he could do was tell the truth; that his sister had been desperately unhappy and he had gone to Hong Kong to see if he could help her. Unfortunately, no one believed him. Of course, he was a good man, they said; his history as an underground revolutionary proved his loyalty beyond the shadow of a doubt, but because he had stayed in Hong Kong, he was suspect. In vain, Ching-chung insisted that he had gone to Hong Kong only for his sister's sake, and that he had worked there only so as to be able to help her. His interrogators persisted in accusing him of having gone on his own account in order to satisfy his need for the comforts of his previous bourgeois existence. And so it was decided that Ching-chung would have to give up his job as an instructor and go to work in the countryside. Only work of this kind could lead to his reeducation, and the extermination of his corrupt bourgeois roots.

Since the incident at the bank, not only had my husband stopped working, but his health had deteriorated dramatically. Liu Yu-huang's illness was psychological. He had entered a period of deep depression, and only with the help of religion did he emerge. For Liu Yu-huang was a Buddhist, and henceforth his life would be reoriented in this spiritual direction. The second floor of the house was converted into a vast prayer room filled with images of several Buddhas: Kuan Yin, the Goddess of Mercy, who witnesses all the evil in the world; Ti Tsang Wang, who cures illnesses and the vices that cause them; and Tao Fu, the First Buddha, who leads the souls of the dead into Paradise. Twice a day, early in the morning, and at night, Liu Yu-huang knelt in the prayer room, lit incense, and prayed for a long time. The rest of the day he spent trying to strengthen his failing health by the customary doses of swallows' nests, ginseng, and vitamin tonics concocted from dried plants.

For this last treatment, the servants regularly filled an enormous caldron with a vast number of plants, sometimes up to a hundred varieties, building a fire in the courtyard. The contents were boiled in the vat for hours until reduced to a syrup, which was then filtered, sweetened with crystallized sugar, and the whole poured into small jars where it congealed so thoroughly that it had to be mixed with water before it could be swallowed. This was a powerful and very expensive tonic, but without it, Liu Yu-huang would not have stayed alive. His condition was in fact so precarious that our doctor ordered me to sleep in a different room so as not to precipitate his death by the exertion of lovemaking. I obeyed, of course, but such a drastic measure was a source of great concern to my mother. For her, sleeping in a different room meant that my life was no longer normal. As for my husband, he was fully conscious of his frailty and, despite his depression, was more concerned about my condition than his own.

"Ching-li," he said gently to me one day, "let me speak frankly. Let me give you all the money you need and the child as well. Perhaps you would like to find another husband..."

The idea had never occurred to me, but once it had been mentioned, I rejected it outright. To abandon a sick husband, particularly one who continued to be so deeply concerned with my welfare, to let him die of grief and depression and to give my beloved Paul a different father—such notions were unthinkable. Nothing would ever make me consent to such an idea; besides, although I had entered my marriage unwillingly, I had now developed a deep affection, if not love, for my devoted and kind husband. I begged Liu Yu-huang never to mention the subject again.

On the other hand, my mother was still worried about my "abnormal" situation. So worried, in fact, that one day she sent a fortune-teller to me who was well known for her exceptional skills as a medium. I was now seventeen years old, and I remember the whole experience vividly. The woman appeared at the door wearing a blue jacket and trousers, her hair pulled back into a neat bun behind her head. The servants showed her to the living room, where she asked me to light incense in order to facilitate the evocation of the spirits.

I can see her now as clearly as I did then—seated, her eyes closed—first yawning, and then even letting wind pass repeatedly, as if to empty her body. She seemed to be in pain, and began waving her arms in the air. Suddenly her head fell forward onto the table and she seemed asleep. A few moments later she woke, got to her feet, her eyes tightly closed. She was calm, as if invested with some presence, and she began to speak in a quiet voice, answering my unspoken questions.

The Goddess of the Flowers had entered her.

"I see flowers in a pot of jade," she murmured. "In a pot of jade before Goddess Kuan Yin . . ."

According to tradition, flowers defined the individual's character, and the container the condition of his existence. An earthenware pot signified poverty, a jade pot wealth. And the presence of Kuan Yin meant that she was my protector.

"There will be much money in this woman's life," the fortune-teller went on, speaking of me in the third person. "She is beautiful, intelligent, and has good parents. She will have exceptional children, one a girl, but in her previous life she was poor, she abandoned her husband and children. Later, she begged for forgiveness, she came to the temple, to embroider a whole Kuan Yin with a heart of gold threads. The work took her a lifetime, and she prayed for beauty, intelligence, and wealth in her next life."

So that had been my previous existence! What struck me was less my poverty than my sin, especially when I firmly believe that our present life is modeled on the errors of our former existence, and that all life is but an expiation of earlier wrongdoings.

Then, abruptly, the old woman stopped; she did not want to go any further. At the time I had no idea why, and it would be some years before I learned the reason why she had remained silent about what would be one of the most painful episodes in my life.

13

By 1953, only three years after China's Liberation, life in cities like Shanghai had become unrecognizable. The imposing buildings, built with foreign gold and Chinese blood, had remained untouched, but the teachers, the missionaries, the bankers, the businessmen, and the adventurers from Europe and America were now only a memory, and although the streets were as crowded as ever, even the type of traffic had undergone a radical transformation. For, along with their foreign owners, the big imported cars had disappeared. The aim of the new government was to free China from its dependence on foreign commodities. Vast quantities of bicycles appeared; it seemed as if each car had been replaced by a thousand two-wheeled vehicles.

In addition to being purged of its gangs and prostitutes, Shanghai also had much cleaner streets. As a result of several long-range campaigns launched by the new leaders, all of China's population—from old men to children—had begun a ferocious cleanup, pursuing such scourges as rats, flies, and mosquitoes. Each family was asked to give the authorities a weekly quota of one rat tail per family member. Those who surpassed their quota were entitled to fly a small red flag on their front door. The country literally blossomed with red flags, and children everywhere vied with one another to see who could kill the greatest number of flies, rats, and mosquitoes. Indeed, more of these troublesome pests were undoubtedly done away with by children than by all the pesticides and traps put together! Even today, when I go back to visit my country, I am astonished when I see the incredibly clean streets and alleys, and remember how overwhelmed we once were by vermin and insects.

Another change which struck me even more forcefully was the disappearance overnight of beggars, hitherto a perfectly ordinary sight at every street corner—mothers squatting with babies, alive or dead, the blind, the maimed exposing their stumps, the elderly who had simply been consigned to the sidewalks to die—all had vanished.

The government also set about distributing the educated more evenly throughout the rest of the country so as to spread out the advantages of their education. Even members of the government were not exempt from this reshuffling; a large number of government functionaries were required to change their place of residence. My eldest sister-in-law, Liu Yu-ying, who now had a baby of her own, and her beloved Jim, who had been obliged to go to work in an office, were invited to move to Peking. For a woman used to all the comforts money could buy and who in marriage had had to live far more modestly than before, this exile from Shanghai brought on further tears and hysteria. Since Yu-ying could scarcely expect help from her parents, my husband secretly gave her some money before she left.

During the following year, my in-laws began sending urgent letters to us from Hong Kong. They were desperate to see their grandson, and given the fact that they were aging quickly, partially the result of living so far away, I made up my mind to satisfy their wishes. I applied for visas. Both Paul and I received ours almost immediately, but my husband's was refused. This meant that I would have to go alone with my son, a prospect that terrified my parents. My father made up dozens of name tapes, complete with our address, which were sewn into all of Paul's clothing in case he should get lost en route. And in addition to a trunkful of clothes, we had to add an enormous cotton bundle containing provisions for my in-laws, including some traditional Ningpo dishes. One way or another, we finally got to the station, where little Paul turned to my parents and asked them please to take good care of his father. Ah-ching, his nurse, kissed him tenderly, for she too was leaving Shanghai, taking advantage of our absence to pay a visit to her native village near Saochin.

This second trip to Hong Kong was quite different from the first. Instead of the hard benches in third class, we now had seats in a first-class Pullman car. And whereas the first time we had traveled for thirty-six hours straight, this time we left the train at Canton and spent the night in a hotel. In order to get back on the train the following morning, however, the passengers had to go through the Luhon customs. There, the Chinese customs officers searched all our baggage with great meticulousness, opening and shutting the trunk and the bundle. Finding nothing of any value, they then asked for my visa. Frantically, I searched everywhere, but couldn't find it. Meanwhile, we could hear the train hissing and whistling on the platform; Paul was getting nervous as I rummaged through pocket after pocket of my Mao suit. And then, suddenly, there it was. In my panic, I had overlooked one of my pockets! Thus, when we were safely back on the train, Paul demanded to keep the visa himself, much to the amusement of the other passengers.

When we arrived in Hong Kong, my in-laws were so overjoyed to see their grandson that they insisted we stay with them. My mother-in-law was so amiable and affectionate with me that I hardly recognized her. A month later, when my return visa was about to expire, she became so depressed that I applied for a renewal. At the same time, two of my sisters-in-law, Yu-chi and Yu-sao, who had been studying at the university in Peking, arrived in Hong Kong to visit their parents. Both were besieged by my in-laws, who wanted them to leave Peking and finish their education in the United States. Although both were devout Liberationists, they obeyed their parents' wishes and went to America, eventually marrying American Chinese.

As we waited for our return visas to be renewed, Paul began to show definite signs of boredom.

"You must have a second child," my mother-in-law urged me. "One is not enough."

Remembering the abortion of my second child in 1953, I replied that as far as I was concerned, one child was just fine, and that in any case, Liu Yu-huang's health was already sufficient cause for worry.

"You mustn't be concerned about that," she remarked. "You must simply fulfill your destiny."

Madame Liu, who had now become an ardent Buddhist and whose advice in any case I had never taken lightly, went on to tell me a curious story.

"When your husband was born," she began, "at the very instant of his birth, I had a sudden vision of a monk. He looked about forty years old, and I felt sure this meant that a monk's soul had been reincarnated in the body of my son. A few hours later, one of my aunts, an extremely pious Buddhist, came to visit me. She told me that she knew I'd had a son, for she, too, had had a vision, a vision of a monk being carried by a white stork and deposited on the roof of my house. But then, three days after your husband's birth, something even more bizarre occurred. An alms seeker, an old monk dressed in black, knocked at our door. He was offered some money, which he refused, then a meal, which he also refused. He asked for one thing only, to see the new baby. The servants were frightened, not only because my son was clearly the most precious thing in the house—after all, I'd already had four girls and one of them had died—but also because Liu Pin-san was very rich and they thought the monk might be a bandit in disguise attempting to kidnap the child for ransom. They refused his request and asked him to leave, but he wouldn't move. The servants began arguing among themselves and finally the noise reached my bedroom, where I'd been confined to my bed. I demanded to see the man. When the servants brought him in, I asked why he was so anxious to see my son, and he replied that the child who had just been born had once been his inseparable friend and companion.

"'We both lived in a temple in the mountains of Szechwan,'

he told me, 'where we had pledged to live a hermit's retreat for a period of twenty years. We were waited on by younger monks in the order, and we spent our days in prayer and meditation. But whereas I remained faithful to the vow we had made together, my friend was constantly tormented by temptation and, at least, he broke his vow and left the monastery. But he was so ridden with guilt he fell ill and died shortly thereafter. I knew, because of his fundamental piety and goodness, that his next life would be comfortable and protected, like a prince's, and that he would have a good wife and beautiful children. But I also knew that since he had broken a sacred vow, his next life would be tormented by ill health, in expiation for his sins. He would be born and die like a king, but his life would be filled with suffering. Your son is my friend, and I tell you these things so that you will watch his health carefully and bring him up under the sign of the Buddha.'

"When he'd finished," my mother-in-law went on, "the monk knelt and prayed, pronounced a blessing over my son, and left without accepting anything at all from me. I remember his face well, and his bare feet. He had come from very far away and was exhausted by his trip. I had no doubt whatsoever about the truth of his tale."

I must admit that I was as convinced as my mother-in-law. I now knew that Liu Yu-huang had been destined to suffer, but that he could live and have children without fear. No matter what he did, his destiny had already been determined.

As the days passed and I waited for news of my visa, I went on long shopping excursions with Madame Liu, during which she purchased quantities of clothes for me to take back to her other grandchildren in Shanghai. For my own child, however, there was nothing—unless I counted some old childhood clothes of Liu Pin-san's which had been cut down and mended for the occasion. I accepted them without a word, although I couldn't help wondering why she was buying all those expensive gifts for the others and none for Paul, who was, after all, her true grandson. In China, only the son of a son may be called grandson. The son of a daughter is referred to as the "outside grandson," as the parents of a daughter-in-law are called the "outside grandparents." Finally, however, my mother-in-law detected my resentment.

"When someone is born," she said to me, by way of explanation, "his destiny has already been determined down to the least detail, even for little things like clothes. I know Paul has a remarkable destiny, but he must be careful not to spend his happiness too soon. If he wears his grandfather's old shirts, he will be *economizing* his destiny."

Contrary to what I had imagined, I discovered that she loved Paul even more than the others, and that the very fact that she was giving them such sumptuous gifts meant they were not nearly as important to her as my son. Moreover, I had thought that this new affection she was showing came from the absence of her beloved son; but now I saw that her concern for me was genuine, if somewhat puzzling.

The days drifted by and still my return visa had not yet arrived. I began to feel nervous and impatient to return to Shanghai, for I was scheduled to give a concert that had been organized by my piano teacher, Mr. Hsiang. I was worried that this delay would mean the end of my concert, as my fingers were becoming more and more rusty with each piano-less day in Hong Kong.

Finally, thanks to one of my in-laws' neighbors who had a piano, I was able to practice a few hours from time to time, although not nearly enough to keep me in condition. And while I practiced, my mother-in-law took long walks with her grandson, who soon began praying fervently to Buddha for a little sister.

In the end, it was four months before my return visa came through. Our departure from Hong Kong was accompanied by tears and lamentations, particularly on the part of my father-in-law. Indeed, it was tragic to see the once-powerful Liu Pin-san, hopelessly withdrawn, cut off forever from his homeland. Only his little grandson kindled a spark of life in him during these past few months, and when we departed on the ferryboat for our journey back to Shanghai, his eyes filled with tears of despair.

204

We may have left Hong Kong amid tears, but we were met in Shanghai with happy smiles.

Once things returned to normal, I applied myself with a frenzy to Rachmaninoff's Piano Concerto, which I'd been working on for some time now in preparation for the recital.

My piano teacher's apartment was filled with people, and although the piano was in the living room, he had opened all the doors so that guests could sit in the other rooms and still hear. One of the guests was a Mr. Fang, who also happened to be the head of the Shanghai Conservatory, and whom I hoped to impress. After I'd finished playing, his only comment was to ask how long I'd practiced. I replied eight months. Without another word, he turned around and left.

I'd already forgotten the incident when a few days following the concert, I discovered I was pregnant once more. My husband and I had followed the doctor's orders and slept in separate rooms, but on my return from Hong Kong, we'd been so glad to see each other that we'd relaxed the rules a bit. Paul was thrilled when he learned he might get a little sister—he was absolutely certain that the baby would be a girl.

On the fiftieth day of my pregnancy, I gave myself a test to verify the child's sex. I'd learned it from my mother, and had used it when I'd been pregnant with Paul. According to this procedure, one must turn over on one's back in bed at five o'clock in the morning. The baby will then rise to the surface of the mother's stomach, and if one presses down carefully, one can feel the child's outline. If the shape is oblong, like a finger, the baby is a boy; if it's spherical, a girl. When I performed the test on myself, I felt a round ball, which immediately slid away. I must admit to being skeptical, but when I reported the results to my mother, she was convinced I was carrying a girl.

This pregnancy was as pleasant as the first had been difficult. I was in good health, my life was peaceful, and I was still able to devote a great deal of time to the piano. The only problem was the house. Liu Pin-san had stubbornly refused to leave this house on Nanking Road, which he had occupied since he was poor, simply because a fortune-teller had declared the house lucky. Through the years, the place had grown more and more shabby. Rats and cockroaches had even taken up residence in the rotting floorboards. One day, I heard Paul screaming from the kitchen below. I rushed downstairs. On a shelf in the pantry was a glassed-in cupboard which held the statue of a kitchen Buddha. Every morning, Paul and a servant placed the traditional incense and cup of tea before it, but in order to do so, Paul had to climb up on a stool. On this particular morning, an enormous rat had sprung out of his hiding place next to the Buddha and begun rushing around the kitchen. That was the last straw. I had no desire to bring up my second child in the middle of all this squalor.

Clearly, it was time to move.

I had heard of an apartment on Hung Chiang Road in the middle of what had been the International Settlement. The apartment had been occupied by a doctor who wanted to retire and move to Suchow. A duplex, it was located in a building coincidentally owned by my father-in-law, Liu Pin-san, although we were not shown any favoritism because of the relationship. The apartment was perfect for our needs, so we paid the doctor a token fee, or deposit, known in China as a "doorstep," enabling us to cross the threshold. Spacious and modern, the apartment included a Western-style bathroom with running water and a *genuine flushing toilet!* No more wooden excrement buckets like the ones we used in that awful house on Nanking Road!

As soon as we moved into our new apartment, I elatedly purchased two grand pianos, a Bechstein and a Steinway, for the drawing room (in the house on Nanking Road, one alone would have caved in the floor!). Then I installed my old upright piano in our bedroom and purchased two more—one for the guest room, where I hoped my sister would stay on visits to Shanghai, and the other in the nursery, for my future child. Excessive, yes, but I was still in my teens, reacting to the deprivation at Nanking Road. Fortunately for me, Yu-huang was a most indulgent husband.

One day I received a phone call from the conservatory; it was one of the officials, inviting me to come for an interview. I was thrilled and immediately began calculating my chances of acceptance. For one thing, my sister, Ching-ling, was now a pianist at Radio Peking, and she was known even in Shanghai. Such a connection was obviously not unfavorable. For another, it was just possible that my Rachmaninoff recital had not entirely displeased Mr. Fang, the conservatory director, even though he hadn't commented at the time. My heart pounded with excitement.

Prior to the liberation, the conservatory had been a closed, exclusive establishment, accepting only those students already educated with sophisticated backgrounds in the history and theory of music. Talent alone did not suffice. Now, however, the government was as interested in the training and formation of artists as it was in the training and formation of scientists and engineers. Artists were, in fact, referred to as "engineers of the soul."

My early marriage at thirteen had of course precluded any possibility of pursuing any musical studies, and I had abandoned all hope of qualifying for the conservatory. But since the Liberation, the conservatory had added a course of studies whereby gifted students lacking the proper academic background in music—whether for financial or other reasons—could now complete the necessary studies and take the baccalaureate exam.

Nervous and excited, I arrived at the conservatory for my interview, and was told that one of the piano teachers in the secondary school was about to have a baby and would be taking a two-month leave of absence. Could I possibly replace her during this period? I agreed immediately.

My husband, however, was not so pleased with the news. It was all very well to stand in for a pregnant woman, he declared, but perhaps I had forgotten that I too was pregnant, and that the conservatory was quite some distance away in the suburbs. I replied that this was a unique chance for me to get into the school and eventually, perhaps, be able to study there. I finally managed to convince him, and once I had taken up my new post I applied myself so diligently that when the teacher I replaced returned, my students petitioned the administration to keep me on. There was no question of my replacing the teacher permanently, of course, but I was informed that I could be given another class, and then become an assistant teacher. I could hardly believe my ears! They were offering me a position as a state instructor—not merely that of a substitute! I blessed this new China where I could at last enter the conservatory that my mother had so vehemently denied me.

Life proceeded smoothly enough until the seventh month of my pregnancy, when the necessity of getting up at dawn and taking several buses to work began taking its toll. With terrible regret I had to stop working, but Paul was delighted to have me at home, as were my parents, who came by frequently to visit. I was only eighteen, however, and filled with the energy of youth. I found it difficult to remain sedentary. I fidgeted like an impatient child as I waited for the baby to be born.

One day it occurred to me that I might be able to speed up the delivery by playing the piano frenetically—Chopin's *Polonaise*, for example. I sat down and played it over and over again for hours, pounding on my Bechstein like a madwoman in the absurd hope of hastening the arrival of this recalcitrant baby. I never dreamed I'd be successful, but at two o'clock in the afternoon, I was suddenly seized with violent stomach pains and had to lie down. The bedroom had already been prepared, for I had decided that this baby would be born by natural childbirth at home. The obstetrician was alerted and at seven in the evening, as my parents sat by my bedside, the pains started up again. Only now it was worse than before; I moaned and cried and vomited, but still labor did not begin. Terrified, my husband locked himself in his prayer room, while Paul alternated between praying with his father and pacing in the hallway, his hands clasped behind his back, just like an expectant father.

"I don't think my sister will arrive until tomorrow," he declared solemnly to my mother at eleven o'clock that night. "So I think I'll just go to bed."

Chung-ai smiled and tucked him in; but my son was not mistaken. It was two in the morning before the baby decided to make its appearance. To my delight, it was indeed a girl. I was given a few drops of ginseng, for the long labor had completely exhausted me. The baby had not cried at all; I looked down and saw that she was contentedly sucking her thumb,

208

her big black eyes wide open. It was only after the doctor gave her the traditional slap on her buttocks that she began to bawl.

Unlike most Chinese babies, whose skin is usually reddish at birth, my daughter's was white, and her head was covered with a pale, downy fuzz, a single strand of white hair sticking straight up in the middle of her head—a sign, my mother informed me, that my daughter would live to a very ripe old age.

We named her Liu Sun-ling, Sun being her generation name—which she shared with her brother, Sun-po, otherwise known as Paul (a transliteration of Po)—and Ling her given name, meaning "of great intelligence." Much later I would call her Juliette, simply because I liked the name, and it reminded me of Shakespeare's *Romeo and Juliet*. Possibly I hoped that as Juliette, she might find the love, romance, and happiness that had eluded me.

It was now December, 1955. Paul's former nurse, Ah-ching, had returned from Saochin to take care of the baby. And, fortunately, since she herself had had another child, she was able to nurse Sun-ling.

I went back to work at the conservatory. Mr. Fang, originally so silent about my performance at the Rachmaninoff recital, now encouraged me to train as a concert pianist, and thought I might acquire some valuable experience—as well as make myself useful—as an accompanist. Thus I began working with violinists and flutists who were busy preparing for their own annual term concerts.

At the same time, Mr. Fang insisted that I continue in my own studies, and he sent me to study under a woman whom I shall call Madame Liang, at that time the foremost pianist in China.

When I first appeared at her home on Szechwan Road, a servant answered the door and led me into an elegant drawing room, wherein the most spectacular object appeared to be Madame Liang herself. At a time when anyone with an ounce of sense was wearing blue Mao suits and white shirts, this incredible lady was wearing a luxurious silk *cheong-sam*, slit up to her thighs, heavy makeup, and a particularly vivid red lipstick reminiscent of Joan Crawford in the thirties.

Two mahogany grand pianos were placed at opposite ends of the drawing room, and Madame Liang motioned me to one of them, suggesting I play something for her. I chose a Liszt Étude. Throughout she kept up a running commentary, relieved from time to time by lifting her arms skyward, or occasionally chirping in French instead of Chinese, as if to prove that she had in fact studied in Paris.

As far as I was concerned, our meeting was a disaster and so was she. But I had no say in the matter; I was to study under Madame Liang, and I would become a concert pianist.

However, talent as a soloist is not synonymous with talent as an accompanist; they are, practically speaking, a contradiction in terms. Thus, although I was forever practicing with each artist, I was something less than a success.

In fact, I was terrible.

My first rehearsal as an accompanist was with an excellent violinist who, in the middle of a Mendelssohn Concerto, was so displeased with my performance that he stopped playing in the middle of the concerto, put his instrument in its case, and stalked off the stage, all the while screaming threats of resignation to the concert director, Professor Chen. The same scene repeated itself with a well-known flutist.

It became quickly clear to me that *I* was the one who should resign.

Professor Chen, however, surprised me by advising me not to be so easily discouraged, reminding me that I was, after all, myself a soloist, and would therefore have to discipline myself against my own egocentric desires, learning to work in concert with the other artists. After all, that was also the teaching of Mao.

Inspired, I resolved to persevere. The situation, however, got worse and worse. All the soloists I accompanied demanded instead that they be accompanied by someone else. Discouraged and certain I had no talent whatsoever, I again resigned. Professor Chen again refused, this time commenting that while there were better accompanists, they were also more experienced, and that since I had greater potential as a soloist I should perhaps concentrate on my own career—but I still needed to learn discipline. He added that he himself was preparing a concert for violin and orchestra by Wieniawski, and suggested that I might perhaps acquire some good experience by acting as his accompanist during the practice sessions. Having lost all confidence during my short career as an accompanist, I accepted with some hesitation, but finally applied myself happily to the task.

Professor Chen's patience and confidence eventually bore fruit. Not only did I regain confidence, but he kept me on as his accompanist, even demanding that I accompany him in a recording of Beethoven's *Springtime Sonata* and Franck's Sonata for Violin and Piano. I also accompanied him in an important concert given at the former Majestic Theater, for which he received excellent critical notices. There was also a tiny mention of me—sufficient to restore the confidence of the conservatory students.

The only problem with success is that it also attracts envy. Rumors began circulating that it was not so much my talent that interested Professor Chen as my person, and if he was offering me so many opportunities, it was only because he was in love with me. These rumors were particularly ugly because Professor Chen was a man of impeccable honor, who saw me only as a pupil and musician. In return, I had enormous respect for him, and even today I am cognizant of how much I owe him.

During this period, a great many musicians from other Communist countries—particularly Czechoslovakia, Rumania, Poland, and, of course, the Soviet Union—began performing at the conservatory in Shanghai. One of them, a Russian, was a well-known orchestra conductor who wanted to perform Tchaikovsky's First Piano Concerto with a Chinese orchestra and soloist. I was asked to audition, but when Madame Liang discovered that I might perform with such a famous conductor, she was overwhelmed with jealousy. In my naïveté, I failed to notice her reaction, although a blind man couldn't have missed it at a hundred paces.

"Ching-li," she said to me one day, "there is really only one person in all of China who can play that concerto as it ought to be played. And that is I. Before you try it, I just want to make sure you realize that you're gambling your whole career on this one throw of the dice. If I were you, I wouldn't risk it. You should step aside and let me take your place. Believe me, I suggest this only in your best interests, which I'm sure you'll realize and thank me for one day."

"But Madame Liang," I protested, "the conductor was very pleased with my audition. How can I go back and tell him I don't want to go ahead?"

"That's no problem," she replied. "All you have to do is say you're ill."

With a heavy heart, I did as she requested, and Madame Liang performed the concerto in my place. It would be unjust of me to deny how good she was, for at that time everyone said that she was definitely the best. And I was, after all, only beginning my career. But the whole unpleasant incident served as a good lesson to me, for it taught me to recognize the difference between a man like Professor Chen, who thought of others before himself, and a woman like Madame Liang who was mean-spirited and too selfish—or insecure—to help new talent. I hoped I would always emulate Professor Chen.

A few weeks later I was offered the opportunity of performing a Mendelssohn piano concerto in public. I accepted with enthusiasm and posters bearing my name sprang up all around Shanghai. Once again, Madame Liang tried to frighten and discourage me. I told Professor Chen what she had said.

"Nonsense," he smiled, "I know you will do well."

His reply bolstered my morale but did not entirely relieve my anxiety. The concert was to take place at eight o'clock in the evening in the conservatory auditorium. When the time came for me to leave home and catch the bus, my stomach was so tied up in knots that I was sure Madame Liang was right, that my budding career was about to come to an abrupt and inglorious end. But my mother popped a piece of ginseng in my mouth and off I went anyway. In a cold sweat when I sat down at the piano before all those people, I soon relaxed and got through the piece with what was later termed by some as "inspired" playing. As I took my bows, I realized that I was perhaps on my way to becoming a concert pianist.

I now had developed sufficient confidence to do something I had been considering for a long time. As in every other Liberation school, the conservatory's administration included a certain number of political commissars in charge of indoctrination through ideological remolding and thought reform. Some were military men, a few even veterans of the Long March, and they were wholly dedicated to the spreading of Mao's teachings. Gathering up my courage, I requested an interview with one of them in order to discuss the matter of my brother, Ching-chung. I was received by a man whose job was to help the conservatory staff with their political problems. Two or three times a week, he met with the professors to discuss the best ways of working in conformity with Mao's philosophy and to analyze certain of his writings. Indeed, such meetings were going on all over China, but here as elsewhere the undertaking was both difficult and delicate. It was a matter of teaching a person to abandon the idea of working for himself, and helping him understand a world where the individual was unimportant as compared to the benefit of the community as a whole. The bourgeois mentality, with its vanities and jealousies, was however thought to be deeply rooted in the artist, and even if he was working for the state, he was suspected of acting largely for egocentric reasons. There was therefore nothing unusual about my asking for an interview with one of these commissars. In a newborn country where the principle enemy was individualism, those officials responsible for the reeducation of us artists were always available to discuss our problems.

During my interview, I poured out the whole story of my brother's visit to Hong Kong and the Party condemnation of him which had resulted. I also explained how Ching-chung had been dedicated to the Party from the start, had even been chosen to instruct others, but was now undergoing a "retraining period" in an agricultural cooperative near Peking. I suggested that since his visit to Hong Kong had been motivated solely out of concern for my welfare, Ching-chung, in all fairness, deserved an immediate reinstatement. The official listened patiently and assured me that he would examine my brother's case personally. A few days later he summoned me to his office for further questioning. Then he said he would write directly to Peking.

A few weeks later, I received a letter from Ching-chung informing me that he had returned to Peking and had been au-

213

thorized to resume his job teaching English. His reinstatement had been swift, and to this day, he knows nothing of my intervention.

I applied myself even more diligently to my job, for now I was serving a state toward which I felt an immense gratitude.

The newspapers and wall posters continued to carry articles about peasants in the most remote regions organizing themselves into agricultural collectives under the First Five-Year Plan. The land revolution—that is, the redistribution of privately owned land among the proletariat and the landowners themselves—had already been completed, and now the government had commerced the second phase of reform: agrarian collectivization. The goal was to raise production, achieve greater agricultural specialization, and move more quickly toward social transformation through communes.

From what we read, it was clear that these heretofore remote and undeveloped regions of our vast country were the real centers of our new world, and that the peasants were the primary agents of a colossal transformation, which is why many bourgeois from the cities were sent out to work on the land for anywhere from two to eight months, depending upon the individual's ability to be reeducated; for in addition to working the land and living together in communes, each person—peasant or bourgeois—had to attend self-criticism groups that encouraged a new life-style, the development of the individual into a new Socialist man.

But although shopkeepers, factory managers, and functionaries of all kinds had been required to work in the fields for some time now, artists and intellectuals had been excused. Now, however, our turn came to undergo *hsi-nao*, or "brainwashing"—a term having negative connotations in the Western world, but which was commonly used in China without any negative associations whatsoever.

If artists were sent to the fields only after all the others, it was because they were considered more fragile, both physically and spiritually. In spite of this, they too wound up serving their term, precisely because Mao Tse-tung considered them vital to the life of the community. Before the Liberation, artists of all kinds were considered unnecessary, their work

214

unproductive and self-indulgent. Now, however, Mao insisted that they receive an education commensurate with the eminent place they would fill in the new society. Movies and plays were felt to be crucial instruments in guiding the public down the correct path of Maoist thought, and thus artists were referred to as "engineers of the soul."

The members of the conservatory were not *forced* to go, however. Instead, the administration launched an appeal and asked for volunteers. There were a good many, although some were obviously reluctant. Only then did the real screening begin, for not all would be accepted and one had to wait one's turn.

As in every other school, there were two sorts of students at the conservatory: those with real talent and a great capacity for work and those with neither, but who were difficult to get rid of. Here, as elsewhere, the second group compensated for its mediocrity by becoming more actively political than the other, using politics rather than talent in pursuit of personal advancement. I do not mean to imply there were no serious artists among those who were politically involved, but in general it seemed that the least talented were the most political. In one of our study groups, for example, there was only one girl out of thirty who felt called upon to stand up and make a dramatic speech extolling the joys of working the land. Not only had she always been ostentatious, but she also happened to be a strictly mediocre pianist. She wasn't content simply to monopolize the meeting with her interminable harangue, but, noticing my silence, she immediately made me her primary target. "And you, Ching-li," she declared. "Why are you so quiet?"

"Because I'm not planning to volunteer," I replied simply.

"Precisely!" she exclaimed. "And we know why this nasty little bourgeois doesn't want to leave! She doesn't like the idea of being reconstructed, does she? She doesn't realize she'll never play the piano well without a Maoist education!"

For a long time now, this girl had taken no pains to hide her jealousy of me. In fact, I suspected she had been responsible for all the ugly rumors about Professor Chen's interest in me. Now she had found the perfect opportunity to attempt to humiliate me in public. I didn't bother to answer her, however, and instead turned to the commissar who was attending the meeting.

"I have never objected to the idea of reeducation," I said. "But if I'm *forced* to go to work in the fields, I'd undoubtedly spend most of my time crying, and I think it would be best if I waited until I was a little more mature before volunteering."

I was being as honest as I could, but this didn't stop the girl from continuing to criticize me; in fact, she did everything possible to turn the whole group against me. Finally, the Party official intervened and took over the meeting himself, declaring that he felt I had been honest and sincere and that it would surely do no one any good to reeducate me by force. I lowered my head modestly, but secretly I was proud of myself for having dared express my real feelings in public.

A few days after this meeting, a huge poster was put up in one of the corridors of the conservatory with the names of half a dozen staff and assistants who had been chosen to work the land for a month in a particularly impoverished area. The first name on the list was that of the girl who had been so vociferous. When she saw her name, she burst into tears and fled. As it turned out, all of those who had so loudly demanded to be reeducated had their wish granted.

The seriousness of the Party's concern for artists was evidenced not only by the privilege of being sent out to work the land, a task synonymous with self-betterment, but Party officials had also begun searching for new talent in places other than the universities, art schools, and conservatories. It was important to show that the artist did not necessarily come exclusively from the bourgeoisie, but could also be found among the peasants and workers as well. Thus it happened that some musicians who were working the land in the region of Fukien discovered a young farm boy, Yin Sen-son, who seemed talented. He had no education whatsoever, and was unable to read a single note of music. Brought to the Shanghai Conservatory, he studied the piano, and in less than two years' time was already playing solo concerts. He went on to study in the Soviet Union, where he won the Tchaikovsky prize, and eventually he became one of the leading concert pianists in China.

216

14

The year 1956 began well.

No one was without work and women began wearing brightly colored skirts and blouses again, for the state was encouraging people to vary their clothing styles so as to make the cities more attractive.

My two children were growing up strong and healthy; my husband was warm and affectionate; and we still had the income from my father-in-law's businesses. We did not even have to endure the scorn typically attached to capitalists, for I was, after all, an Artist of the State.

In addition, I had my parents close to me at last, for the government had begun implementing its program for equality in housing by decreeing that all those families whose houses were excessively large as compared to the number of inhabitants would have to share their homes with others. Our apartment was one of these, and since we did not want to live with strangers, my parents turned their own house over to the state and moved in with us on Hung Chiang Road, bringing with them my little brother, Ching-chang, and my little sister, Ching-ching, both of whom were now going to school. In sum, I had everything to make me happy, and so I was, for a while.

But in the spring of 1956 commenced what was known in

China as the period of the Hundred Flowers. As Mao had proclaimed: "Let a hundred flowers blossom; let a hundred schools contend!" Or, put it another way, let the most diverse opinions be permitted free expression. Presumably our leaders could be criticized in the interest of improving the government. This sudden freedom of speech was in part an attempt to attract the intellectuals, even non-Communists, many of whom had already protested against the tight controls and excessive censorship that had gone on for seven years now. The invitation was issued cautiously, however, and the government recommended a certain moderation in such criticism, hoping that the campaign would be, as they put it, like "a gentle rain and a soft breeze."

And so it was—in the beginning.

Short satirical plays were performed on the radio, one of which told the story of a functionary so obsessed with the planning ahead that he drew up a plan every morning for his afternoon's work, and another in the afternoon for the next morning, and so on, until he wound up spending his whole week drawing up plans and doing no real work whatsoever. Soon enough, however, such mild criticism paled and the press began publishing articles attacking the Party and its leaders with an unprecedented virulence. Then the masses followed suit. They had been prevented for so long from voicing any opposition to their managers or commissars that now all their grievances poured forth, until they went far beyond constructive criticism and began instead to use criticism for the settling of personal scores.

Unfortunately, both my brother and father allowed themselves to be swept unwittingly into this rising tide.

My brother, Chow Ching-chung, was teaching English in Peking when the period of the Hundred Flowers began. The director of my brother's school decided that this would be the perfect time for him to settle certain scores of his own, and he would steer the school's debates into an attack on those who opposed him, enlisting the aid of Ching-chung, a known devout Party member, in order to strengthen his own position. In his naïveté, my brother thought it both correct and proper to

218

support his superior—a mistake that cause Ching-chung to be later classified, along with the director, as "right-wing."

At the same time my father, Chow Hui-i, himself the director of another school, proved to be as naïve and undiscerning as his son. There were two distinct factions in his school: the teachers on the one hand and, on the other, the cadres responsible for political reeducation. When the period of the Hundred Flowers, or free speech, was encouraged, my father took to task certain members of the cadres, most of whom were peasants by birth. Not only did he question their competence, a fair enough criticism, but he went even further—much too far for a man of bourgeois origins—and reproached them for their negligence in dress, their sandaled feet, and for their peasant habit of urinating when and where they pleased, despite the fact that the school had its fair share of toilets.

My father hadn't really meant to ridicule them; he merely hoped to persuade them to change their ways, much as they might wish to change his. What he so obtusely failed to see, however, was that it was *he*, a bourgeois, who was obliged to change, and not they. And so Hui-i, too, became labeled as "right-wing."

By this time, however, because of the surprisingly excessive and virulent criticism taking place, the Hundred Flowers campaign was already being discouraged. And by the summer of 1957, the government launched a "Socialist education" movement, unfortunately accompanied by a severe anti-rightist backlash which struck my family. Both my father and brother lost their jobs. Ching-chung was sent to a corrective camp in a remote region outside Peking for "rehabilitation," while my father, Hui-i, after signing a "self-reform pact" was permitted to remain at his school, reduced from director to janitor.

In any case, it was clear that two "rightists" in the same family were two too many, and as a result, my younger brother, Ching-chang, would also suffer. At sixteen, he was an excellent student, having received top grades in his baccalaureate exam, showing a particular gift for science and mathematics. In spite of his record, however, he was not permitted to enroll in the university.

Priority was now being given to the children of workers, then peasants, and finally bourgeois nationalists. But there was no way for children of any "rightists" to qualify.

But Ching-chang was too courageous to become discouraged. Instead, he found a job as a worker in a small sheet-metal factory not far from Shanghai. Tears came to my eyes as I watched him go off, knapsack on his back, but at least this was better than his staying at home doing nothing. On the other hand, he was convinced that taking such a job would redeem his honor in the eyes of the Party. Perhaps when he showed them that the son of a "rightist" could be a good worker, they would let him return to school.

He had been working in the factory for a few months when the government circulated an order to all young people who had been refused admission to colleges and universities to proceed at once to the miserable and poverty-stricken region of Tsinghai in western China, where a university had been built especially for the children of the bourgeoisie. Apparently the government felt that forcing these particular students to live under the most primitive and difficult conditions would speed up their reeducation. This university in fact accepted all "rightists," regardless of class, for when it came to punishment, the government made no distinction between those who had strayed from the path and those who had never taken the path at all. Ching-chang was ready to go to Tsinghai, even if it turned out to be hell itself. And in spite of his grandmother's tears and pleas, he returned to Shanghai to register. My parents, depressed by their own situation, said nothing at all, but grandmother begged him not to go and began a long period of fasting, spending her days praying to Kuan Yin.

On the morning of his scheduled departure, Ching-chang rose early and went to the bathroom, only to find that his urine was spotted with blood. My mother immediately called on a neighbor, who was a Party member, to witness Ching-chang's condition. The woman confirmed in writing that Ching-chang couldn't possibly travel, and the officials allowed him to stay behind.

Ching-chang was immediately hospitalized, where his condition remained unchanged for several days. The doctors believed he had some sort of kidney infection, but the results of the endless tests made were inconclusive.

And then, as suddenly as it had begun, the bleeding stopped. My grandmother was convinced that a miracle had been brought about by her prayers to Kuan Yin.

As the year wore on, Liu Yu-huang's health grew more precarious. Since visas were being issued without any apparent difficulty, Madame Liu began urging Yu-huang to come to Hong Kong to consult with heart specialists there.

However, when Liu Yu-huang applied for his visa, it was denied on the ground that as there were perfectly good specialists in China, there was no need for him to go elsewhere.

In desperation, my in-laws asked me to apply for a visa for myself and the children, convinced that once we were in Hong Kong, Yu-huang would have a better chance of getting there too. Their logic escaped me, but I agreed to do as they asked.

As a state musician, however, I had to first receive the permission of the officials at the conservatory. In applying, I explained that since I had two small children and the burden of a sick husband, I was no longer able to do justice to my job. I suggested that if I were to go to Hong Kong with my children, and leave them in the care of my in-laws, I could return to Shanghai better able to concentrate on my work.

The commissars refused. I insisted. Finally I was told that "in the opinion of the Party you are a good, healthy girl, loyal to the Party. And we thus cannot let you go into an unhealthy society. If you go, we know your husband's parents will not let you return to China. We are refusing your visa only for your own protection—you are a talented artist and cannot let your family destroy your future."

It was useless to argue, and I gave up trying.

15

In February, 1958, heady with the success of the First Five-Year Plan, the National People's Congress started the Second Five-Year Plan with the Great Leap Forward, a movement which was to last three years, most of it disastrous.

At the start, the Great Leap Forward was welcomed with frenzied enthusiasm by the people. From school to factory, from city to countryside, everyone was mobilized in a tremendous effort to catch up with Western industrialism. Within the next fifteen years, the slogan ran, we must equal, even surpass, Britain!

Accompanying this fanatic drive for industrialization, the government also created the people's communes to step up farm production. We must walk on two legs, another slogan went, one leg being industrial, the other agricultural.

In the countryside, the peasants were first organized into communes, then work brigades, and finally production teams, each composed of approximately forty families. And while they went off to the fields singing and chanting, groups of workers crisscrossed the cities carrying banners, and enthusiastic posters were plastered all over Shanghai.

Unfortunately, China was not yet ready for industrialization, and quantity could not replace quality, nor energy natural disaster. And soon we found ourselves short on supplies of all kinds.

When ration books were issued, I was permitted a few extra tickets as a state pianist. Several other categories of workers, such as teachers and engineers, were also given larger allowances. But with all the new restrictions, my husband's health continued to decline, as did my father's. At the same time, Shanghai was ravaged by a virulent epidemic. One day, Paul came home from nursery school with a high fever and fell asleep immediately. I woke him several times during the afternoon and evening to feed him, but each time he dropped back dazed and heavy onto the pillow. The whites of his eyes had turned yellow and when the doctor finally arrived, he took one look at him and declared it to be his liver, adding that he had seen many other cases of the same kind and that all had begun with a three-day period of total somnolence. Then, forty-eight hours later, Juliette was showing the same symptoms. I was extremely worried as rumors had already begun circulating about several deaths in the city as a result of this mysterious ailment.

There were now three sick people to nurse and, one way or another, I got no sleep at all, limiting myself to a few spoons of rice in order to increase the others' rations. While my father was getting ready to go to work in the morning, I would slip some meat or preserved eggs under the rice and vegetables in his lunch box, but when he came home at night, he never failed to make a scene about it and would always inspect his lunch carefully before leaving the following day. Perhaps other families were fighting with each other over food, but with us it was the opposite. We had always been a close-knit family, and all of us, including my husband, looked for ways to deprive ourselves so that the others could have more.

This period of penury, with a desperately ill husband and two sick children, lasted three long months. In the end, I could hardly stay on my feet. The conservatory had given me a leave of absence, but I could now see no other solution than resigning, for I could not go on with my work and care for my family at the same time. Depressed and unhappy, I handed in my letter

223

of resignation. Once again it was refused. This time, however, I was determined to quit with or without authorization, an act that was of course a grave offense. Both my sister Ching-ling, still a pianist with Radio Peking, and my brother Ching-chung, who had by now been released as rehabilitated, were adamantly opposed to such a move, insisting that an unauthorized resignation would ruin me. But I didn't see what else I could do; my husband and children came first.

Given the difficulty of life in general, it was not long before the black market surfaced once again. Peasants came into the city selling poultry at exorbitant prices, a practice dangerous for both the seller and the buyer. I ran the risk, however, and bought a live hen to begin a chicken coop, and then another. Soon we had a dozen hens providing us with a regular supply of eggs. In addition, from time to time packages containing food arrived from Hong Kong, for it was still legal to send and receive such items.

We were not alone, of course, in our preoccupation with the problem of food. For three somber years, the entire country hung suspended on the edge of disaster. Droughts, floods, the failure of the Great Leap Forward—all of these catastrophes contributed to the general depression. But the Chinese had had long experience with poverty and famine, and their ingenuity wrought miracles. Chicken coops and rabbit hutches sprang up all over the city—on balconies, in courtyards, even inside apartments. Vegetables were raised on soccer fields and in public parks; group forays into the countryside were organized to gather berries and edible grasses. Virtually everyone was engaged in this struggle for survival. Collectives fixed the rations for each of their members; campaigns were launched to limit the consumption of staples. At one point, Mao decreed that all schoolchildren who had not yet reached their maximum height were entitled to consume more than their parents. Desperately concerned by the seriousness of the situation, the government continually exhorted the population to work harder, and that included nonworking housewives who stayed home and concerned themselves exclusively with their families.

I could see the time coming when I would have to do as the

224

others and go out to work, in a factory if necessary. In all honesty, I must admit that the idea of factory work seemed highly unattractive to me, yet I dared not try to return to the conservatory. I had been absent for eight months, and my unauthorized resignation following the visa refusal had scarcely left the door open for an easy reentry.

Concerned about my situation, my sister Ching-ling wrote one day with the news that six European musicians, all soloists and all from Communist countries, had just arrived in Peking to give a series of concerts, and because Peking was short of pianists they were searching desperately for a decent accompanist. The Peking Conservatory had suggested Ching-ling herself, but she already had so much work that she had to refuse, whereupon she had proposed my name. I was accepted, despite my unorthodox resignation from the Shanghai Conservatory.

Ever since my brother's censure, I had been very anxious to go to Peking. One disaster after the other had befallen him since his encampment. For one thing, he had taken a serious fall one day while driving a cart, and despite a knee injury, had refused to stop working. Knowing him as I did, I was sure that this former underground revolutionary was struggling to save face and to regain his honor. I also know that life on his agricultural cooperative was far from being a bed of roses, and it had occurred to me more than once that I might be able to help him. I now had the perfect excuse; since I had to rescue these foreign musicians, I could take advantage of my visit to see Ching-chung. And so I accepted the offer, deciding to take Paul with me, leaving my husband behind with Juliette and my parents. Liu Yu-huang was not at all happy with the prospect of my trip, but the idea of my doing factory work seemed worse still, and he was finally obliged to accept my proposal.

The journey to Peking was a strange one. To begin with, our first-class car was filled with important government officials and high-ranking officers of the Red Army. Little Paul, who was now a big boy of seven, endeared himself to everyone and there was a great scramble to see who would play with him and who would offer him the next piece of candy. When they learned that Paul was not, as they had thought, my little brother but my son, they were stunned, and I was treated to a chorus of exclamations and compliments. As the trip wore on, the atmosphere in the car became increasingly casual and friendly, until one Party dignitary even asked me whether I would like to make movies in Shanghai! When I replied that I was a pianist, an officer from Tientsin offered me a job as a music professor at the conservatory there. I was indeed flattered and became more cheerful than I'd been in a long time.

Seated at a table in the dining car, I became aware of a noisy group nearby who turned out to be professors from the Shanghai Conservatory. I knew them all, of course. They were going to meet the same six foreign musicians as I, and when they heard why I was going to Peking, they were shocked.

"What an absurd idea!" they all exclaimed. "Why go to Peking for work when you can work with us? You must come back to Shanghai; we need you!"

Surprised and embarrassed, I reminded them that I had broken a regulation and, under these circumstances, I could not possibly ask for my old job back. One of the commissars from the conservatory swept my argument aside with a wave of his hand, assuring me that such things were of no importance and that I must stop worrying about them at once. Given the exceptional circumstances of our meeting, everything he said seemed unreal. Was the man in fact offering me my old job back? In any case, they all insisted I make no long-range plans in Peking; that once I had finished my assignment with the European musicians, I should come back to Shanghai where everything would be taken care of. Stunned and delighted, I promised to do as they wished. My whole life had suddenly turned around, and for the first time in a long while, things began to look brighter.

My sister Ching-ling was waiting for me at the railroad station, along with a group of colleagues from Radio Peking who wanted to meet me. Ching-ling took me back to her house and I was welcomed with great warmth by her husband and two children. Then we settled down to wait for my brother's arrival. When he had learned that I was coming to Peking, he had asked for a few days' leave.

According to my sister, Ching-chung's situation was even

226

worse than I had imagined. For now the hostility of his wife added to his difficulties. The student with whom he had fallen so deeply in love had turned into a heartless wife; she had left their children in Shanghai with her parents and no longer wanted to have anything to do with a poverty-stricken husband, whose life had become so complicated. My sister told me that Ching-chung had arrived home in Peking late one Saturday evening and his wife had refused to let him in, shouting that she didn't want any "rightists" in the house. It was one o'clock in the morning, and since he had felt too humiliated to disturb Ching-ling at such an ungodly hour, he had spent the night wandering about the city until morning, when he could take the train back to his collective farm. Since then he had not returned to Peking and was here now only to see me.

On learning this, I was filled with rage. At midnight, Ching-chung appeared. At the sight of him, I couldn't help bursting into tears. Only twenty-eight, he had aged terribly. His face was lined, his hands blackened, the palms heavily calloused, and his clothes tattered. Indeed, he was so exhausted that he went to sleep immediately, lying down on the floor next to the bed I shared with Paul. I spent the night weeping. Where was that young man, so strong and full of life, the big brother who had watched over me, who had told me stories about the heroes and heroines of old China? The companion who had taken me for walks in Jessfield Park and taught me monkey boxing? Where was Ching-chung, the boy I had known and loved so dearly?

My brother stayed with us for two days. On the second day I decided to go with him to see his wife. To my surprise, she invited us in.

"Sister-in-law," I said gently, "you are very advanced politically, and I'm proud to be related to you. But I'd like to ask you if the Party has ever asked a wife to turn her back on a husband who has made mistakes? Has the Party ever asked her to slam the door in his face? No, I don't think so. All you've done, it seems to me, is demoralize and discourage your husband. I hope with all my heart that you'll reconsider and will try to act differently toward my brother in the future."

She remained silent for a long time. Finally, embarrassed

and ashamed, she stammered out a few words as I made my exit, leaving the two alone.

When I returned to my sister's, I saw that Ching-chung had brought with him from the commune a huge bag of dirty laundry. There was no hot running water in China at that time, and when you wanted to wash, water had to be heated on the stove. Ching-chung had so much laundry, however, I decided to wash it all in cold water. I nearly froze my fingers. It suddenly occurred to me that I had come a long way; not long ago it would have been unthinkable for me, a bourgeois, to do laundry. But here I was, working joyfully, and even though it was for my brother, I wondered too if it might not be possible to work for the state with the same joy.

Thus it was during my visit to Peking that I finally realized what was happening to China.

Once back in Shanghai, I discovered that the promises made to me on the train had been neither idle nor fanciful. When I presented myself at the conservatory, I was put to work immediately, as if nothing unusual had ever occurred. I was overjoyed.

Two months later my sister-in-law Liu Yu-ying returned to Shanghai with her two children. Her Jim had been killed in an automobile accident. She had, unhappily for me, installed herself in an apartment building right next to ours on Hung Chiang Road. It didn't take long for Yu-ying to begin poisoning my life once again. Even though her brother was now seriously ill, she could think of nothing more original than to accuse me of having lovers, the idea for this having been suggested by a new Party campaign.

This was not the same kind of official campaign as the others, but rather a general movement aimed at maintaining certain moral standards among the population. Everyone was invited to ferret out adulterous relationships in the interest of protecting the sacredness of marriage. Admittedly, several men had been attracted to me at one time or another, but although I had occasionally enjoyed these flirtations, my real affection for my husband and concern for my parents were more than enough to keep me from doing anything dishonorable. My sister-in-law knew perfectly well that despite the frequent visits of singers and musicians to our house, I had remained irreproachable. But none of this kept Yu-ying from making insinuations which unfortunately affected my husband's morale, even though he knew she was lying.

My sister-in-law was not our only problem, however. Still short on food, we now had a permanent colony of a dozen hens in the courtyard. But since the hens too had to be fed, their part of the rations eventually became too large for us to manage, and my mother decided that all of them would have to be killed. The idea of killing these poor hens that had already supplied us with so much food horrified me, and so I arranged to have them given to friends who promised not to kill them, but would only keep them for their eggs.

Packages from my in-laws fortunately continued to arrive—ample compensation—but I insisted on keeping one of the hens for myself, a red one, the first we had bought, and who had survived all the calamities which from time to time had afflicted our poultry population. I never left the house without giving her a little goodbye pat, and I always brought home a jar of insects for her to eat, which I caught in the conservatory gardens. The only trouble was that my little red hen was now quite old, and although she had once been an excellent layer, she no longer produced any eggs at all. But I kept her anyway, for sentimental reasons.

One night, as I lay sleeping, I heard a voice say that the red hen would die within a week. The next morning, I asked my servants to keep an eye on her because I thought she might be ill. One week later, my husband telephoned me at the conservatory to tell me that the red hen had indeed died. I buried her in the fields and offered up a prayer that her soul might go to heaven. For, according to the Buddhist doctrine I was taught, those who are guilty of serious sins are condemned to reincarnation as an animal; all Buddhists are therefore vegetarians. After the death of the red hen, I announced that henceforth no animal would be killed on our premises; and in restaurants I refused to eat the meat of any animal that had just been

229

slaughtered. It might have been simpler to become an outright vegetarian, but I hadn't yet attained the spiritual maturity to do so.

Although the year had been an extremely difficult one for our family, one bright note appeared: Ching-chang, who had been denied entrance to the university because of the "rightist" sins of his older brother, Ching-chung, and father, Chow Hui-i, was now granted permission to continue his studies at the new Institute of Agronomy in Peking.

That was the only happy event of 1959, however. Fate would turn against us once again. For as the year drew to a close, the further deterioration of Liu Yu-huang's health propelled us into one of the most tragic periods in my life.

16

By the end of 1959, my husband's condition had become hopeless. And, if that weren't enough to bear, my mother-in-law's health had also taken a sudden turn for the worse. Her prospects were in fact so bleak that my father-in-law, Liu Pin-san, wrote a detailed letter to his son, asking Liu Yu-huang to begin the search for a suitable resting place, giving his precise instructions for the burial procedure in the event of Madame Liu's death.

Liu Pin-san's request was hardly unusual. All Chinese prepare for their burial long before the possibility of death arises; and the richer the family, the more elaborate the preparations. Madame Liu, for example, had years ago supervised the construction and completion of both her and Liu Pin-san's coffins; in addition she had already selected her burial costume and chosen the material goods—gold coins, jewelry, and the like—that she wished buried with her in order to accompany her into the next world. The only peculiarity was that neither had yet selected their place of burial.

Although Liu Yu-huang was scarcely strong enough to undertake such a task, no one could have persuaded him to turn this sacred obligation over to someone else. And since his parents had come from Ningpo, it was there—a day's trip by boat from Shanghai—that he began the search.

Finding what he considered an appropriate piece of land on the top of a hill, he consulted the best specialist in the area, a venerable old man who found the location so favorable that he predicted it would attract good fortune to the descendants of anyone buried there. When construction of the tomb was begun at the chosen location, a swarm of snakes slithered out, confirming the old man's prediction. Contrary to Western thought, many Chinese believe snakes represent good fortune since a snakepit signifies warm earth, and warm earth represents a promise of wealth for several generations to come.

When the tomb was ready, Liu Yu-huang had photographs taken and sent to Hong Kong. My in-laws were completely satisfied, and delighted with the episode of the snakes. Only then did Liu Yu-huang return to Shanghai, satisfied that he had fulfilled his filial duty. Little did he suspect that he himself would be buried on the hillside in Ningpo long before his mother or father.

After this trip, Liu Yu-huang hardly ventured out of our apartment on Hung Chiang Road, spending a good deal of time in the prayer room. Our son Paul was now nine years old and attended primary school, but Juliette, who was only four, stayed at home with her father. They adored each other, playing, eating, and even sleeping together.

Paul had been born during the year of China's Liberation, and his reeducation began in the schoolroom. Already, children of his age were being taught the "correct" way of thinking, particularly the necessity of contact with the working-class world. A few years earlier, my son would undoubtedly have attended a private school run by foreigners, one reserved exclusively for the rich. Now, however, he went to a public school and, like all his little classmates, was taken to a factory two or three times a week where he helped cut out and paste together various cartons and packaging materials. Paul was not exactly proficient when it came to manual labor. And so before long, he was transferred to the delivery service where the cartons were piled up on a rickshaw, driven by an older boy, and my son sat on top of the heap. He was rather pleased with this new position, and he helped with the loading and delivery of the cargo. His job may have seemed trivial, but he was beginning to learn what it meant to work. He was also learning songs and mimes which inspired further productivity and praised the exploits of the Red Army during the Long March. I was pleased to see that Paul often won the red scarf which was awarded to outstanding students.

Between factory and schoolroom, my son spent the better part of each day with the children of workers, and those of peasants too. The first noticeable consequence of this association was a sharp increase in vulgarity. Insofar as their education was still in its early stages, working-class children continued to speak a fairly vulgar idiom, and Paul was not slow to pick it up. This particular problem caused teachers no end of difficulty, and I did my best to reprimand my son severely when he brought his new verbal acquisitions into the house.

One day, a classmate of Paul's knocked at our door and showed me his torn pants, including a portion ripped out of the seat. It was Paul who had done it he said, adding that he was a poor boy who owned only one pair of pants and he was more than a little concerned about his parents' reaction. At that moment, Paul arrived and I scolded him roundly, accusing him of having acted like a hooligan. His version was different, however. It seemed that for some time now this particular schoolmate had been calling him a "dirty capitalist." Paul claimed he had ignored the taunts, but that today the boy had added a singularly uncomplimentary obscenity about me.

"I never did anything when he insulted me," Paul argued. "But I won't let him insult my mother! So I knocked him down and his pants got ripped. But he was asking for it!"

And so I was forced to scold someone else's child, but the boy soon apologized and promised he would try to behave in the future. I gave him a pair of Paul's pants, and a few days later the boys were friends again. In fact, like beggars, prostitutes, and pickpockets, badly brought-up children were fast disappearing from the People's Republic.

Early in 1960, a letter arrived from Hong Kong informing us that my mother-in-law had had a severe stroke; her right side was completely paralyzed and she was unable to speak.

The news came as a terrible shock to my husband. After he

read the letter, he went straight into his prayer room and remained there for such a long time that I began to worry. When he emerged, I asked him if he was all right.

"Perfectly all right," he replied. "But I must tell you, Ching-li, that I've made an important decision."

He talked for a long while about his parents, reminding me of how diligently they had cared for him since his birth and how his debt to them was too vast ever to be repaid.

"I know my mother is going to die any time now," my husband went on, "which is why I've been praying to Buddha. You see, I've made a pact with him: ten years of my life for ten more for my mother."

My husband's declaration moved me deeply. I knew how strong his faith was, and I myself believed that his request would not be refused. Yet I could not help protesting to him. What right had he, I asked, to give up ten years of his life to his mother if it meant abandoning his wife and children? What would happen to us, I cried, when *he* died?

"I've given it a lot of thought," Liu Yu-huang replied. "You're still very young, Ching-li. What kind of life is this for you, spending all your time with a sick husband? An eighty-year-old man is stronger than I. No, believe me, it's better that I die. It will be a deliverance for both of us. As for the children, I can go in peace. I know you love them and even if you remarry, I know you would never neglect them."

I didn't know what to say; all I could do was cry.

Among very pious Buddhists, there is a traditional ceremony called the rite of Water and Earth, the purpose of which is to offer up prayers for the souls of all creatures who suffer because of their sins. Solemn and elaborate, this ceremony lasts a full week and is accessible only to the very rich, for it necessitates the participation of a hundred monks, and the offering of gifts.

Liu Yu-huang desired that such a ceremony be performed for the benefit of his mother, hoping that it would reduce the importance of any sins committed, and thus improve her health on earth. Indeed, before the Liberation the Liu family

234

celebrated this rite every year, but since then they had done so only two or three times. My oldest sister-in-law, Liu Yu-ying, had always made the arrangements before, but since she herself was now ill and couldn't undertake such an enormous task, and since my second sister-in-law, Liu Yu-chen, had been authorized to care for her parents in Hong Kong, the job of organizing the ceremony fell naturally to me.

Liu Yu-ying was furioius.

"You can't turn over such a responsibility to Ching-li!" she complained to my husband. "She's too young. She doesn't know anything about it, and she's not even a Believer. If she does it, the rain will never fall."

She was alluding here to one of the most important parts of the ceremony. The first and second days are spent imploring the gods in heaven to enter the temple; the third day is devoted to begging the assembled gods to save the souls of those who have not yet been reincarnated. All those lost and abandoned souls desperately need the prayers of their children, their parents, and their friends so that even if they are not destined to go to heaven, they can at least begin their new life on earth with the least sins on their account. Thus it was crucial during the third and fourth days to lure all the spirits of the earth, the sky, and the water into the temple, and it is during these two critical days that an abundant rain *must* fall, or the spirits will not appear. Prayers for rain would surely go unheeded if the speaker was not a sincere Believer.

Liu Yu-huang stood firm against his sister's objections, however, declaring that no one but I would be responsible. And so I asked the conservatory for a week's leave of absence, choosing the temple of Tien Tai, called the Temple of the Eight Hundred Buddhas, where the monks were famous for their saintliness. This particular monastery had come through the Liberation unchanged. The monks of Tien Tai were too old and the ground around their temple too barren for them to change their way of life.

Liu Yu-huang was too ill to undertake the trip, and since the region was in too remote an area for me to travel alone, I was accompanied by two cousins and one of our servants. Before leaving, I gathered together large quantities of cotton cloth, towels, napkins, and some basic medicines—aspirin, various pomades, and tiger balm—to offer as gifts to the monks.

By the time we were ready to leave, we had a dozen large packages. The trip was arduous, a two-day train ride, followed by a bus which took us to the foot of the mountain of Tien Tai. A young monk was waiting for us with several litters. I let my servant and all the luggage be carried by litter, but I wanted to climb the treacherous and narrow pathway to the temple on foot. My cousins did the same, and after a six-hour ascent along a rocky trail we arrived at the monastery.

Worn down by the centuries and about to fall into ruin, the venerable old temple of Tien Tai was both vast and austere, lacking the sumptuous ornamentations that graced other sanctuaries of its kind. But even though its enormous Buddhas had lost their gilt, they remained imposing. Whole sections of the walls had crumbled, leaving holes and cracks through which the cold wind easily penetrated the temple. Inside, there were a few barren rooms used to shelter pilgrims. As for the monks themselves, some lived in small wooden houses nearby, others in caves where they lived on wild fruit, grains, and edible leaves. Their black robes, torn and mended countless times, had become stiff and hard. And on each shaved head were six scars, signs that all attachments to flesh, love, and money had been forsaken forever.

It was autumn when we arrived. The weather was mild and the sky especially clear and blue. The ceremony began the following day. Nearly a hundred monks gathered together, this time in their yellow robes. One of their superiors led me to the middle of the sanctuary, where I stood, then knelt, stood again, then knelt, according to the monk's instructions. From the first, I felt myself filled with such fervor that the world I had left behind vanished.

By the evening of the second day, I began to worry about the third, that crucial day when the gods would gather and the spirits of the dead would meet with them in the temple. The sun had to be hidden by clouds so that the gods would consent to appear. The first two days had been beautifully clear, and I

236

began to wonder if Liu Yu-ying had not perhaps been right after all.

The moon was shining in the sky that second evening when I went out for a walk. Encountering an inhabitant of the region, I asked if he thought it might rain tomorrow.

"It will be a clear day," he replied. "Look how the mountain stands out against the moonlight. There's not a single cloud anywhere."

All this was obvious and extremely worrisome. What if the spirits didn't come, I thought, returning in anguish to my room, where I began to pray ardently for rain—or at least a cloudy sky.

The third day opened with a radiant sun. We prayed all day and all night, but the moon still shone brightly, the silhouettes of the mountains standing out clearly in the dark. The possibility of rain had never seemed so remote. At last, the fourth day arrived and it was still sunny. I locked myself into my room and prayed desperately to Buddha.

In the temple, the time had arrived for the gathering of the spirits. It was noon, the curtains were pulled tight against the light and the candles lit. The monks began to pray, invoking first all those spirits imprisoned in hell and guarded by secondary gods. Just then, my servant entered the temple, hurried up to me, and whispered:

"The storm is about to break!"

And as grateful tears poured from my eyes, the rain began to fall. It rained without pause through the following morning, and I gave thanks to Buddha for having heard the voice of an insignificant creature. This was the beginning of my own conversion. Henceforth I followed the teaching of Buddha. Not only did I abstain from eating either meat or fish for two weeks out of every month, but I began to understand the true meaning of our terrestrial existence. We are alive only because we are guilty, and we must never lose sight of this in our relationships with ourselves and with others.

Liu Yu-huang listened with pleasure when I returned to Shanghai and recounted the details of my extraordinary week in the mountains. I sensed his inner happiness. From then on

237

my husband seemed to submit to his suffering without resistance. His condition deteriorated rapidly, and when he began cortisone treatments in 1961, his body became swollen and he could hardly walk. His health became worse with every passing day, and by the end of the year we could no longer even bolster his health with ginseng and other Chinese herbs and medications. There was nothing to be done to alleviate his suffering.

Again and again he would apply unsuccessfully for a visa to Hong Kong, pleading that he needed the medical care of specialists there; secretly, though, he knew he was dying and wanted to be with his mother and father when it happened.

From time to time he would stop breathing completely, his body breaking out into a cold sweat; then we would call an ambulance, and he would be hospitalized for a few days. My mother, terrified that Yu-huang would soon die without having seen his parents, urged us to try again for a visa and finally, in July, 1962, two were granted: one for Liu Yu-huang and the other for our son Paul.

Although I could not accompany them, I was nonetheless happy that Yu-huang would at last be able to rejoin his parents. Soon after purchasing their tickets, however, we heard the news that there had been a tremendous flooding in the south. Since the colony of Hong Kong is located on the coast just south of the city of Canton, I called the railroad station there to find out if the flood would affect Yu-huang's and Paul's trip. Typically it took several hours to get through the busy lines and finally, when I did, no one knew anything. I tried to dissuade Yu-huang from taking the train until we knew for certain what was happening in the south, but he refused even to consider delaying the trip by one day.

Exhausted and worried, I lay down on my bed and closed my eyes. Suddenly I heard a voice say distinctly, *The day after tomorrow, at 8:30 in the morning, Liu Yu-huang will arrive in Canton.*

I had no idea whether I'd been dreaming, but when I mentioned it to my father, he merely shrugged, saying, "Mei-mei, when will you stop all this nonsense?" I put the incident out of my mind.

238

I won't go into the details of our parting, but we had each of us been in tears since early morning, and when the train pulled out of the station, we all wondered whether we would ever see Liu Yu-huang alive again.

Two days following my husband's departure I called the hotel in Canton where Hong Kong-bound passengers spent the night before taking the morning ferry and I was told that no one by the name of Liu Yu-huang was registered. I was panic-stricken, berating myself for listening to silly "voices"; instead, I should have insisted that Yu-huang and Paul stay in Shanghai until we were certain the floods had receded.

The telephone rang. It was Yu-huang. "We arrived at 8:30 this morning," he said, "but there was some sort of mix-up about the reservations, and we've been put up at another hotel instead. What's the matter with you—why are you crying?"

"Oh, it's nothing," I said, promising myself that in the future I would indeed have more faith in voices and visions.

17

I continued to work at the Shanghai Conservatory, while news of Paul and my husband arrived regularly from Hong Kong. Liu Yu-huang was spending every day with his paralyzed mother, and although she was unable to speak, it was obvious that the presence of her son and grandson was a constant consolation, especially now that Liu Pin-san, my father-in-law, was in the United States. Since being accepted on the immigration lists, Liu Pin-san was obliged to go to the States every two years.

In spite of a healthier diet and the attention of the best doctors, Liu Yu-huang continued to deteriorate. One day, I received an urgent phone call from him.

"I think of you and Juliette so often," he told me. "Please, I beg you, do whatever you can to join me."

And so once again I applied for a visa. This time, however, the authorities understood the urgency of the situation. My visa was immediately granted.

At the conservatory, the same political official who had denied my earlier request now admonished that "we are letting you leave because of the state of your husband's health, but I repeat what I told you once before. You are a good woman and you are about to enter a corrupt society. We hope you will return here as quickly as possible."

Before leaving, however, I decided to confirm my faith as a Buddhist, an act analogous to the Christian baptism. Taking Juliette with me, I went to the venerable city of Suchow in the valley of the Ling An, where I had gone as a schoolgirl on an excursion with my class. There I went to see Ta Sen, a mountain hermit whose reputation had spread far and wide. When we arrived at his hermitage, I prostrated myself at his feet, as did Juliette. Ta Sen was a man of about eighty, radiating strength and goodness. He performed the ritual of my confirmation, blessing my husband and my family. After the short ceremony, he made me promise to observe the Buddhist commandments rigorously. When I left he remarked that this was the first time he had been so moved by one of his "children." I myself felt that there was some kind of a deep and mysterious rapport between us. He told me I must be strong and follow my destiny courageously. It was as if he knew that I would soon confront the saddest and most difficult period of my life.

After Suchow, I went to a second holy mountain near Hangchow, where there was an abandoned temple at the top of a steep and sinuous path in a completely deserted area. I took a large sum of money with me, both for the poor and for the restoration of the temple, which had fallen into ruin. Accompanied by Juliette and Ah-ching, I was making my way up the path when suddenly the odor of incense filled the air. The other two smelled it also, but we had no idea where it could possibly be coming from. I looked around; there were neither houses nor trees, only an old and empty temple. I gave the money to the monks who lived at the top of the hill, asking that they build shelters for themselves, the pilgrims, and for the poor woodcutters who came to the mountain for wood and had to carry it down regardless of the weather. While talking with the monks, I asked about the incense.

"Buddha is moved by your generosity," one of them explained.

I later learned that the venerable Ta Sen died a few days later; I had been the last of his spiritual children.

Now confirmed as a Buddhist, I felt free to leave with Juliette for Hong Kong on October 1, 1962. Although I was miserable at having to leave my parents once again, I was also looking forward to seeing Liu Yu-huang and Paul after such a long separation.

My second sister-in-law, Liu Yu-chen, was to meet us at the border town of Sham Chun, but when we arrived I learned that we would not be able to cross the frontier right away. A tighter immigration control had been established by Hong Kong because massive emigration from mainland China had created an incredible population problem for Hong Kong, and the immigration officers were now being extremely careful in checking visas—making certain that only those with good reason for returning to China, or those wealthy enough to take care of themselves in Hong Kong, were allowed through.

Juliette and I had just settled ourselves in the noisy waiting room when Liu Yu-chen arrived, her face streaming with tears.

"He's dead," she said simply.

"Who?" I replied, knowing, but unwilling to accept it.

"Your husband."

Numbed and dry-eyed, I said nothing.

Then Juliette began screaming and crying.

"It's not true! It's not true!" she sobbed. "Papa told me he wanted to be a grandfather! He promised to wait until I grew up and had lots and lots of children! You're lying!"

I was barely conscious when an immigration officer, who had witnessed the whole scene, took pity on us and let us pass through without waiting.

On arriving at the Lius' apartment in Hong Kong, the first person I saw was my mother-in-law. I was shocked by her appearance. Wasted away and paralyzed on one side, she lay on a sofa, surrounded by relatives and friends. Ignoring them, I ran to her side and embraced her, tears coursing down both our faces. Then my little Paul appeared, trying to hold both his grandmother and me in the circle of his little arms. He was crying, too.

"You mustn't cry," one of his aunts said gently, "otherwise you'll make your mother cry even more."

Poor little Paul made a superhuman effort to stop; then, on a

242

pretext, escaped to his room. When I went in later, I found him hidden under the bedcovers, crying. On the table next to his bed was a photograph of his father, and on the back, Paul had written "October 3, 1962" the date of Liu Yu-huang's death.

My husband had died in the hospital. While he was there, although Paul was attending school, he made it a point to visit his father twice a day. It was on his last visit that Liu Yu-huang had died. Unbelieving, Paul had rushed home, lighting three sticks of incense to Buddha, praying desperately that his father be brought back to him.

I saw Liu Yu-huang for the last time at the morgue. According to Chinese custom, there was a large photograph of him placed on a white cloth and surrounded with flowers; to one side there was a long band of white cloth on which a poem of Paul's had been written.

When my husband had left Shanghai, his body had been terribly swollen with cortisone. Now he was thin again, his skin clear and light, his features in repose. When I looked at his body and realized, finally, that he was truly dead, I fainted. My sister-in-law Liu Yu-lan had some smelling salts, and I returned to consciousness sitting on a chair. A man's hand held mine. It was Yu-lan's husband, Feng.

A short time later, I found myself seated in the back of a large car next to Liu Yu-lan. Her husband, Feng Chou-chai, a well-known Hong Kong architect who had come from a very wealthy family, drove. Only later did I learn that both of them had cared for Liu Yu-huang during his last days, and now they went out of their way to make things easier for me.

We had just returned to the apartment when a heated argument broke out between Liu Pin-san's brother and my two older sisters-in-law, Yu-ying and Yu-chen. The two women wanted a modest coffin, while their uncle demanded an expensive one made out of the best wood. My brother-in-law, Feng, took the uncle's side, but in the absence of Liu Pin-san, who was still in America, the family purse strings were controlled by Liu Yu-chen, my second sister-in-law, and she defended her position fiercely. Paralyzed, my mother-in-law was helpless. The once strong and dignified woman, who had always been able to impose her will on everyone around her, was now reduced to tears, her only recourse in this petty and ignoble dispute. Fortunately, thanks to Feng's insistence, an expensive casket was finally ordered.

Before my husband's body was placed in the coffin, Paul brought all the clothes he was to wear. As I watched this serious little prince and his small sister who, despite her age, was trying so hard to imitate her brother and maintain the dignity befitting the occasion, I realized that only these two children were giving me the strength to go on.

Finally, Liu Yu-huang's coffin was nailed shut and placed in the back of a limousine. A large crowd had gathered in the street, for my father-in-law, himself still unaware of his son's death, had many friends among the Shanghai rich who had settled in Hong Kong. All had come to my husband's funeral and thus there was a long procession crossing the city slowly behind the hearse, a traditional procession which would never have been permitted in liberated Shanghai. Liu Yu-huang was given a temporary grave, against the day that his body could be transported to Ningpo, to lie at rest on the hillside he had chosen for his parents.

During the funeral, my mother-in-law remained at home with an aunt, and as I followed the hearse with my two children, I thought of the story she had once told me about the monk's visit on the morning of my husband's birth. The monk had told her that Liu Yu-huang would life a life of suffering, although he would always be surrounded by wealth. "He is born and will die like a king," the monk had said.

And in fact, as we crept through the streets of Hong Kong, people turned to stare at this impressive and kingly funeral procession of a man who was now delivered from the pain and suffering of his terrestrial existence.

18

Looking back after the death of my husband, I now realized how tragic had been my fate. As a thirteen-year-old schoolgirl I had in effect been sold to a wealthy family, albeit under the guise of marriage, and condemned to live with a stranger I didn't love—a man who bore no resemblance whatsoever to the romantic heroes of the Chinese legends, European novels, and American movies who, I had been led to believe, would be the Prince Charmings of my grown-up life.

I had resisted, but the child I was could not hold out against either my own family's greed or, more important, the ancient and rigid tradition of strict obedience to your parents, regardless of their wishes.

Liu Yu-huang had been kind, and he loved me; in this I was lucky. In such arrangements kindness itself is unusual. Finally resigning myself to the fact of our marriage, I accepted Liu Yu-huang as my husband, and I even grew fond of him. But I never loved Yu-huang, and the two children he gave me were my only love and pleasure.

Moved by his frail health and physical suffering, I had promised and was ready to take care of Yu-huang forever, but thirteen years after our marriage he died, leaving me alone—

twenty-six years old, and the mother of two school-aged children.

Now my primary duty was to remain with my mother-in-law while she mourned her eldest son and favorite child, able to bear her grief only because of the comfort of her two grandchildren. It was obvious that Madame Liu should not be deprived of either Paul or Juliette, and so I decided to stay in Hong Kong until my father-in-law returned from the United States and my mother-in-law could accept the fact of Liu Yu-huang's death.

In addition, as the widow of the eldest son, and in the absence of his father, I had inherited Liu Yu-huang's family position along with his responsibilities. Oddly enough, my eldest sister-in-law and past chief tormentor, Liu Yu-ying, ceased to persecute me; instead her role was quickly taken up by my second sister-in-law, Liu Yu-chen.

Possibly this behavior was due to the fact that Liu Yu-chen was herself so unhappy, having married a ne'er-do-well with pretensions to being an artist, but who actually earned his keep by having established himself, Liu Yu-chen, and their children in Liu Pin-san's household under the guise of taking care of my sickly mother-in-law, thus insuring that all his family's expenses would be paid for by Liu Pin-san. My arrival, however, would force Liu Yu-chen and her husband to pack up and leave since, as the eldest son's widow, it became my responsibility to take care of my in-laws.

Meanwhile, the ritual prayers for the dead continued on behalf of my late husband. A short while after Liu Yu-huang's death, I received a letter from my own father, informing me that he had gone to visit the monks of Tien Tai in order to arrange the celebration of Earth and Water for my husband's soul. Apparently, my father wrote, the monks had refused to accept any money from him, claiming they were doing this in memory of my own generosity to them so many moons ago.

In Hong Kong, I took care of the more traditional prayers. For, according to Chinese belief, the souls of the dead drift about, lost and confused, for forty-nine days, and in order to orient them the family must pray once a week for seven weeks. Since Paul and Juliette were still in school, I went to the temple

246

with my two sisters-in-law for the first prayer, where, according to tradition, we were given small sheets of thin paper covered with lead paint; these were folded into the shapes of coins, then burned, symbolically sending to the dead their money, otherwise known as "dead man's money."

By the time we left the temple, it had grown chilly. It was only October, but winter comes early in Hong Kong. I thought about the coats I would have to buy for myself and the children, for we had left Shanghai only in our light Mao suits—which in themselves created some curiosity and staring in the streets. Since I had also left Shanghai with little money, in accord with regulations, I mentioned my dilemma to Liu Yu-chen, keeper of the family treasury. To my astonishment, she replied that my husband's illness and death had already cost her father a tidy sum and therefore she could not allow me any more of my father-in-law's money for myself or my children!

Feigning sympathy for my predicament, she suggested that she would be only too happy to lend me some money from her personal account. Smiling conspiratorially, she lowered her voice and whispered, "Ching-li, you must realize you can't expect anything whatsoever from my father. Besides, you already have everything you need. You're still young and pretty, so why not start looking around for a man? If you catch another husband, your future will be absolutely secure!"

It was a shocking suggestion. In China, especially among Buddhists, a widow must remain faithful to her late husband. The idea of remarriage was scandalous. And since Liu Yu-chen herself belonged to a generation that strongly believed in widowhood-to-death, she was not only being insulting, but was obviously hoping to persuade me into an act that would ostracize me and my children from the family, thereby leaving her in control.

Thus my widowhood began badly. My father-in-law was still in the United States; my mother-in-law was too ill to know what was going on, and couldn't have done anything about it even if she had known. Therefore, the only thing I could do was to make myself financially independent by giving piano lessons.

247

Searching desperately for students, I finally found four: two neighborhood children, a cousin of my mother's, and the niece of an uncle. The difficulty was that I spoke Shanghainese and the dialect of Chao-chou, but no Cantonese. Gradually, however, I began to learn Cantonese from my students.

I also had to learn how to find my way around this unknown and complicated city, whose buildings reminded me so much of Shanghai—or at least of the old Shanghai, with its endless fancy shops and tourist attractions. In a way, I *felt* Hong Kong more than I knew it, for I went out only for specific errands and always followed the same short itineraries. We lived on the Kowloon side of the peninsula, and my in-laws' apartment at 58 Granville Road was only five minutes from the dock of the Star Ferry which ran back and forth to the island of Hong Kong. My farthest student lived in Victoria, and so three times a week I took the ferry. It crossed the harbor in fifteen minutes, and for quite some time this was the longest distance I ever traveled from my home.

As I waited for my first payment, I dressed my children as best I could in several layers of clothing. At last the time came when I could buy them warm clothes and abandon the Mao outfits. My uncle on my father-in-law's side had boutht us some things as well, for he understood the situation and found Liu Yu-chen's attitude profoundly shocking. From time to time, some of Liu Pin-san's friends, recent arrivals from Shanghai, came to see us. They regarded me with a mixture of astonishment and curiosity: the concert pianist reduced to giving lessons to children; one of the richest women in Shanghai on paper now fallen into poverty.

Fortunately, during this lonely and difficult period, I had one true friend, Barbara Fei, a famous opera singer in Hong Kong, who helped me find pupils and regularly invited me to her home. I met Barbara when I first arrived in Hong Kong, and our rapport was immediate; she soon became my confidante and her loyalty was a constant support and consolation. As for material concerns, I was soon managing quite well on my own. My lessons brought in 4,000 Hong Kong dollars a month, or $800, enough to supply my children with the necessities. Fortunately, Paul and Juliette were no problem; they were doing well at school, and at twelve, Paul was already a mature and serious boy. Only Juliette, who was only seven, voiced any complaints. Used to our easy life in Shanghai, she was now no longer able to have whatever she wanted, and when her requests were denied, she would begin to cry for her father, which made it even more difficult for me to refuse her.

We continued to go to the temple once a week to pray for my husband's soul. On our third excursion, I was in the midst of imploring the Buddha Ti Tsang Wang to free Liu Yu-huang from his sins so that he would not suffer in the next life, when suddenly I caught sight of Juliette, sitting immobile on her chair, her face as white as a sheet. When I asked her what was wrong, she replied, with some hesitation, that she had gone into the outer room of the temple and had seen a monk with a tall hat and a long robe embroidered with squares. Carrying a stick in his hand and with Juliette behind him, he had entered the inner temple where I was praying and had stopped behind me as I knelt. Then he had suddenly disappeared, like a mirage, and the poor child was terrified. I did my best to calm her for I was certain that this wasn't just the figment of a child's imagination. As far as I was concerned, the monk had been the materialization of Ti Tsang Wang, and his apparition meant that my husband's soul had been saved.

My children and I did not take up very much space in the house on Granville Road. In fact, we occupied only one room, next to the communal bathroom.

Mercifully, my children spent most of their time at school and I most of mine running back and forth between my pupils' houses, returning home only at night to sleep. My children and I had only one visitor: the architect Feng, the husband of my sister-in-law, Feng Yu-ming.

Quick-witted and intelligent, Feng had rapidly won the hearts of both Paul and Juliette, and he spent hours talking to them or helping them with their homework. This left me some free time to sit with my mother-in-law, for I knew Liu Yu-chen was not sincere in the affection she pretended toward her invalid mother.

And so, every evening after I'd finished practicing on my

piano, the only gift I had left from my husband, I sat down with my mother-in-law and recounted what had happened during the course of the day. Even though she could not reply because of her stroke, I knew that these moments were as precious to her as were the times when Paul and Juliette came to see her. With her one good hand, she would awkwardly caress their heads.

As my oldest sister-in-law, Liu Yu-ying, had returned to her children in Shanghai, I remained alone at Granville Road with Liu Yu-chen, her "artist" husband, and their two children. Unfortunately, the oldest of her two children, encouraged by his mother, took great delight in hitting Paul when I was absent. More than once I had to speak severely to the "artist" about his son, as I still preferred to have as little as possible to do with Liu Yu-chen.

And then one day, after quite some time had gone by without our speaking to one another, Yu-chen appeared suddenly in the kitchen while I was preparing lunch for my children, and asked if I had made any progress in my search for a new husband. I was so outraged that the knife slipped from my hand and sliced my finger to the bone. As I sat there with blood spurting out and the children running frantically around trying to find a bandage, my sister-in-law calmly left the room just as Feng arrived. In the twinkling of an eye, he had found the gauze and the alcohol and had fashioned a sturdy bandage which stopped the flow of blood.

"What happened between you and your sister-in-law?" he demanded.

I replied that I'd been nervous and when Yu-chen had said something a bit disagreeable to me, I'd lost control of the knife. Feng did not seem at all surprised, as he and his wife had long been aware of Yu-chen's attitude.

"There's only one thing to do," he told me. "You mustn't stay here any longer."

Which was precisely what I myself had begun to think.

When Liu Pin-san finally returned from the United States, the tone and tempo of warfare increased dramatically. By this time, the seventh week of prayer had gone by and we were almost at the end of the year. I went alone to the airport to meet my father-in-law, for he still did not know that his son was dead. When I saw him, I began to cry, and he realized immediately what had happened.

And so he returned from America—where four of his children as well as numerous relatives were living—only to find a paralyzed wife and his eldest son dead. The shock coupled with the poisonous family atmosphere transformed him into a feeble old man, no longer resembling the powerful and commanding Liu Pin-san whom I had first met at the Green Pavilion so long ago.

With the return of her father, however, my sister-in-law Liu Yu-chen saw that her days were numbered. It was clear that she and her family would have to go, leaving me as rightful mistress of the house. It was Liu Pin-san's brother who gave him a detailed account of Yu-chen's behavior, but as my father-in-law had never seen his daughter treat me other than kindly, he refused to believe his brother's stories. Instead, Liu Pin-san called me into the room and, in the presence of his wife, demanded to know what was going on. I replied that contrary to what his daughter may have said, I had no intention of encouraging him to turn out a couple unable to earn their own living; but since I was perfectly capable of taking care of myself and my children, I would move out and take an apartment of my own.

My mother-in-law was clearly in anguish. She had only limited means of expressing herself, but her tears and groans left little doubt about what she thought. When I mentioned taking an apartment for myself and the children, she moaned loudly, obviously not wanting us to leave. And whenever Liu Yu-chen's name came up, she made an odd gesture with her one good hand, as if to chase Yu-chen away. Instinct told me that Liu Yu-chen had mistreated her mother when they were alone, and since the poor woman had no way of denouncing her, Yu-chen could continue to play the part of the devoted daughter publicly.

The house filled with tension. One after the other, my husband's uncle and his wife and my brother-in-law, Feng, came to argue my case before my father-in-law. Following one of these heated sessions, Feng telephoned me from outside and asked me to meet him, for he had something important to tell me. I agreed, joining him in his American car, which he had parked at the corner.

"I have some bad news," he began solemnly. "But you may as well know the worst now. My wife tells me that your father-in-law is completely under Liu Yu-chen's control. He's even been influenced to make a will leaving you and the children out altogether. You're on your own now, and if you want to plan a future for yourself and your children, I think it might be best for you to go abroad."

I was grateful to Feng for his concern and advice, and asked him to thank his wife for me. Although unpleasant, his revelation neither came as a surprise nor did it upset me. My Buddhist training and beliefs had taught me to be fatalistic. In any case, how important was the inheritance when I was still young enough and strong enough to take care of myself and the children?

Feng is undoubtedly right, I thought. I will have to leave Hong Kong. My first impulse, of course, was to return to Shanghai. But I also knew there was a strong possibility —perhaps a certainty—that Liu Pin-san, because of his wife's health and attachment to my children, would insist on keeping Paul and Juliette with them. And, because of Chinese tenets of behavior, I would not be able to defy them.

But since my in-laws would clearly never return to China, how could I go back to Shanghai? Visa controls were becoming tighter and tighter, and it would be a long, long time before I could be allowed to return to Hong Kong to see my children.

Lacking the courage to defy my in-laws or, for that matter, to be so cruel as to tear the grandchildren away from two old people who had just lost their beloved eldest son, and unable to abandon my own children, I simply decided to do nothing, at least for the time being. Surely Fate would show me the way out.

At the same time, the prospect of continuing to live with a sister-in-law who spent her time dreaming up ways of getting rid of me was not exactly appealing. Thus I continued to give piano lessons, putting away money for our eventual departure.

And I also began to think seriously about taking up my ca-

252

reer again as a concert pianist. It struck me that I could both get away from my sister-in-law and enhance my career by emigrating—either to Europe or America.

America came first to mind simply because Liu Pin-san had so many children and relatives there. After all, they were my relatives as well, were they not—even if only by marriage. I therefore wrote to my brother-in-law, one of the four Liu children living in the United States, who was an engineer with the Ford Motor Company. Although we had never met, he seemed the most likely candidate for the sponsorship necessary for all immigrants to America. I made it perfectly clear in my letter, however, that his sponsorship would be only a formality, and not a responsibility, as I had some money of my own and fully intended to earn my own living. The reply came in due course. In spite of my assurances, he seemed fearful that he would end up having to support me and my children; he therefore refused with regret, stating that there was no way in which he could help. Thus ended my dreams of America.

During this terrible period in my life, Barbara Fei's friendship became even more precious, if that is possible. The evenings spent in her company were my only relief from the difficulties of the day, and the hours were always pleasurable and entertaining.

In Hong Kong, Chinese of the upper classes do not receive a woman such as I, a widow who has lost her fortune along with her husband. Barbara, however, was cut from a different pattern. Pretty, distinguished, and elegantly simple in her tastes, she and her husband, a well-to-do jeweler, judged and collected people on the basis of intellect, interest, and personality. The Feis accepted me into their circle and introduced me to their friends, primarily journalists, music critics, and talented and successful musicians such as Morya Ray, the first violinist of the Hong Kong Symphony.

These introductions were not made casually, for it was Barbara's idea to introduce me to people who might be helpful in launching my career as a concert pianist. Talent and influence aside, in Hong Kong one still needed money to rent an auditorium for a debut, and I of course had none.

One day I went to visit Morya Ray to play a César Franck Sonata with her. During a break, we discussed my dismal-looking future, and she suggested that I might consider trying my luck in Paris. Although my ultimate intention was to return to China, any training I might receive in Paris or Vienna would give me the necessary cachet to succeed in Shanghai.

Others felt this a good idea as well, but I knew no one in Paris, nor could I speak French, and I wasn't certain how I could manage such a move. But I was determined to continue with my career, and I knew how badly I needed proper training—talent alone is not enough. Still, I did not yet have the courage to make so drastic a change.

Outside of Barbara Fei's circle, I was snubbed outright; the old Chinese prejudices still held sway and conspired to imprison me. Each time I went to Barbara's, for example, my in-laws made an incredible scene. I was not observing the laws of mourning, and my mother-in-law showed as best she could the signs of extreme distress, while my father-in-law emerged from his torpor only to watch and wait for my return. But as I had stayed in Hong Kong for my in-laws' sake, I felt little guilt.

One evening I received a letter from my father with news of the family. Ching-ling, still a pianist for Radio Peking, was living happily in Peking with her husband and children. My brother, Chow Ching-chung, "rehabilitated" and forgiven by the Party, had now returned to his original work as Party instructor, and was also living in Peking.

To my chagrin, however, my father's letter was also full of advice on the reserved and decorous conduct befitting a young widow like myself, who must under all circumstances remain "as pure as a lotus flower." He even went so far as to remind me that, as a widow, I must carefully abstain from even laughing in public!

Thus passed my first miserable winter in Hong Kong. Then in the early summer of 1963, Paul, now twelve, offered me the first real moment of happiness I had had since the death of his father. Having finished primary school with honors, he received a Hong Kong government scholarship—an incredible feat for a child who knew neither Cantonese nor English, who had learned to write in Shanghai according to the simplified

254

system, and who had had to relearn classical and traditional Chinese in Hong Kong! The problem now was how to find him a good secondary school in an overpopulated city with a limited number of schools, all of them filled.

My generous brother-in-law, Feng, who still inquired after us daily, suggested an excellent and well-known high school in the suburbs, but which accepted only boarders. As I had already applied to a private Baptist school in Kowloon because it was near our apartment, and Paul could continue to live at home, I wasn't pleased with Feng's suggestion. But Feng insisted I at least look into it, as the school had such an excellent reputation, and he offered to drive me there that very day for a visit.

I hesitated. Apart from my indecisiveness about Paul's future, I had for some time now become quite uneasy in Feng's company. Over the months I had noticed a subtle change in his attitude, and there was something about the way he looked at me that made me uncomfortable. And so I replied that I had no time at the moment to visit the school, and that in any event I wanted time to think things over.

The next day his wife, Liu Yu-lan, telephoned me quite early in the morning.

"I don't understand you, Ching-li," she complained. "We're trying so hard to help you, and you turn your nose up at us!" She then went on to argue so persistently about going to see the school that I finally gave in, promising to join them at the ferry in an hour.

Feng was waiting for me when I arrived; he had left his big American car behind and was driving a little Volkswagen. And he was alone.

"Where's Yu-lan?" I asked, immediately suspicious.

"Taking care of the children, of course," he replied calmly. "Something came up at the last minute, and she couldn't come."

We left Hong Kong, heading south. It was June and extremely hot. The humidity, fearsome in Hong Kong, made both of us uncomfortable, and we stopped several times at Feng's suggestion, in the shade on the side of the road. Finally parking in front of a hotel, Feng proposed that we go in for a cooling drink. I followed him to the bar, where he ordered some iced concoctions.

"It's so hot," he said, "perhaps you'd like to rest a while, and take a nap. I could take a room . . ."

Shocked, and horrified to realize that my suspicions about Feng were not figments of my imagination, I told him I wasn't in the least bit tired, that I hadn't come with him to have a nap, but to visit the school. We finished our drinks in silence.

Once back on the road, Feng made several feeble attempts at jovial conversation, but I remained unresponsive. At long last we arrived at the school, where the director received us, introducing me to several of the teachers, and guiding me on a tour of the school. After a lengthy discussion with the staff about the suitability of the school's curriculum and about Paul's qualifications, we left.

By now the heat had become unbearable, and Feng was perspiring perceptively. Uncomfortable myself, I suddenly realized that we were not returning via the same road we had come by, but that in fact we were at a beach.

"This is Repulse Bay," Fong announced, stopping the car.

Despite its ugly name, Repulse Bay is one of the most beautiful spots in Hong Kong. Not only does the beach defy description, but the area is dotted with incredibly elegant homes and, here and there, the most incredible hotels in the Far East—but not so many as to mar the landscape.

"This time I am really dying," Feng said. "Let's stop for a little while. It's so beautiful, and I absolutely must have something to drink."

I myself was dying of thirst, and hungry as well. It was nearly three, and I had not had any breakfast. I readily agreed.

We seated ourselves at one of the tables on the beach, near a snack bar. Because of the extreme heat and time of day, there wasn't a soul about. Feng wandered off in search of a waiter; he found one, giving him some money. Returning to the table, Feng beckoned me to follow him, saying the waiter had a better table for us. Only when we reached a row of cabanas did I stupidly realize what was happening. Before I could get away, Feng had shoved me into one of the open dressing rooms.

Pinioning my arms behind me, he began to kiss me passionately about the face and neck. Still holding my wrists with one hand, he freed his other to tear the front of my dress and fondle my breasts.

I wrenched one of my arms free, hitting him about his face and pushing him away, screaming at him to stop, to think about what he was doing.

But all my efforts were in vain; instead, he knocked me to the floor, pulling my dress up over my arms and tearing off my undergarments until I lay before him naked.

"Please," I gasped. "Let me go, Feng, please! Please!" I was in anguish. Whether it was what I said, or the anguish in my voice, he stopped, relaxing his hold.

"All right," he panted. "All right, I'll let you go . . ."

Sighing deeply, half-dead from exhaustion, I raised myself to the bench, reaching for my dress. Just then, when I thought I was safe, the wretch threw himself on me, pinning my arms against the bench. And then I felt the gush of him in me.

Insulted, dishonored, and disgraced, I wanted only to die. As soon as he lifted himself from my body I ran from the cabana, naked and weeping, through the deserted beach to the sea. I had only one thought: to die.

I threw myself into the waves, but the horrible Feng caught me, pulling me back to the beach, begging me to forgive him.

How could I?

Feng pleaded that he had misunderstood, that at my age he thought I needed and wanted a man to hold me in his arms, that he hadn't meant to dishonor me, that he was obsessed with me, and that anyway I had no right to kill myself. What would happen to my children?

At the thought of Paul and Juliette I stopped struggling, and asked the wretch to bring what was left of my dress from the cabana. Pulling it about me, and filled with embarrassment at the possibility of running into anyone, half-clothed as I was, I somehow made my way back to the car with that horrible man.

Spending the return trip huddled on one side of the car, I somehow managed to get into my in-laws' apartment and back into my own room without being seen. Filling the tub, I washed myself over and over again in a vain attempt to cleanse myself of both Feng and the memory of what had happened.

For a week afterward, I lived in a daze. Calling some students, I cancelled their lessons, pleading illness; others I forgot altogether. Spending my days cloistered in my room, I appeared only for dinner, and even then I found myself only staring at my chopsticks, not knowing what to do with them.

The shock was both emotional and physical. When my period failed I was in panic. Unwilling and ashamed to reveal the rape to my gynecologist, I consulted instead various women of dubious reputation who sold forbidden drugs guaranteed to advance or retard one's period. The drugs were dangerous, but I felt it would be better to die than to carry Feng's unwanted baby.

In the end, I was not pregnant; my period eventually arrived and, on the surface at least, things returned to normal.

But I still could not get over the event; it pains me even now to think of it. What was particularly strange was that the evening before the terrible excursion to Repulse Bay, I had dreamed that my husband was lying in an open coffin, and that he suddenly rose to embrace me protectively.

Fear of pregnancy had now given way to violent hatred; all I wanted was revenge, and I began to fantasize ways to create as much pain and humiliation for Feng as he had for me.

Feng, on the other hand, had dropped out of sight, but only for a week, resurfacing as if nothing at all had happened. But by that time I was ready for him.

"You have hurt me deeply," I told him, almost sweetly. "I trust you're sincerely sorry for all you did?"

"Yes, but I want you to understand why," he responded. "My wife and I have nothing in common. But with you, the second I met you, I knew you were everything I've ever wanted in a woman. I love you," he continued extravagantly, "and I thought I read reciprocation in your eyes as well . . ."

"*My* eyes?" I repeated, uncomprehending.

And then I understood. He had conceitedly mistaken my gratitude for his generosity toward the children as "love."

I had now found the way to make Feng pay for his actions at Repulse Bay, and I weighed my words carefully before replying.

"Feng," I finally began, "since you claim you acted out of

love, I am touched, and I could forgive you—but only if you are sincere and don't consider me a passing flirtation." My eyes lowered coyly. And I sighed.

With these words I suggested that I understood and was flattered by the fact that he was a lover driven mad by passion, indicating that he could have me if he truly loved me.

I wanted to make him hope for the impossible—a love affair with me—and then, just when he thought the impossible could happen, I would reject him, humiliate him, crushing him like the cockroach he was. I had no idea when I would tell his wife, but that was also part of my plan.

First, however, I had to make Feng understand that I refused to be his secret mistress; that he could only have me if he undertook full responsibility. I wanted to test his willingness to accept the risk of a scandal. And then I would kick him out, treating him with the scorn he deserved. I have never before or since felt such hatred for anyone.

And so I continued to see Feng, remaining distant and yet friendly, in carefully measured doses. He and Yu-lan often invited me to their home for dinner, and not a day passed without, in one way or another, Feng seeing or hearing from me. I could see that he was falling more and more deeply in love with me. And he was becoming very sure of himself.

Eventually it was not enough for him to see me only once a day. He began to follow me everywhere, waiting for me outside my pupils' homes. At that point my diabolical plans began to weaken as I came to my senses. Hate had made me overlook the terrible consequences of my actions.

What if Feng really did mean to leave his wife and get divorced? Then there would be two unhappy people. Liu Yu-lan had never harmed me, and she *was* his wife.

The sudden realization of what I was doing prevented me from revealing anything to Yu-lan, and made me give up my ugly plans. I had never forgotten my own father's affair, when I was a little girl, and the suffering it had caused my mother; at least my father had loved his mistress, while I loathed Feng. Also, the idea of becoming a homebreaker myself filled me with disgust. Thus, just as I neared my awful goal, I pulled back.

Hoist with my own petard, I was now unable to get rid of Feng. He became ubiquitous, following me everywhere, telephoning me daily, begging me to see him. What was I to do?

Until now my plans for emigrating had remained vague and confused. My dear friend Barbara Fei, fully aware of what was going on (she had originally tried to dissuade me from my plans), now took the opportunity to suggest what she had been urging me to do for years—fulfill my dreams of becoming a concert pianist by going to Paris to study.

It seemed that, without telling me, Barbara had written to a friend of hers in Paris, Diana Wang, whose husband was a violinist, inquiring about the possibilities of my studying and being able to earn a living in Paris. Diana had answered, saying I had passed the age limit of eighteen for study at the conservatory, and that the private music schools were not only expensive, but of questionable quality. However, since Diana knew the musical world in Paris extremely well, she advised that I come and study with the famous pianist Marguerite Long. Madame Long accepted only a handful of students, but it would do no harm to apply. All that was required was that I make some tapes of my work and send them to Diana, who would take them to Marguerite Long.

Thrilled, I began practicing for hours daily, hardly stopping to eat or sleep. I intended to send Bach's Chaconne for Piano, adapted by Liszt, as well as Liszt's own *Sospiro*. Practicing for days on end, I was finally satisfied with the results and, two weeks later, took the tapes to Barbara, who was equally satisfied and forwarded them immediately to Diana Wang.

It seemed an eternity before we received a reply. But I was accepted! I would have to leave Paul and Juliette temporarily behind in Hong Kong, which was the most painful part for me; but Diana convinced me that if I really intended to remake my life abroad, I would have no time to concern myself with worry over the children. After all, they were far better off with their grandparents, and it was because of my in-laws' demand to keep the children that I couldn't return to Shanghai. But if I were successful in Paris, I could come back for visits often and, eventually, take Paul and Juliette with me to Paris—which is in fact what I was able to do less than two years later.

To be accepted by such an illustrious pianist seemed to me an impossible dream come true; and for the first time in the two lonely years following my husband's death I saw a gleam of hope for another life.

At the end of September, 1964, we were all standing in the drawing room of Barbara's apartment. In just a few minutes I would be leaving Barbara and her husband, perhaps forever. Barbara gave me a little purse containing five small pieces of paper, folded in quarters, each with a friendly address in Paris in case I should run into trouble and need help.

And so I left my dear friend, Barbara Fei, she who had been my friend through the most trying period of my life, and who had encouraged me—indeed, had mapped out my route to that magical city I had dreamed about so long ago in Shanghai.

Leaving the Feis' apartment, I went home to pick up Paul and Juliette, who were to see me off at the airport, accompanied by my father-in-law. As the taxi pulled up to 58 Granville Road, I looked up and saw Liu Pin-san on the balcony, holding his wife so she could have a final look at me. Her one good hand waved feebly. I wanted to cry.

Juliette, now eight and wearing the pretty dress I had made for her myself, and Paul, tall at thirteen and already looking like the head of the house, jumped into the taxi. Then, all too soon, we were at the airport. Amid tears and kisses I bade my two darling children goodbye, promising to send for them shortly.

As the plane departed down the runway, I thought of my parents, Chow Hui-i and Chung-ai. Both knew the day and hour of my departure, and were surely crying a silent farewell to me in Shanghai.

And then the image of the MacIntyre School came into focus, the young choir girls singing; and Jessfield Park, where father had taken me for walks and Ching-chung had taught me monkey boxing. I saw them all—my parents, my brothers and sisters—and to each I bade a farewell, saving the most painful one until last. In my mind's eye I could see Juliette and Paul waving to me, Paul's arms around Juliette, both blowing kisses to me, and I to them.

The plane gained altitude as Hong Kong spread out beneath my gaze, and just barely on the horizon, the coast of China, where all the happy and sad moments of my life were being left behind.

And now there were no more tears, for I had none left to shed.